The Continental Commitment

Recent debates about British political and military strategies, derived in particular from dissension about Britain's relationship with Europe and from disagreement over the Iraq war, have led to a greater awareness of the problematic nature of the concept of 'national interests'. This book provides a historical perspective on this issue as the twin strands of the question are captured by the consideration both of the Continental commitment and of British interventionism in the eighteenth century. It discusses the extent to which Britain's rise to superpower status in America and Asia was related to the Continental connection and to the Hanoverian interests of the dynasty, and considers the relationship between the domestic position of the Crown and its interests as Electors of Hanover.

By also focusing on the wider public debate on foreign policy and its consequences, Jeremy Black sheds a new light on the relative weight of dynastic, strategic, colonial, religious and political interests in the formulation of eighteenth-century Britain's foreign policy.

This book, written by one of the world's leading authorities on the subject, will be essential reading for students of international history, British diplomatic history and European history in general.

Jeremy Black is Professor of History at the University of Exeter.

The Continental Commitment

Britain, Hanover and interventionism, 1714–1793

Jeremy Black

Routledge
Taylor & Francis Group

LONDON AND NEW YORK

First published 2005
by Routledge
2 Park Square, Milton Park, Abingdon, Oxon OX14 4RN

Simultaneously published in the USA and Canada
by Routledge
270 Madison Ave, New York, NY 10016

Routledge is an imprint of the Taylor & Francis Group

© 2005 Jeremy Black

Typeset in Sabon by RefineCatch Limited, Bungay, Suffolk
Printed and bound in Great Britain by
Antony Rowe Ltd, Chippenham, Wiltshire

British Library Cataloguing in Publication Data
A catalogue record for this book is available from the British Library

Library of Congress Cataloging in Publication Data
A catalog record for this book has been requested

ISBN 0–415–36292–X

For Karl Schweizer, a toiler in the same vineyard, and an old friend

Contents

Preface

Recent debates about British political and military strategies, derived in particular from dissension about Britain's relationship with Europe, and also from disagreement over the Iraq war of 2003, have led to a greater awareness of the problematic nature of the concept of national interests. The purpose of this book is to offer a discussion of strategy and policy that provides a concrete instance of the past debate within Britain over the notion of national interests. This offers a historical perspective that is also a contribution to contemporary discussion, indicating, as it does, the extent to which interventionism – an active foreign policy focusing on a determination to direct the course of events abroad – has always been controversial. The twin strands of this – policy and strategy – will be captured by the consideration of both interventionism and the Continental (in the sense of the European mainland) commitment. The remainder of this synopsis will address the historical dimension. It is necessary, however, to bear in mind the contemporary position at all points, as it helps set the resonance for the book; although it is also pertinent to recall the specificities of particular historical episodes. *Old England*, a London newspaper, in its issue of 20 October (os) 1744, commented on 'the way in which we are too apt to reason, without paying due attention to the difference of time, situation, motives, characters, and a thousand other circumstances which we ought to have considered'.

The extent to which Britain's rise to super-power status in America and Asia in the eighteenth century, so that by 1763 Britain was the most powerful Western state, was related to the Continental connection, as well as to the Hanoverian interests of the dynasty, is a central theme of the book, as is the relationship between the domestic position of the Crown and its interests as Electors of Hanover. After the accession of the Elector of Hanover to the British throne as George I in 1714, Hanover was used as a political locator for the debate with Britain about the value of Continental intervention. In the late 1720s, this process was furthered because interventionism was based on the Treaty of Hanover of 1725 and Britain's alliances reaffirmed within the resulting Alliance of Hanover. Thus, running together concern about the domestic situation with anxiety about interventionism, George

Clarke, a jaundiced Tory MP (the varied governments under George I and George II were Whig), complained in 1726:

> there seems to be little occasion for Parliament, for it is a sort of resolving all power into one hand . . . It was pretty plainly insinuated that this money that's wanted, is to induce people to accede to the Hanover Treaty and it is as plain that none of the German princes will accede without money, when they know that the Parliament will pay what they require.[1]

The use of Hanover as a locator for interventionism is understandable, as there was considerable overlap between policies for the benefit of Hanover and the cause of British interventionism. This does not mean, however, that modern commentators should fall into the mistake of running the two together, nor that contemporaries could not distinguish between the two. There could also be important clashes between Hanoverian and British policy.[2]

Here we are moving into the field of polemic, because the informed attempt to distinguish between the variations encompassed by the term interventionism did not readily find a place in a partisan debate in which it was helpful to smear opponents with the charge of betraying national interests. This smear, when directed by opposition writers and speakers at Hanoverian concerns, especially in 1717–20 and 1742–4, was not without some point, but it permits a modern misinterpretation of the debate, for critics from within government ranks were not apt to go public, and yet their criticism was informed and significant. As a result of failing to devote sufficient attention to critics within government ranks, it is possible for modern defenders of the Hanoverian connection, and, more generally, of Continental interventionism, to present criticism largely in terms of the public debate, and therefore both as factious and as flawed by this partisanship. This risks falling into the trap of treating the bounds of parliamentary contention and the culture of print as the parameters of debate, which was not the case. Instead, the range of criticism included factious attacks, not all of which were misguided, yet also far better-informed, but more private, criticisms.

The issue of Continental interventionism also opens up the question of how alliances generate their own pressures, at the same time that they are supposed to help overcome challenges; while, in addition, indicating how the domestic support for alliances shifts, creating political dynamics that, in turn, affect the international dimension. The collapse of the Anglo-French alliance in 1730–1, which owed a lot to domestic political pressures in Britain, was a good instance of the latter. This collapse also exacerbated Hanover's vulnerability, although that of the Hanoverian dynasty in Britain was threatened even more by the risk of French support for Jacobitism, the cause of the exiled Stuarts.

The subject also leads to consideration of the processes of academic activity. Indeed, the study of *ancien régime* international relations has been affected by a move in the culture of higher education. The striving for significance has taken the form of assuming that the long-established, accretional, but arduous, world of archival scholarship not only can, but should, be replaced by the search for long-term activating forces. These structuralist accounts variously look to supposedly inherent characteristics of politico-economic systems, with the enhanced capability allegedly result-ing,[3] or to the world of ideas as manifested through the study of texts, with these ideas reified and given explanatory force.[4] The modishness of some accounts lend themselves to the strategies of publishing houses, while their archive-'lite' quality make the research easier, if that is not too grand a term for the deductive character of much of the argument. However crabby, if not ungenerous, these remarks may seem, it is difficult to know how else to address the disparities between the clarity of the presentation of the past in much of the literature, and, on the other hand, the complexities and prob-lems that concerned the ministers, diplomats and commentators of the period, and the different ways they understood and confronted them.

The perception that foreign policy has somehow been done, and, anyway, that it is part of the 'stuff' of history that modish scholars had best avoid, in their quest for intellectual significance and career advancement, is well established in the profession. Foreign policy in fact was one of the most important aspects of state activity, and also one that revealed the operation of the political system and what were believed to be the key factors affecting national policy and capability. Foreign policy was also significant as the forcing house of notions of national interest: the debate over policy led to the articulation of ideas, and helped associate them with political groupings, although that, in turn, made the analysis and articulation of concepts of national interest far more complex. To fail to allow for the importance of foreign policy is to offer an unbalanced account of eighteenth-century British politics. Furthermore, in discussing the rise of empire, the fashion-able presentation of identity, and of views of the 'other', in terms of eth-nicity, gender and sexuality needs to make due allowance for the real issues that were at stake: to discuss 'genderised' concepts of Britannia without assessing what contemporaries were being asked to die and pay for, and why, is unhelpful. Methodological and archival issues are not avoided in this book because they are important to the framing of the modern debate about eighteenth-century policy and discussion.

I am most grateful to those who have supported archival research, not least the German Academic Exchange Scheme and the University of Durham for funding German archival trips. The hospitality of Hilmar Brückner, Gerhard Menk and Armin Reese on these trips was most welcome. I benefited from discussing this topic at length with a number of scholars, particularly David Aldridge and the late Uriel Dann, and would like to thank Brendan Simms for inviting me to a colloquium on the Hanoverian dimension in British foreign policy and domestic politics, 1714–1837, held at Peterhouse, Cambridge in 2004. I would like to thank Jane Olorenshaw for being an exemplary copy-editor. It is a great pleasure to dedicate this book to a fellow scholar in the field, and, with that, to mark over twenty years of friendship and co-operation on a number of projects, as well as my respect for the detailed archival research that is the basis for his major contribution to the understanding of Anglo-Prussian relations.

Notes on dates, spelling and titles

The New Year is always taken as starting on 1 January. Until the reform of the calendar in 1752, Britain conformed to the Julian Calendar. Dates recorded in this calendar are referred to as old style and designated (os). All other dates are new style, the Gregorian calendar, which was eleven days ahead. Spelling and punctuation have been modernised, except that the older, Danish, form Sleswig is used, as that is appropriate to the period. Where possible, well-established anglicised forms have been used for both place and personal names. The length of noble titles and of titles of offices has dictated their shortening. Place of publication is London unless otherwise indicated.

Abbreviations

Add.	Additional Manuscripts
AE	Paris, Ministère des Relations Extérieures
AN	Paris, Archives Nationales
Ang.	Angleterre
AST	Turin, Archivio di Stato
Aylesbury, Trevor	Aylesbury, Buckinghamshire Record Office, Trevor papers
Bayr. Ges.	Bayerische Gesandtschaft
BL	London, British Library
Bod.	Oxford, Bodleian Library, Department of Western Manuscripts
Br.	Brunswick-Hanover
Cal.	Calenberg Brief Archiv
Chewton	Chewton Hall, Chewton Mendip, papers of James, 1st Earl Waldegrave
C(H)	Cholmondeley Houghton papers
Cobbett	W. Cobbett (ed.), *Cobbett's Parliamentary History of England* (36 vols, 1806–20)
CP	Correspondance Politique
CRO	County Record Office
CUL	Cambridge, University Library
Darmstadt	Darmstadt, Staatsarchiv, Gräflich Görtzisches Archiv
Dresden	Dresden, Hauptstaatsarchiv, Geheimes Kabinett, Gesandschaften
Eg.	Egerton Mss.
EK	England Korrespondenz
FO	Foreign Office
GK	Grosse Korrespondenz
Hanover	Hanover, Niedersächsisches Hauptstaatsarchiv
HHStA	Vienna, Haus-, Hof-, und Staatsarchiv, Staatskanzlei
Ing.	Inghilterra
KS	Kasten Schwarz
LM	Lettere Ministri

Marburg	Marburg, Staatsarchiv, Bestand 4: Politische Akten nach Philipp d. Gr.
MD	Mémoires et Documents
Munich	Munich, Bayerisches Hauptstaatsarchiv, Gesandtschaften
Münster	Münster, Staatsarchiv, Archiv Nordkirchen, Plettenberg papers
NA	London, National Archives, formerly Public Record Office
NAS	Edinburgh, National Archives of Scotland
NLA	Canberra, National Library of Australia, Department of Manuscripts
os	old style
Polit. Corr.	R. Köser (ed.), *Politische Correspondenz Friedrichs des Grossen* (46 vols, Berlin, 1879–1939)
RA	Windsor Castle, Royal Archives
SP	State Papers
Weston Underwood	Iden Green, Mill St. House, papers of Edward Weston
WW	Sheffield, Archives, Wentworth Woodhouse papers

1 Britain and the rise to world empire

Why were his territories invaded, his cities plundered, his palaces rifled, his country laid waste, and his subjects butchered? Not because he was Elector of Hanover. Neither the Court of Vienna, nor Versailles, pretended to have the smallest demand upon him as such. It was because he was King of England; and the French ... thought that the King of England would favour the Electorate of Hanover.

(*Westminster Journal*, 29 December 1759)

It is fair to assume that many out of each generation of scholars feels disappointed in its successors, concerned about novel assumptions and methods, happy to dismiss new enthusiasms and fads, and keen to express a sense that their own contribution has been neglected. Yet, at the present moment, there seems particular force to such complaints, because the emphasis on discourse has led to a sea-change in historical method. The older stress on primary research was essentially incremental, and thus led to debate with earlier contributions, and, while that is not absent from the emphasis on discourse, it is not central to it. Instead, there is the claim that a particular scholar, or group of scholars, has unlocked the mindset of the age in question, and, by doing so, has cast in the shade other approaches. In doing so, the emphasis on discourse offers a reification of that most misleading idea, the *zeitgeist* (spirit of the age), one that inherently clashes with the complexity that primary source-based scholarship is at pains to delineate and dissect.

This emphasis on discourse and the *zeitgeist* has made deep inroads in cultural studies, helping to ensure that much of the subject becomes an extended paean to theoretical knowledge, or at least massing of theoretical references; and also in social history. In the political sphere, the emphasis on discourse has been less insistent, but it has nevertheless made an impact. As far as military history and international relations are concerned, the subject and method of structures of argument and language seen with the emphasis on discourse are apparently less pressing than the structural accounts deployed in systemic analyses. In fact, the two are related, not least with the distinction between an essentialist dimension, supposedly approached by analysis of underlying structures, and another dimension. Fernand Braudel, with his preference for the *longue durée* over the *histoire événementielle*, described the latter in terms of epi-phenomena.[1]

Furthermore, the eighteenth-century use of structural terms and mechanistic concepts, particularly the language of natural interests and the balance of power, readily lends itself to this modern neo-Platonic emphasis on underlying reality.[2] It also has the comforting consequence that the apparently boring world of past scholarship, suffused in archival references, can be slighted, or even ignored, in favour of a more accessible world of, for example, treatises on diplomatic or military method. Why study the complexities of the consolidation of British control in Bengal, when you can read a few pamphlets about drill and argue that its capability for mechanistic efficiency ensured Western success? Why bother to understand the complexities of policy debates among ministers, politicians and diplomats, when it is possible to abstract a few speeches by William Pitt the Elder from their parliamentary background and specific political context, and demonstrate that this shows that he had an accurate, coherent and consistent schema that ably integrated British commitments and opportunities? And all this before, on the basis of a particular reading of texts, we treat the rise of the British empire as an essay in masculinity or racial exploitation.

In practice, to enable us to understand texts as they were intended, it is not only necessary to read them extensively, locating them in terms of the details of contemporary debate, but also to be conversant with the range of established scholarship, so that the selectivity underlining both the creation and survival of texts, and our reading of them, can be appreciated. This affects the discussion of the obscure process by which ideas on foreign policy developed in the eighteenth century. There is a lack of clarity in particular over how far the ideas had an independent existence, and how far debate related largely to the particular political context of the moment. In practice, the latter helped account for partisan bite and political sponsorship, leading to the re-formation of existing ideas for particular contingencies.

An understanding of this requires what is an equivalent to the source-based and cumulative scholarship that is also necessary for diplomatic history. A fascination with discourse as subject and approach can, unfortunately, lead to an abandonment of source-based and accretional methods, and, instead, to a mishandling of texts, such as pamphlets and speeches. There is a tendency to place too much weight on particular texts, for example specific passages from parliamentary speeches, without considering them within the wider state of the debate on foreign policy at that moment. Secondly, there can be a failure to explain adequately the links between a climate of opinion, itself an inadequately defined concept, and the formulation of policy. John, Lord Carteret, Secretary of State for the Northern Department, and an experienced politician, observed in 1743 that British government was not despotic and that it was necessary to lead and satisfy 'the people',[3] although, within the constraints of the political system, he was to fail to do so, and even fell from power in 1744 as a result. However contentious in practice, the theory outlined by Carteret established parameters that it is difficult to evaluate. Thirdly, there is a tendency to overstate the extent to which there was only one climate of opinion, and a reluctance to probe the consequences of divisions in opinion, not least about operative assumptions. This is understandable from the perspective of discourse studies, as the assertion of the existence of a dominant opinion can then apparently serve to activate the opinion as a causative force. Fourthly, the stress on discourse generally stems from, and ensures, a focus on just one participant in the international system, and thus neglects its multilateral character and rationale, as well as the extent to which policy changed in response to the real and perceived intentions of other powers.

Difficulties are no reason not to attempt a subject, but, rather, serve to underline its methodological problems. The latter indeed ensure that most scholarly comments need to be prefaced by a 'probably'. Yet, the importance of the definition and pursuit of national interests ensures that to neglect it as a subject in favour of a 'safer', more readily bounded issue, would be irresponsible.

The culture of print bulks large in any discussion of the mechanics of debate, but it would be misleading to ignore other ways in which national interest and foreign policy were debated. Important in their own right, they also affected, and interacted with, the culture of print. The most important was individual communication between politicians. The source that best survives for this is correspondence, but this needs to be considered alongside the source for which records are scanty, conversation. The extent to which Britain remained a face-to-face society is generally neglected, as is the degree to which this affected politics. In such a forum, the personal weight of the individual was important in the discussion, but this is an element that it is difficult to recover. Face-to-face exchanges included not only meetings between individuals but also institutional bodies, particularly Parliament and the Cabinet Council.

There were also public forums in which policy was discussed, including taverns and coffee houses. This discussion was satirised, for example, in Henry Fielding's play *The Coffee-house Politicians*[4] (1730) and in the pamphlet *The Dead Emperor: or, Reviving Peace. Being some deep coffee-house speculations on these important subjects* (1745). The London meetings addressed by 'Orator' Henley, an independent and often eccentric preacher on all topics, also reflected the extent to which discussion of foreign policy was regarded as appropriate. In 1744, he was recorded as advocating the medical–political benefits of tar water: 'It might be used, for Court holy water to put St. James's in mind of the navy and the privateers and clear their eye-sight of the films of Hanover.'[5] Henley thus suggested that the Continental commitment was both disease and distortion.

Political correspondence survives in quantities, and provides one of the major sources for the debate on foreign policy. Letters, however, need to be employed with care. The general use of correspondence was to persuade rather than to explicate, and the purpose of persuasion posed specific exigencies that need to be judged in particular contexts, for example the royal supervision of drafts.[6] Furthermore, the survival of correspondence is patchy: some individuals took care to preserve letters, but most did not, and some sought to have their letters burned, as Sophia Dorothea, Queen of Prussia, did for hers to her father, George I.[7] Because of her reluctance to entrust herself to the page, Sophia Dorothea also made British envoys pass on messages verbally.[8] The government itself faced problems because of the failure to save material. Former officials retained correspondence to a degree that would not be permitted today.[9] There is also the problem of secret correspondence, with the relationships of commission and omission that it established. The deliberate exclusion of others from such correspondence was a particular aspect of debate, because the process of drawing boundaries and deciding whom to include helped establish the parameters of discussion.

An analogous situation was provided by manuscript newsletters, which contained more information than (printed) newspapers, but from which most readers were excluded by factors of cost. In the first half of the century, these newsletters provided more information on parliamentary debates than the newspapers. These debates themselves were an important aspect of the public discussion of policy, especially because they represented the way in which it most readily impinged on the policy-making process. This owed much to the government's desire to avoid difficulties in Parliament, and, instead, to have its backing.[10] The parliamentary debate over foreign policy had a close relation with the culture of print, and, in the second half of the century, Parliament provided much of the material for newspapers. Earlier, the meeting of the session led to an annual highpoint in the publication of political pamphlets, as efforts were made to delineate the political landscape and to define the key topics for discussion.

The analysis of printed debate faces several problems. The most serious are omission and commission. Under the first head, a large number of newspaper issues and pamphlets that are known to have existed do not survive. Were the survivors to be a representative cross-sample, the issue would not be overly serious, but this is not the case. Instead, due in large part to governmental action, the non-survivors are particularly marked among opposition works, especially those of a seditious character. Secondly, there is the problem of commission. The very number of works that survive pose difficulties for any individual researcher, one that is exacerbated by the lack of any systematic system of headlining in newspapers or of indices in pamphlets. In addition, the practice of anonymous or pseudonymous authorship makes it difficult in many cases to trace authorship. Irrespective of survival and identification, there is the issue of apparent significance. Certain newspapers, pamphlets and writers have attracted attention, but, conversely, others have been neglected, often unduly so, with serious consequences for the manner in which the public debate is considered. Partly this reflects the pressure of space, and the desire to present a clear account, but there is also the issue of celebrity status.

The mechanisms of debate were far from constant. During the period, the role of pamphlets declined, although 5,750 copies of Israel Mauduit's influential and critical *Considerations on the Present German War* (1760) were printed in five editions within a few months.[11] As the role of newspapers became more important, and the format of the press changed, the lengthy disquisitions that had advanced arguments in pamphlets (and also in newspaper essays) became relatively less important. Instead, such length was principally offered by the newspaper reports of parliamentary speeches. Greater freedom in reporting Parliament increased its centrality in the public debate, while it also bridged this debate with the world of discussions between politicians. Earlier, Parliament provided another focus because of the practice of printing instructions to MPs, such as those from the Common Council of London in October 1742 which, in turn, led to a pamphlet: *Seasonable Expostulations with the Citizens of London; upon their late instructions to their representatives on postponing sending of supplies to Continental allies* (1742).

Censorship and manipulation both played a role in the public discussion of foreign policy. This reflected the views and interventions of government, and also pressure from foreign powers. Constraint, however, was less important than the active patronage of particular arguments, although the process by which this took place is frequently obscure, and it is not always possible to establish the accuracy of claims to that effect. The nature of support for writers varied greatly. In some cases, there was direct payment, but in others authors were themselves prominent politicians. Indeed, the world of print led to an overlapping milieu of well-informed élite writers, such as Horatio Walpole, and hacks, such as John Shebbeare, a bitter critic of the Hanoverian connection.

While the mechanisms of debate were not constant, the political context also altered with the rise of empire. Nevertheless, throughout the period, interventionism in Europe remained a key issue in British foreign policy. Debate over the latter indicated the contentiousness of the notion of national interests, and that this remains the case today is not alone due to the exceptional character of present circumstances.

To assess the rise of Britain to become the world empire, and the contemporary debates over policy, is to be returned to the uncertainty of contemporaries. There was no confidence that this rise would occur or that it could be sustained. In 1738, William Hay, a ministerial Whig MP of independent mind, told the House of Commons that it was important to keep up the army: 'I never think on this subject but I consider this island as situated in the neighbourhood of France. I consider France as its natural enemy, and at the same time as the most powerful of all nations.'[12] With Napoleon dominant in Europe as late as the retreat from Moscow in 1812, there was, indeed, scant reason for confidence. In about 1810 appeared a flysheet entitled 'Warning and admonition to the People of Great Britain, published by the Commission of the General Assembly of the Church of Scotland and ordered to be read by the Ministers of that Church, from their respective Pulpits, on the Day appointed for a National Fast', that included a passage:

> the war is not on our part a matter of choice. It is a war which the first law of nature, the great duty of self-preservation, renders just and necessary: it is a war not for wealth, for distant possessions, for commercial advantages: it is a war in defence of all the blessings, which we have received from Heaven, in defence of the honor, the independence, the existence of the nation.[13]

Repeatedly, informed commentators were concerned that the government was not up to the challenge. In 1807, George Gregory, a writer and cleric, wrote to his patron Henry Addington, the former Prime Minister, that Napoleon was likely to invade Britain as, due to the military collapse of Britain's alliance system, there was nothing to distract his efforts, and that, anyway, the Continental Blockade of Britain's trade mounted by France would 'produce discontent and calamity':

> For this awful crisis we are unhappily more unprepared than we were four years ago, and the spirit of the nation checked by discordant plans, instead of invigorated by a steady, persevering government is now evaporated, or almost annihilated . . . neglect of internal defence. There are some Martello towers erected and erecting on the coast of Kent; but not many of them are finished, and if they were, what is to be done when the enemy advances further into the country? Not one measure of precaution is there taken . . . Even the measures so wisely ordered under your Lordship's administration [1801–4] have been put aside or perverted. Instead of being preserved in the national archives, and not inspected by any one, I am told the military surveys that were taken have been published for the emolument of the surveyors, and the information of the enemy.[14]

As we are now, correctly, encouraged to see empire from the periphery as well as the metropole,[15] and to consider the extent to which those who experienced imperialism helped shape the process, it is important to appreciate that this uncertainty was not limited to Britons contemplating French invasion preparations, as in 1744, 1745–6, 1759, 1779, 1797 and 1805, and alleged preparations on other occasions, as in 1731 or 1756, or the loss of Minorca in 1756 and of the American colonies in 1775–83, or setbacks and defeats in India at the hands of Mysore in 1769, 1780, 1782, and the Marathas in 1779, or rebellion in Ireland in 1798; but was also perceived elsewhere. Rulers, merchants and others had to make informed judgements about whom it was prudent to co-operate with; and, in some cases, for example both around the Plate Estuary and in Egypt in 1807, or in the Low Countries in 1809, or at New Orleans in 1815, it would have been mistaken to bet on British success. Thus, the structural interpretations of British success, which ascribe it, for example, to the strength of public finance or to naval superiority, are at odds with contemporary concerns, expectations and, on occasion, experience.

As British success in large part rested on co-operation, the foreign perception was also important, providing, as it did, both a key to British capability and an explanation of the limits of successful British force projection. Co-operation was indeed seen as important. Those who advocated particular conquests tended to present them as likely to be successful due to local support as much as British military effectiveness. Thus, in 1738, James, 2nd Lord Tyrawly, the splenetic envoy in Lisbon, suggested annexing the Mediterranean island of Majorca, not only because it would be easy and profitable to conquer, but also as the population would accept the change, 'from the happiness they see their neighbours of Minorca enjoy under our government, at least to my certain knowledge they were in this way of thinking when I was at Port Mahon',[16] the major British base on Minorca, which had been controlled by Britain since its capture in 1708. Proponents of operations in Latin America erroneously argued that much of its population would help Britain against Spain.

Co-operation was also seen as particularly important in maintaining control in Scotland and Ireland, in short in seeing that Britain itself worked, without which foreign policy, and, even more, wartime strategy would be gravely weakened. Thus, in 1807, Edward Lee wrote about Ireland to Addington:

> except there is a large French invasion the People will not rise, although partial disturbances ever have, and ever will exist, and which are to be attributed to religion, to tithes, and to the educated style of the lower orders of the People; if the People were not directed on account of religion, and if the Protestant religion had never been introduced, or being introduced, it had been *taught and prosecuted with effect* in this country as it has been in England, we should now have been one of the richest and happiest parts of Europe, for we have everything to make us so, except the mind and disposition of the lower orders of the People.[17]

To emphasise co-operation and consent is to reverse the usual structural reading of British success – from inherent qualities, particularly in public finance and naval management, to consequences in terms of resources, especially money and ships, to victory;[18] but that reading fails to allow for the many failures of government to provide the necessary resources,[19] as well as the multiple nature of contingencies that affect their successful application.

Thus, it neglects strategy and policy, more particularly policy choices, diplomatic proficiency and military skill, and ignores, or, at least, underrates the factors that contributed to the latter two. The military ones are well rehearsed, and include strategic insight, operational skill, tactical effectiveness, unit cohesion, and morale.[20]

Their diplomatic counterparts are less frequently discussed, but were important. At the outset, it is necessary to counter the essentialist, or structuralist, caveat that defeats and checks did not lessen the nature of British power, so that, for example, failure in Egypt in 1807 no more disproved Britain's great power status, than the retreat from Kabul in 1842 was to undermine Victoria's empire; or, to employ a modern analogy, that failure in Vietnam and setbacks in Iraq meant that the USA was a weak power. While not without some force, if weak is replaced by limited, this argument ignores the extent to which defeat and setbacks not only helped shape empires (both geographically and by altering the attitudes that set parameters), but also provides a way to analyse their strengths, as well as weaknesses. In particular, a consideration of failure challenges the argument that structural factors inherently led to success.

To turn to diplomacy is to be reminded again that empires developed in co-operation with others, and that this played a major role in shaping military tasking. At the periphery, co-operation entailed relations with colonists, with conquered peoples, and with those beyond the pale of control, a category that ranged from Native American or Australasian tribes, to sophisticated Indian principalities. This process was not free from considerable difficulty. In 1719, when Charles Delafaye, Under Secretary in the Northern Department, drew attention to the threatening position for the British colonies in North America, and suggested that the plan for a seizure of St Augustine in Florida from Spain (with which Britain was at war) had merit, he wrote:

> It is the common cry that the French [then Britain's ally] by their new settlements [Louisiana] will quite surround our plantations in America, and may be soon masters of them when they please. Some little effort on that side, if it were feasible, would perhaps allay that clamour and also do real service. Mr. Secretary Craggs is charged to consult some of the Admiralty upon it. I verily believe our own colonies might furnish out such an expedition; but they are a pack of people envious of one another and rather seeking each others destruction than any public service.[21]

Indeed, it proved difficult to negotiate the desired level of support from the North American colonies. Nevertheless, co-operation from the colonists helped ensure the eventual defeat of France in Canada in 1758–60. Aside from the specific commitment of the colonies, in manpower, shipping and logistical support,[22] the knowledge that such help was an option encouraged the British government to act. There was no equivalent, however, to provide backing for the ideas that were floated for conquest of the Spanish colonies in South America, and this gravely weakened the 'Blue Water' strategy of trans-oceanic conquest as far as that area was concerned. The contrast between this and the successful conquest of Canada from France underlines the variety encompassed within particular strategies.

In considering co-operation within the Western world, there was also the important level of relations not simply with powers that were usually, yet not invariably, Britain's rivals, namely France and Spain, but also with states that might be willing to co-operate with or against these rivals, especially Austria, Prussia, Russia, Portugal and the United Provinces (Dutch), as well as with states that were unlikely to do either but that might still play a role, for example, from 1783, the USA. The analytical problems posed by this crucial irruption of contingent challenges and skilful or maladroit responses into the world of schema and structure[23] are for many resolved by the notion of the balance of power – so that other European states co-operated with Britain against the hegemonic threats posed by Louis XIV or Napoleon, with the British trying to do the same against France in the War of the Austrian Succession (1740–8). Other scholars similarly employ easy theorems to offer guidance through the complexities of international power politics: for example arguing that William Pitt the Elder conquered America (in fact, New France: Canada) in Germany, i.e. that co-operation with Prussia in the Seven Years' War (1756–63) brought victory.

These arguments are generally misleading, first, because they simplify national interests and, secondly, because they mistake the assertion of a policy for its analysis. To turn indeed to discourse, the balance of power was used for normative as much as, if not far more than, for descriptive purposes: it was an aspiration and a call for action in the polemic of public politics and the interplay of diplomacy, rather than an analysis of what had, was, or was likely to, occur.[24] In short, it offered neither policy nor strategy, and, outside the realm of public debate, could not readily link Britain's European and trans-oceanic interests. Furthermore, many did not accept the call for action against hegemony. Paul Schroeder was spot on in drawing attention to the willingness of rulers to accept defeat by Napoleon and to seek to co-operate with him,[25] and the same was the case with Louis XIV of France (r. 1643–1715), while the anti-Austrian league of despoilers created in 1741 were happy to pursue their own ends even if they led to a French-dominated Europe. During the Seven Years' War, France, Austria, Russia, Sweden and most of the Holy Roman Empire were willing to co-operate against Prussia, France indeed abandoning its alliance with the latter in 1756 in order to co-operate with the far stronger Austro-Russian alignment. Later in the conflict, Spain joined with France against Britain.

This willingness to ignore the theory of the balance of power created serious problems for British ministers opposed to France, and was an issue for commentators. For most of the period 1756–1813, as earlier in 1736–40, Britain was not part of the alignment of the most powerful European states, and had to decide whether, and how best, to respond: whether to be pro-active or re-active, and how to do so. The language of the balance of power was part of this response.

A structural approach to the problems facing Britain would focus on the search for a countervailing alliance by Britain, and there has indeed been useful discussion of what has been termed the Continental commitment.[26] This discussion has frequently been critical, with the argument that British ministers failed to appreciate developments in Continental power politics that made other states both disinclined to see French power and intentions as the prime challenge and unwilling to co-operate with Britain against them. From this perspective, Britain was weakened by the lack of an ally during the War of American Independence (1775–83),[27] but subsequently saved as Napoleon's inability to accept limits provided Britain with allies, so that the neutrality negotiated with Revolutionary France by Prussia and Spain in 1795 could not be sustained. The eventual victory of Britain's allies in 1813–14, particularly of the Austrian and Prussian forces that invaded France in 1814, ensured that, in the eventual peace settlement negotiated at the Congress of Vienna in 1814–15, Britain would be able to retain its colonial gains from France and its allies, as it had not been able to do with the Peace of Amiens with Napoleon in 1802.[28] In this approach, diplomatic skill was a matter of the coalition building that was unsuccessful or absent in 1763–86, and Britain's eventual global success was dependent on victory in Europe. As John, 2nd Earl of Stair claimed in 1743: 'Great Britain bestows the many millions she advances with no other intention but to secure herself and all the rest of Europe against the dominion of France.'[29]

This is a proposition worthy of consideration, but it needs to be debated rather than simply asserted. In particular, it is necessary to assess the argument alongside the suggestion that the Continental commitment was a cause of weakness, and that skill was best shown in limiting engagement with European politics; a very different relationship between policy and strategy to that generally advanced. From this perspective, the decision to abandon the Prussian alliance in 1762, in the closing stages of the Seven Years' War,[30] emerges as a wise move, as, for example, does the refusal of William Pitt the Younger's ministry to join Austria and Prussia in fighting Revolutionary France in 1792.[31] The latter indeed is an instructive commentary on misleading claims that Pitt was keen to commit Britain to Continental concerns and alignments.

The arguments in favour and against intervention require a willingness to engage with the politics of Continental states in order to assess the viability of an alliance, and, more particularly, of the prospect of the alliance serving British interests. From this perspective, British interventionism appears misplaced as, despite Britain's great naval and financial strength, the value that British commentators placed on alliance with Britain was not generally shared abroad. Indeed, it was weak and vulnerable powers, such as Portugal in 1735 and 1762, and the Dutch in 1747–8 and late 1792, who were most willing to seek assistance and to pursue alliances; while others, such as Russia in the 1760s, were only willing to offer terms that were unacceptable to Britain, with reference to both the subsidies expected and the guarantees demanded.[32]

A defence of non-interventionism has to address British failure in the War of American Independence, as well as the question whether it would have been appropriate for Britain to let France dominate the Continent and, in doing so, be in a position both to seek to deploy the navies and colonial resources of other Continental powers, the Dutch, Spain and Portugal, a goal sought by the French Revolutionaries and Napoleon, and also to block trade with Britain. In the case of the War of American Independence, the impact of the lack of an ally to engage France, however, should not be stressed because Britain had failed anyway to win prior to French entry into the war in 1778: not only had British leaders and forces been unable to translate battlefield success, particularly in Canada and on Long Island in 1776, and at Brandywine in 1777, into an ability to impose their will on their opponents, but they had also experienced serious setbacks, especially being obliged to abandon Boston in 1776, and surrendering an army at Saratoga the following year.

Although French intervention was to lead directly to British defeat at Yorktown in 1781, it is unclear that Britain could have won irrespective of French participation in the war and, indeed, Yorktown. Thus, the claim that, had Britain had Continental allies, they would have distracted France provides no guidance to the course of the war in North America. Instead, a war on the Continent involving Britain might have exposed Hanover to threats, as in 1741, if not invasion, as in 1757. In the event of such a conflict, the alliance between Austria and France would have left Hanover very exposed, and, anyway, there was little prospect of refighting the Continental stage of the Seven Years' War. A wider war might also have led to the Bourbons putting pressure on Portugal, as in 1762.

Indeed, when Britain did have Continental allies, that did not prevent French preparations for intervention in the British Isles: on behalf of the Jacobites in 1744, 1745–6 and 1759, and, after a failed attempt on Ireland in 1796, a landing in support of Irish rebels in 1798. This intervention was not successful, which suggests that too much should not be made of the French role in the War of American Independence; although, in each case, it is necessary to allow for specific factors, and it is difficult to read from one instance to another. It is certainly inappropriate to contrast British success in North America during the Seven Years' War with failure in the next conflict, as if the former proves the value of allies. In the first, the outnumbered French in New France (and the West Indies, India and West Africa) were, like the British, an imperial force heavily dependent on maritime links that could be severed, and vulnerable to amphibious operations, whereas, in 1775–83 in the Thirteen Colonies, Britain was opposed by indigenous revolutionaries who could lose port-cities, such as New York (1776), Newport

(1776), Philadelphia (1777), Savannah (1778) and Charleston (1780), and still fight on. A more appropriate comparison with the War of American Independence is with Pontiac's War with Native Americans in 1763–4, which indicated the limitations of the British army in operations in the interior; as, later in the decade, did British setbacks in India in the First Mysore War of 1767–9.

A focus on India is instructive, as it draws attention to the weakness in the Europe-overseas link offered by pro-interventionists who claim that strength in the former, in the shape of an effective alliance system, led to success in the latter. The French were able to mount their most convincing challenges to the British in India in the late 1740s, under Dupleix, and again in the early 1780s, under Suffren. In neither case was France troubled by conflict with any European ally of Britain (although Britain had such allies in the late 1740s), whereas Britain was able to defeat Tipu Sultan of Mysore in 1799, and to force the Marathas to peace in 1806, when France was otherwise engaged in Europe. As already mentioned, this kind of approach, however, is flawed because it misleadingly isolates one element and fails to offer comparisons with due caution. Irrespective of France's Continental commitments, there were important constraints on her intervention in India, most particularly the strength of the British navy, the logistical problems facing intervention (including the high death rate among French troops shipped to the Tropics), and the availability of naval bases en route and in Indian waters.[33] The role of the British navy was readily apparent in the destruction of the French fleet in the Battle of the Nile on 1 August 1798, a success that, like Nelson's other victories, did not stem from contributions from Britain's allies; although Egyptian and Turkish forces played an important role in opposing French moves in Egypt and Israel/Palestine. Nelson's victory in 1798 isolated Napoleon's force in Egypt, and thus wrecked plans for a France–Egypt–India axis that pre-dated the French Revolution.

The alliances that were most useful in British imperial expansion were not those with European powers, but rather with Indian ones (and certainly not the improbable alliance with the Moors that Tyrawly proposed in 1738, with the navy to ferry over a Moorish army to recapture Granada).[34] British commanders in India needed to be able to recruit local manpower and required local logistical support. In addition, they were, in part, dependent for cavalry on local allies, while, even more, they needed to prevent native princes from co-operating against them. Thus, in the 1790s, it was necessary in the two wars waged with Tipu Sultan of Mysore (1790–2, 1799) not also to have to fight the Maratha Confederation and/or the Nizam of Hyderabad at the same time. The sequencing of conflict was important.

The intricacies of Indian politics did not, however, recommend themselves to commentators in Britain who preferred to debate policy within a world defined by rivalry with France; a parallel to the somewhat implausible character of part of the debate in the Warren Hastings case (1788–95) over the ethics of British rule in India (as if Western moral guidelines provided clear indications). The definition of policy in terms of rivalry with France, in fact, provided few guidelines for British policy in India. This definition also helped cause confusion when the British government focused on hostility to other European powers, as then there was little basis in public politics for defining policy goals and appropriate courses for action. This was particularly the case with the Ochakov crisis with Russia in 1791, but was also seen with discussion about the response to the First Partition of Poland in 1772. From the perspective of most British commentators, these were unexpected irruptions into an established diplomatic world arranged in terms of rivalry with France and Spain, although, from the 1710s, there had, in fact, been periodic concern about Russian expansion and intentions, especially in the late 1710s and the 1720s, but also in 1762.

Worry about Russia by 1791 related to the fate of the Ottoman (Turkish) empire, and, looking forward, to the concerns of the nineteenth century. This was already linked to anxiety about the route to India. In the 1710s, the situation had been very different, for public concern had focused not on that very specific issue, but, rather, on the more general question of the impact of Russia's rise under Peter the Great (r. 1689–1725) on the balance of power and on British trade with the Baltic. Driving Russia from its Baltic gains could be justified from the British perspective by arguing that it should be denied the chance to be a naval power.[35] Between the 1710s and 1791, the geopolitics of British concern altered dramatically; and this shift toward India was also associated with the transformation of the amorphous entity that can be defined as the British imperial state. Furthermore, the interests of 'Hanover', in other words of the King as Elector of Hanover, played a major role in the government response to Russian power in the late 1710s and early 1720s, but was not a comparable issue in 1791, although George III's hostility to Catherine the Great was believed to play a role in Anglo-Russian relations.

Both cases indicated the role of politics. In 1791, the Russian envoy, Count Vorontsov, found willing allies among the opposition for his attempt to stop Pitt the Younger's policy of intervention against Russian expansion at the expense of the Ottomans.[36] In the late 1710s, the Hanoverian concerns of George I, particularly his desire to secure the acquisition of the duchies of Bremen and Verden from Sweden, and his fears about the consequences for Hanover of the hostile links and intentions of the Russian-backed Dukes of Holstein-Gottorp and Mecklenburg, helped not only to determine British policy but also to divide the British ministry. This is a reminder that the role of contingency was intertwined with the character and extent of the foreign policy debate.

In both the cases cited, there have been attempts to defend government policy that make the opposition appear opportunistic, if not worse. This indeed is a process that goes back to the period when the governments of George I and George II sought to link foreign rivals and domestic critics, and further to condemn both by arguing that they sought to foster a Jacobite return. In addition, in 1791, the government, correctly, drew critical attention to links between the Foxite opposition and Catherine the Great, not least with reference to the mission of Robert Adair to St Petersburg. These criticisms had considerable weight, and indeed drew attention to a major area of constitutional uncertainty – the conduct of opposition in foreign affairs, indeed its legitimacy in this sphere; but they deliberately underplayed the extent to which government itself was divided over policy. The determination of George I to pursue Hanoverian goals split his ministry in 1717, provoking a serious opposition by hitherto loyal ministers – Charles, 2nd Viscount Townshend, and Robert Walpole; while the Ochakov crisis led to a Cabinet crisis, a change in policy, and the resignation in protest of the Foreign Secretary, Francis, 5th Duke of Leeds.

Thus neither crisis can be seen, without serious qualification, in terms of an informed ministry, conversant with national interests, and prescient about the danger from Russia, but opposed by factious politicians lacking such qualities. This *a priori* assumption about debates over foreign policy badly fails to understand the views of critics and to appreciate the extent to which ministries were split or put under tension by foreign policy. Divisions and tension indeed helped jeopardise Whig unity, and, at times, stable ministerial control, under George I and George II. This accounts for the importance of George III's abandonment of his grandfather George II's strong psychological commitment to Hanover, a shift that was made clear in his lack of interest in territorial acquisitions for Hanover at the close of the Seven Years' War.

George III was subsequently to show support for Hanoverian interests, for example with his membership, as Elector, in the Fürstenbund (League of Princes) of 1785, but never with the intensity, nor divisive consequences, seen under his two predecessors. There has been valuable scholarship on the Hanoverian dimension of his policy, but it needs to be put in context. Not only is there the obvious contrast with his two predecessors, but also the episodic nature of the King's interest in Hanover was different in kind to his far greater concern to defend his royal prerogatives and self-image as King in response to demands for, first, clear self-government for the American colonies and, later, Catholic Emancipation. George III's emphasis on order, authority and the position of the Church of England made these issues particularly important to him.

Reviving interest in debates over policy, specifically the value of an interventionist foreign policy, helps link the eighteenth century to the position today, and serves as a reminder that the course of policy was by no means clear. Some of the debate was, to a degree, abstract, as, in many cases, there was scant sign that it would lead to action. Indeed, a problem with the discourse approach is that it can devote not only disproportionate attention to conventional remarks, that were essentially platitudinous, but can also fail to appreciate what were key debates and contributions, in part because they were atypical. The same, of course, can be true of analysis of the documents: ministers lost nothing in instructing diplomats, who were anyway at their post, to express a desire for better relations. To castigate this as a foolish misunderstanding of possibilities can be to devote disproportionate weight to such conventional remarks. At the same time, a need-to-have approach to policies has to take note of the extent to which ministers felt it necessary, within a general context of uncertainty, to prepare for eventualities.

Difficult as it is to analyse the ministerial and public debates over policy, these debates serve as a valuable reminder of the need to consider the processes of policy-formation and evaluation, rather than the structures that can be made to appear to have pre-determined policy and success. The weakness of the determinist approach, indeed, has several facets, not least a lack of clarity as to whether it was descriptive or, indeed, prescriptive. Whichever view is taken, needs to confront the difficulties contemporaries encountered in understanding pressures and processes.

Furthermore, aside from the important role of politics in contemporary perception, understanding and analytical concepts, this was not a static situation. Aside from the unpredictability of events, an interest in Britain especially in the closing decades of the century in reform contributed to a sense of flux, and to an idea that varied judgements and criteria were possible, even if only some were presented as normative.[37] In addition, there was a general downgrading of theory during the period, with facts (and thus the perception of what had happened), instead, becoming more important, not least as the notion of applied knowledge acquired definition and prestige, especially thanks to the development of political arithmetic and political economy. Rather than taking the state as the prime mover in the world of information flow and debate, it is appropriate to note the extent to which government was responding to wider social, cultural and intellectual currents. In particular, there was a intellectual shift towards a situation in which information, rather than received wisdom, had greater currency, both as a source of authority and as a practical guide to policy-making. This shift is generally treated as an aspect of the history of science, but in fact was far wider in its sources and applications. In the British case, what was termed political arithmetic was particularly important. It served as a valuable guide to policy formulation, execution and explication in the world of public politics that followed the 'Glorious Revolution' of 1688–9 and the subsequent creation of a politico-governmental system in which annual sessions of Parliament were a central aspect of the political process, while accountability to Parliament became more significant for government.

Numbers acquired a set of connotations that made them central to what counted as knowledge in numerous domains, for example, in the case of international relations, the balance of power. Irrespective of popularity and acceptability, however, the shift from using information in policy discussion to policy prescription was but partial, particularly prior to the nineteenth century.[38] The popularity of the policies advocated, and of their sponsors, was more significant. For example, whatever the information offered, one limitation greatly affecting critics of the 'Blue Water' emphasis on naval strength and, increasingly, trans-oceanic interests, was the widespread sense that war was likely to break out with the Bourbons (the rulers of France and Spain). There was little emotional support for the notion of preparing, either in diplomatic or in military terms, for conflict with any other power.

The social dimension of the information flow was a broadening of the tranche of society that comprised the 'political nation': those who expected to be aware of, and to have a view on politics. In part, this was due to the political transformation resulting from the 'Glorious Revolution', but, again, far more was at issue, not least a greater sustained public curiosity about the outside world that, in part, reflected a different attitude to news that, in turn, affected the demand for information. In particular, although they remained very important, the role of community agencies – families, kindred, localities, confessional and economic groups – in formulating and disseminating news, became less significant than external agencies. This was a long-term process, to which the role of state-directed religious change during and after the Reformation contributed greatly, but key elements were the increasing literacy that facilitated information demands, and the extent of socio-economic change and opportunity that encouraged interest in the world outside the locality. After the lapsing of the Licensing Act in 1695, the expansion of the press met this need and, in turn, created a daily system of comment on events.

The British state had greater authority than its modern European counterparts, for example in religious and moral matters, but, in many respects, its power was less. In particular, the small size of the bureaucracy ensured that governance depended on co-operation as well as a measure of consent, and, in the field of information, the government lacked the means to dominate the provision of news and opinion. Pro-government newspapers and pamphlets were funded, but there were no opportunities for the totalitarian news-management to be seen in the twentieth century. Instead, government attempts to affect the nexus of news and opinion reflected not its strength, but rather its weakness.

For much of the period, this weakness was accentuated by, and focused on, particular challenges: specifically to the legitimacy of the government and the security of the state from domestic and external threats. In the first case, the key problem stemmed from the 'Glorious Revolution', for the expulsion of the male line of the Stuarts, in the person of James II and VII (r. 1685–8), was far from consensual. Issues of legitimacy were made more serious in security terms when, as with Jacobite plotting, they interacted with specific domestic and/or international crises. The dynastic challenge remained militarily significant within Britain until the defeat of Charles Edward Stuart at the battle of Culloden in 1746 and, in international terms, until the naval victories of Lagos and Quiberon Bay in 1759 smashed a

French invasion plan. This challenge affected British strategy, Thomas, Duke of Newcastle warning in 1757, 'If we should send away a great, and perhaps the best part of our army out of reach, and call, we may not be able to replace them either at home, or from any quarter from abroad'.[39] Issues of legitimacy after 1759 were not dynastic in character, but their seriousness was readily apparent, particularly with the civil war within the empire known as the American War of Independence, and subsequently with the crisis caused by radicalism in the shadow of the French Revolution, especially with the Irish rising of 1798.

For government, influencing the public debate over policy played an important role in confronting crises and in maintaining support for policy. It was also necessary to ensure a positive foreign perception of developments. Furthermore, it was seen as helpful to try to limit accounts of developments abroad that would encourage disaffection within Britain or, at least, challenge the sense of confident power on which the strength, and therefore purpose, of government greatly depended.

The need for information, by both government and political commentators, and for news-management, varied greatly. It was pronounced when Britain was taking an active, interventionist stance in Continental power politics, as in the 1710s, late 1720s, early 1730s and 1740s. Conversely, a relatively isolationist stance, as in the late 1760s and early 1770s, ensured that the need was less. Nevertheless, there was then the requirement for government to demonstrate that its failure to act, when for example the French purchased Corsica in 1768 or the First Partition of Poland occurred in 1772, did not betoken an inability to discern and defend national interests.

Interventionism also required information if the government was to adopt the appropriate policy and to be able to defend it. This was particularly so as such interventionism depended on a successful interaction with other states and on an adroit operation of the mechanisms available for power politics. Both were made more complex for British ministers (and commentators) because in most states there was scant role for public politics. Instead, foreign policy was a mystery of state, formulated in conditions of secrecy in court contexts riven by factionalism. Issues of *gloire* and dynastic interest played a major role in policy. These and their application were difficult to discern, not least given the kaleidoscopic character of alliances. In the case of military strategy, there were also the problems arising from the lack of a peacetime British planning agency drawing up contingency plans. The strategic unity of the disparate problems facing Britain proved contentious and elusive.[40]

The nature of decision-making in foreign states created major problems for British (and foreign) processes of description and assessment, as information was generally unreliable and random, both of which contributed to uncertainty in analysis and debate. Far from recognising clearly the intentions and actions of others in an international system, ministers and commentators operated in a context of opacity. Furthermore, it proved difficult to apply the systematic ideas then available: the balance of power, and the related concept of natural interests.

The ambiguity of these concepts interacted with the difficulty of acquiring accurate information about the plans of other states, and produced a situation of great uncertainty. Looked at differently, this resulted in a wide field for speculation. The flexibility with which information and analysis were employed in political debate helped ensure the value of the systematic ideas available – they could serve all sides – but also created difficulties, as there was a desire for precision. Indeed, the extensive use in discussion of the balance of power reflected in part the fascination with Newtonian physics, and its mechanistic structures and forces, and, more generally, with reason or rationality.

There was, however, an awareness of change and of the role of the vicissitudes of dynastic arrangements, the hazards of war, and all sorts of contingent fashions, all of which made international relations less calculable. The *Plain Dealer* of 7 December (os) 1724 claimed 'The measured lines of human foresight, which are so proudly distinguished by the name of policy are vain amusements and mere cobweb subtleties'. The *Weekly Miscellany* of 27 October (os) 1733 stated 'The great world . . . is of a piece with the little, and we see the sordid motives of present convenience and self-interest, in the one as well as the other, at several foreign courts, take place of a sense of honour and gratitude'.

Ministers and commentators tried to reduce these factors to order, to ensure that international relations could be perceived as calculable. Thus, intelligence and information were designed to provide the necessary level of predictability that would make analysis possible, and thereby validate the contemporary conceptualisation of international relations. Information thus helped make the system seem rational, indeed gave it its systematic character, and, in turn, apparently made it possible to analyse and predict developments rationally: rationality understood in terms of predictable cause and effect relations. If information could provide evidence of passion, greed, inertia and other 'irrational' forces at work, it could also make them comprehensible, and thus manageable within the wider context of a predictable system.

Knowableness was the key, as any emphasis on uncertainty challenged the possibility of ensuring order, peace, and, in British eyes, the national interests bound up with these. William, Lord Grenville, the experienced Foreign Secretary, noted in 1798 that international relations in Eastern Europe, and British policy toward the region, had changed dramatically from the Ochakov crisis of seven years earlier:

> We are concluding an alliance with the Porte [Turks], in conjunction with Russia, which I certainly never thought I should live to see, much less to be an active instrument in, when in 1791 I came where I am. We

are silly creatures with all our deep speculations, and our reasonings, and our foresights.

He then quoted from Horace's *Odes* (III, 29–30): 'God buries in misty night the outcome of future time', adding that it

> is better philosophy than one thinks when one first reads it, full of confidence in all that one is to do, and to see, and to foresee – But then I doubt whether because this sentiment is just, the right conclusion from it is that we have nothing to do in this world but to drink and to – [sic].[41]

Grenville's letter captured the tension between the attempt to shape events and the extent to which they defied shaping, in short the triumph of a realism about the limitations of calculation, over confidence in the predictive nature of developments and policy initiatives. Yet, as he pointed out, as the response could not be to do nothing, so it remained important to use the calculation that information permitted to lessen the odds, or, at least, to counter the sense of uncertainty and helplessness. In terms of the different philosophies of foreign policy, intelligence-gathering therefore played a major role in both Whig and Tory assessments (see pp. 39–42).

If this situation did not present enough of a pressure on the provision of intelligence and the flow of information, it was accentuated by the spreading international concerns of the British state. This was a dual process. First, the European political system changed both to incorporate a relatively distant state (Russia) and to ensure that conflict, or the risk of conflict, with other European powers arose from trans-oceanic disputes (particularly over the Ohio River country with France in 1754–5, the Falkland Isles with Spain in 1770, and Vancouver Island with Spain in 1790). Secondly, it was necessary to consider more non-European powers, as British interests expanded, first, and in particular, in India, and then in the Malayan Peninsula (1786), with, subsequently, in 1792–4, an attempt to improve relations with China.

The resulting pressure on information was acute, and in the case of North America in 1755, the system failed, as the British and French governments found it impossible to agree on the cartography of the area in dispute.[42] Similarly, in the Ochakov crisis with Russia in 1791, there was a lack of clarity about the strategic importance of the fortress of Ochakov, and, in particular, about the extent to which it dominated the estuaries of the Rivers Bug and Dnieper. This led to an attempt to secure expert advice, and to a controversy between diplomats.[43] Given this dissension, it was scarcely surprising that parliamentarians and newspapers also disagreed about the importance of the fortress, as well as about the relationship between Russian gains and the balance of power. The problem facing parliamentarians discussing remote districts was mentioned by Richard Brinsley Sheridan, a leading opposition MP as well as a playwright, who referred to the pro-government Sir William Young as having 'expatiated with as much familiarity concerning the Dnieper and the Danube, as if he had been talking of the Worcestershire canal'.[44]

This dispute looked toward the nineteenth century, as did the Nootka Sound crisis over Vancouver Island of the previous year. Ministers, politicians and commentators struggled to make comprehensible a wider world, and sought to understand its interactions. Existing institutional and intellectual strategies proved to have only limited value. Government responded by leaving a large margin of discretion in policy (and thus policy analysis) to local agents. This was to be characteristic of much of the imperialist age, until the technology of telegraph, railway and steamship encouraged a sense of immediacy that corresponded to Victorian system-building and to the expectation of an application of moral principles, ensuring new ethos and practices of interventionism and a drastically revised demand for, and provision of, intelligence and information.

An emphasis on ideas, as on structures, as if they determined (as opposed to helping to explain) policy and success is wrong, as it rests on a misunderstanding of both policy and success. This is true not only for Britain, but also for other states. Indeed, one of the most important aspects of the re-evaluation of British foreign policy and imperial success is that it needs to rest in part on a more sophisticated understanding of developments in other powers and in what can be termed (although only if not used for structural determinism) the international system. Far too much of the work on Britain treats other states in unproblematic terms and, in particular, there is often a less than adequate assessment of the nature of the French state and the character and contents of French policy-making, and an assumption that British moves determined those of France: in short, that there was a readily manipulated (and analysable) move-and-response process. An instance of this is the argument that, had Britain not sent troops to Germany from 1758 during the Seven Years' War, then the French would have been able to mount a more convincing maritime challenge. In practice, such cause-and-effect arguments, whether employed in the eighteenth century or today, generally rest on an inadequate understanding of the process of French decision-making and the problems of decision-implementation.

A similar process of inquiry needs to be extended to non-European powers, and, in particular, Eurocentric notions of relative capability and preferred development have to be critically assessed. In short, if Britain's rise to world empire is the subject, then the world has to be the object of scrutiny. This is particularly important in relating British policy in Europe to Britain's trans-oceanic position and in discussing the policy and strategy of the former in counterfactual terms.

There also has to be an assessment of the British imperial state which accepts its variety in interest and action. Alongside the consideration of aggregate interest and strength, which is the usual approach, frequently presented in somewhat crude terms of comparative advantage with regard to other states, should come an emphasis on the state as the amalgam of a number of very different constituencies and spheres, a point that emerges clearly in the case of the Continental commitment thanks to the interests, role and contentiousness of Hanover. Government, like information, debate, trade and the use of force, emerges as a dynamic element linking together these constituencies and spheres.

An organic description of the imperial state, like the mechanical (balance of power) one employed by contemporary commentators, poses a problem, however, as it makes the process appear misleadingly easy, which was not how it struck contemporaries. Many, instead, saw political practice, if not the British political system, as a bar to the good government necessary to protect, if not strengthen, the empire. In 1750, Rear-Admiral Charles Knowles, who had been Commander-in-Chief in Jamaica, complained to its Governor, Edward Trelawny, about the difficulties he had encountered in persuading ministers in London about the island's vulnerability to France or Spain, a sensitive point given the ministry's focus on Continental power politics, specifically the Imperial Election Scheme. When Knowles called on Henry Pelham, the experienced First Lord of the Treasury, the latter expressed his concern:

> but said, though the information I had given him was very satisfactory and necessary for him to know, yet it ought to have come through another channel (meaning the Duke of Bedford[45]). I did not think proper to let him know I had been with his Grace as his answer was 'He believed there might be a necessity for fortifying the island but where was the money to be found, for his part he had nothing to do with money matters, that was not within his Department. They lay with Mr Pelham. I must go to him and see what he said, for he would not ask a thing where it might be denied.' . . . animosities at present run so high between the Pelhams [Henry and his brother, Thomas, Duke of Newcastle] and the Duke of Bedford that the disposal of all the great offices vacant is postponed . . . and all other affairs of consequence are at a stand, each side seeming determined to transact no business with the other.[46]

If government was a dynamic element, with its own capacity to generate policy and strategy, it responded to, indeed often countered, other elements within both state and empire, many of which are not helpfully considered as anachronistic or particular. Instead, some of these elements were dynamic in their own way. Indeed, the state, like the empire, understood as both structure and process, has to be considered as deriving much of its activity and energy from its uneasy partnerships with other forces, partnerships that depended on often shifting bases of co-operation and legitimation, and that affected debates over policy. In classic terms, the crucial reconciliation was that of state, commercial interests, and landed orders, and the ability of government to link these different interests gave much of the particular character to the British state, not only in the British Isles but also in the empire, especially in the Thirteen Colonies. This process faced considerable difficulties, but the continued politicisation of social and economic difference, and the ability of government to act both as a sphere for peaceful contention and as a regulator, enabled the pursuit of interest without untoward strife.[47] The equivalent with Hanover was a reconciliation of British ministry and Hanoverian counterpart thanks to the King, and with much of British opinion attracted to this nexus by support for the Hanoverian Succession, but this relationship lacked the institutional framework and socio-economic foundation of that of state, commercial interests, and landed orders in Britain, and never came close to acquiring them.

Modern discussion of the purpose of government offers an instructive perspective for the consideration of the context of eighteenth-century decision-making, not least the role of the monarch and the impact of the Hanoverian link. While progress was understood, as it was for much of the twentieth century, in terms of government-directed reform and the expansion of state power, then the eighteenth century was fitted into this process in teleological terms: indeed the development of modern or more modern state forms appeared its most important aspect in governmental terms, and there seemed to be a clear model set by the economic transformation described in terms of Agricultural, Transport and Industrial Revolutions. Thus, a governmental revolution was discerned, first in terms of fiscal developments and, then, more generally. The navy was described as the largest enterprise of state, and this appeared proof positive of the virtue of big government.[48] Policy and strategy were presented as products of this stronger state, and the capacity to pursue them its cause and consequence.

More recently, however, has come the notion that the size and strength of government are a burden on the productive economy and a problem for society. This offers an opportunity for rethinking much of the narrative and analysis of history, certainly the modernist perspective, and, as yet, this rethinking has scarcely begun.[49] Eighteenth-century Britain needs to be rethought in these terms, for, instead of arguing that early signs of modern government development were crucial enablers, it can be suggested that the state, certainly in the shape of an expensive war machine, the ability to mobilise a higher percentage of loan finance than France, and the resulting rise in the national debt,[50] was a serious burden.

This offers a problematic perspective on eighteenth-century policy and strategy, for their pursuit, particularly that of Continental commitments, can be seen as causing this serious burden. Equally, failures in the successful implementation of policy and strategy could greatly increase the burdens. This offers a way to look at the failure to maintain alliances in the eighteenth century, although some of these can also be seen as creating serious burdens of their own. The inability to secure or sustain alliance with Spain, with which Britain indeed was allied on occasion, for example in 1729–33, ensured that Britain needed to think in terms of a two-power naval standard, which increased the pressure on government finances and, eventually, public indebtedness. Thus, the failure of the state in the diplomatic field led to serious added burdens.

The cost–benefit analysis of the Continental commitment and of empire, and of particular policies and strategies for European relations and for imperial aggrandisement and security, can therefore be refocused, not least by underlining the value of meeting the costs of protection and expansion from local sources. While this was to be disastrous in the case of the North American colonies, it was very important elsewhere, not least in the suppression of opposition in Scotland and Ireland, and in expansion in India. That imperial expansion worked, at least in part, because its structure permitted such sharing, albeit on very unequal terms, and did not require a strong state, is one of the apparently counter-intuitive aspects of the subject. If it contrasts with the usual emphasis on the value of a strong publicly financed military system, that indicates the room for debate on how best to employ modern notions of the rethinking of the state, and also to understand the eighteenth century. An emphasis on the opportunities and problems of shared burdens also suggests a way to approach the coalition-building central to British interventionist policies and strategies for Europe, both in war and peace, not least the provision of military backing.[51] This emphasis also offers a perspective on the isolationist arguments in favour of limited intervention in Continental power politics, including the view that Britain should leave the Continental powers to balance one another.

2 Hanover and the debate over policy

It may be said, 'No party is against our taking a just concern in affairs of the Continent. The opposition that has been made is only to our embarking in them deeply' . . . but I have not yet heard it said; for if I understand any thing of common sense, the arguments of the gentlemen in the opposition to the present measures, tend to dissolve all kind of connections between us and other powers.

(Anon., *Reflections upon the Present State of Affairs . . . In a Letter from a Member of Parliament to a Constituent*, London, 1755, p. 25)

Politicians and political nation in Britain alike faced in the early eighteenth century a situation of great volatility. The benchmarks that had helped define policy and debate in the late seventeenth century – at home, the issue of Stuart intentions and, abroad, the response to the growing power of Bourbon France – no longer served as an appropriate response, although both still played an important role in the debate over policy. Instead, there were different issues: at home the workings out of the Revolution Settlement, the measures that followed the 'Glorious Revolution' of 1688–9, and, abroad, the consequences of major developments in the European system, in particular a shift of relative power east from Western Europe as Austria, Russia and Prussia became more powerful. The political contention over policy that followed the accession of the Hanoverian dynasty to the British throne in 1714 was set in these contexts, and much of the problem that faces discussion about the Hanoverian dimension rises from the difficulty in distinguishing the subject from the issues arising from these changes. This also helps explain why scholars have disagreed in their views, because there is no clear methodology available to address this difficulty. As a consequence, it is understandable that scholars come to clashing conclusions as a result of contrasting cause-and-effect models of the relationship between Hanoverianism and the wider domestic and international contexts.

To turn first to these contexts is not to ignore the role of the individual, the particular and the contingent in the course of British policy, but, rather, to be reminded of the complexity of the issues at stake, as well as the extent to which history did not begin in 1714. In terms of domestic politics, the legacy was a difficult one, and there was no clear, acceptable standard of royal behaviour by which George I (r. 1714–27) could model himself, nor by which he could be judged. The last exemplary monarch in public memory was Elizabeth I (r. 1558–1603), and, aside from the seriously distorting perspective of mythmaking, she had not faced the problems of dealing with a composite state spanning the North Sea, although opposition in Ireland during her reign had served as a pointed reminder of the difficulties of multiple statehood. These had been underlined in the shape of a broader British question under her first four Stuart successors, with the additional problem of serious suspicion about their domestic intentions.

William III of Orange (r. 1689–1702) had 'solved', or at least shelved, the British question through force, but, aside from the controversial character of his linkage of Britain to his interests in his native United Provinces, William's attitude towards his position as King aroused both concern and opposition. This led to a serious political storm in 1700 and, in the Act of Settlement of 1701, to what were intended as limitations on his eventual successors, the Hanoverians, the key one being 'That in case the Crown and imperial dignity of this realm shall hereafter come to any person, not being a native of this kingdom of England, this nation be not obliged to engage in any war for the defence of any dominions or territories which do not belong to the Crown of England, without the consent of Parliament'.[1]

In the meanwhile, Queen Anne (r. 1702–14) was personally more popular than William, particularly because political anxiety and anger were focused on her ministers; but many of the political issues that had faced him in the working out of the 'Glorious Revolution' remained acute. This was particularly true of the collective responsibility of ministers and of the relationships between party cohesion, policy formulation, and the choice of ministers. These issues were to erupt anew under George I, with the Whig Split of 1717,[2] but, although this ministerial and party division owed much to contention about George I's Baltic policy, the constitutional problems posed did not stem from this issue. Of course, looked at differently, political skill involves management within existing constraints, or shifting the parameters of the latter, and George was unable to do either in the late 1710s.

The long-term shift in the international system was the rise of Austria, Russia and Prussia. This receives most attention from mid-century, in particular with the diplomacy surrounding the Seven Years' War (1756–63), and the First Partition of Poland (1772),[3] but should be dated earlier. For Austria, the defeat of the Ottoman Turks outside Vienna in 1683 and the subsequent conquest of Hungary in 1684–99 and 1716–18 were crucial, as were the major gains made from the Spanish Habsburg inheritance as a consequence of the War of the Spanish Succession (1701–14), including Lombardy, Naples and the Austrian Netherlands (essentially modern Belgium). Russia benefited from the extent to which it, and not Saxony-Poland,

Denmark, Prussia nor Hanover, gained most territorially and geopolitically from the Great Northern War (1700–21) with Sweden, not least thanks to its establishment as a major Baltic power with the gain of Ingria, Estonia and Livonia.

The shifts in the international system created serious problems for Hanover, and helped ensure that alongside the theme of Hanoverian expansionism came that of Hanoverian security. Although interrelated, these were also different, and this had important implications for British foreign policy and for the debate within Britain about the impact of the Hanoverian connection. The political placing of Hanover in British public debate owed much to the original character and impact of the connection. A focus on expansionism was initially part of the Hanoverian optimum that began in 1714. That was the period of bright prospects: a new dynasty in Britain, established without resistance, rapidly overcame the attempt at a Stuart *revanche* in the '15. The British ministry negotiated, in 1716, an effective alliance with France that, while pushed hard for Hanoverian reasons, greatly lessened British vulnerability, particularly to further Jacobite conspiracies, but also to obligations stemming from the defence of the Low Countries. The ministers also formulated a peace plan for the Mediterranean that led to a spectacular naval victory over Spain (off Cape Passaro in Sicily in 1718), while Hanover itself looked set to benefit territorially from the partition of Sweden's trans-Baltic empire, a benefit seen not only in the gain of territory, but also in denying territories to other powers, especially Denmark and Prussia, its major rivals in north Germany.

Royal opportunism, however, helped to divide the Whigs, with ministers separating over George I's expectation of support for his Baltic policy; although differences over power in Britain and between George and his heir, the future George II, also contributed greatly to the Whig Split. This division did not stop George and his advisors from continuing with their policies, but the Hanoverian optimum ended in 1719–21, as the Stanhope/Sunderland ministry proved unable to retain or regain control of Parliament, while the bursting of the South Sea Bubble in 1720 caused a political as well as a fiscal crisis, and the attempt to intimidate Peter the Great of Russia into accepting the British peace plan for Northern Europe, and therefore returning conquered Livonia and Estonia to defeated Sweden, failed miserably.

There were parallel problems within the Hanoverian ministry. Furthermore, the Hanoverian acquisition of the duchies of Bremen and Verden from Sweden had proved to be not a speedy and clearly successful move but, rather, one that had led to lasting international commitments that proved difficult to limit, prefiguring the situation when Frederick II (the Great) of Prussia conquered Silesia from the Habsburgs (rulers of Austria) in 1740–1. More generally, from the late 1710s, in response, first, to Russia's Baltic policy, which threatened to exploit continued disputes over Mecklenburg, as well as the unsettled nature of the Sleswig question, and then to the Austro-Spanish alliance negotiated in 1725, there was a switch from expansionism to defence, setting a new agenda for the Hanoverian dimension of British foreign policy and for public debate.

A sense of Hanover as an incubus stemmed directly from the crisis of Baltic policy which began, but did not end, in 1716–17, as this aroused far more ministerial concern than the consequences of the French alliance. This concern also related to the way in which relations were handled, and Townshend complained about what he saw as Hanoverian mishandling of relations with Russia. In domestic British political terms, the French alliance was an embarrassment that in fact owed much to the Hanoverian Succession. However, until the parliamentary storm in 1730 over illicit and illegal repairs to the harbour at Dunkirk (in breach of the Treaty of Utrecht of 1713), that nearly led to the defeat of the Walpole ministry in the House of Commons, the French alliance did not challenge the government's conduct of foreign policy to the extent that Baltic policy did.

During the Whig Split of 1717–20, as well as in the 1740s and the mid-1750s at a time of later Whig divisions, the dynamic tension of interests that can be simplified in terms of Britain and Hanover became the focus of Crown–ministerial relations. It did so, however, in the context not of an established constitution with clear conventions, but of the testing out of new arrangements. When, for example, MPs debated whether Hessian subsidies were a breach of the constitution, on the grounds that British funds were used for the security of Hanover, it was far from clear how assertions to this effect were to be disproved.

Most of the details of Hanoverian commitments had only limited impact in the culture of print, unsurprisingly so as, although newspapers, such as the *St. James's Post* of 15 March (os) 1717, made efforts to provide information about Hanover, the British public knew relatively little about Germany. This did not alter during the Hanoverian period. For example, there was no increase in the learning of German. Indeed, in so far as knowledge of the outer world increased, it was knowledge of the expanding British empire, particularly the North American colonies, the West Indies and India. This needs to be borne in mind whenever there is an emphasis on cultural and intellectual links with the Continent, for example the cultural impact of the foundation of the Georgia Augusta University at Göttingen in 1734–7.[4] These, indeed, were important, but, in terms of the balance of interest, it was the extra-European world that played a greater role. This was an aspect of the expansion of the European imagination, an imagination that was particularly pressing for Britain due to its imperial role.

Thus, the implications of most of the Hanoverian commitments for Hanover, let alone Britain, were not widely appreciated outside diplomatic circles. This can be seen by considering George I's generally poor relations with the Wittelsbachs, the leading family of German Catholic rulers after the Habsburgs. Only one problem in these relations struck a resonance with at least part of the British public: George's championing of the Protestant cause in the Empire. This issue came to the fore in the late 1710s and early 1720s, when the Elector Palatine, Karl Philipp (r. 1716–42), was correctly accused of infringing the rights of his Protestant subjects, and George led the Protestant attempt to put pressure on him.[5] Already in 1716, the British envoy in Paris had been ordered by George, via Jean de Robethon, a Huguenot in the Hanoverian Chancery in London who was the protégé of Count Bernstorff, the leading Hanoverian minister, to back the Count of Hanau's interests in Alsace in which Protestant rights were involved.[6] The other Wittelsbach Electors (of Bavaria and Cologne) lent support to their Palatine relative, and the dispute served to embitter general relations between them and George, whom Wittelsbach diplomats criticised as the most troublesome of the Protestant rulers.[7]

The issue was closely related to another that had a far more tenuous link with British concerns, George's anxiety about the Wittelsbachs' attempts to fill as many German prince-bishoprics as possible: the ecclesiastical principalities were not hereditary, and on the death of each ruler a new one had to be elected by the Cathedral chapter. Clemens August, Elector-Archbishop of Cologne from 1723 to 1761, also succeeded an elder brother as Prince-Bishop of Paderborn and Prince-Bishop of Münster, both of which bordered Hanover. He also added the Prince-Bishoprics of Hildesheim (1724) and Osnabrück (1728), both of which also bordered Hanover. In Osnabrück, which, under the Peace of Westphalia of 1648, alternated between a Catholic and Protestant member of the House of Hanover, the clash between Clemens August's predecessor, George I's brother Ernst August, and the chapter had already led to tension in 1722 over the support the latter was receiving from the Imperial Aulic Council.[8]

Hanoverian attempts to prevent these elections, and Wittelsbach fears, sometimes unjustified, about such attempts, played a major role in ensuring poor relations between the Wittelsbachs and George I.[9] The Wittelsbach presence in the region limited Hanover's influence in the bishoprics, the best chance for Hanoverian expansion after the Great Northern War, compromising its ability to protect Protestant minorities, such as the inhabitants of the town of Hildesheim, whose municipal rights Hanover had guaranteed, blocked possibilities for annexing the bishoprics, and ensured that, in disputes between Hanover and any individual prince-bishop, the latter would be supported by the full weight of Wittelsbach influence. None of this meant much to British politicians, let alone the public, and diplomats regarded these matters as irritants.

A further issue bedevilling relations with the Wittelsbachs, and again meaning nothing in Britain, was the Hanoverian attempt to deprive the Elector Palatine of his office as Lord High Steward of the Empire, a prestigious post that reflected the determination of the rulers of Hanover to obtain the prestige they felt they deserved due to their recent gain of the Electoral honour and their even more recent royal status. This determination was an aspect of how an assertive dynasty irritated other powers.[10]

Given these tensions, it is not surprising that relations between George I and the Wittelsbachs were poor. From the British point of view, these poor relations played a role in helping to ensure the failure of Anglo-French attempts in 1725–6 to recruit the Wittelsbachs, especially Elector Max Emanuel of Bavaria, to the newly created Alliance of Hanover, and thus to weaken Austria. Disputes over the bishopric of Hildesheim, including border quarrels with Hanover, and over the treatment of a Wittelsbach representative in Osnabrück, further embittered relations, while Baron de Beveren, President of Karl Philipp's Court of Justice, who went to Hanover in 1725 when George was there, failed to find a solution to the disagreement over the Lord High Stewardship.[11]

This might seem to be an appropriate indication of the deleterious consequences of the Hanoverian connection for British policy, one moreover that archival research can recover, to lend substance both to contemporary claims of malign Hanoverian self-interest and to modern assertions of the importance of the connection. In 1726, Townshend informed Count Ferdinand Plettenberg, the leading minister of Clemens August, that he could not respond to his request for good offices over the Hildesheim differences as the matter was not within his brief,[12] in other words was a Hanoverian issue, but such differences in fact affected Britain's German policy.

The course of negotiations with the Wittelsbachs, however, also revealed that other issues that had a role independent of Hanover were at stake, serving as a reminder of the degree to which Hanover serves as a term to signify what in fact were the more varied and complex consequences of Continental interventionism. Some of these issues were German in character. Thus, Beveren was also sent to Hanover to prevent George from agreeing to support Frederick William I of Prussia over the inheritance to the duchies of Jülich and Berg, which he was contesting with the Wittelsbachs. George promised he would undertake no such engagements, but, in the fourth separate article of the Treaty of Hanover of 1725, Britain and France in fact committed themselves to the third signatory of the treaty, Frederick William, to support his claims.[13] As far as Max Emanuel of Bavaria was concerned, the more serious issue was a British unwillingness to back his schemes, either for his branch of the family acquiring the Imperial dignity after the death of the Emperor Charles VI (who had no male heirs), or for gaining territory from the Habsburg succession.[14] Furthermore, the refusal of the British government to meet Wittelsbach expectations of peacetime subsidies was also a major problem. Horatio Walpole, envoy in France as well as the brother of the leading minister, Robert Walpole, indeed claimed that such subsidies would be unconstitutional.[15]

Thus there was a range of reasons, each more important than the Hanoverian issues at stake, why the Wittelsbachs decided in August and September 1726 to accept Austrian offers. The vulnerable position of Bavaria vis à vis Austria was crucial in the decision of Charles Albert, the new Elector, while Clemens August had to consider Imperial support in further episcopal elections.[16] This underlines the multi-causal nature of relations.

Nevertheless, issues that can be categorised as Hanoverian were pushed hard. In late 1728, Townshend observed to Horatio Walpole, 'Your Excellency knows sufficiently already by all that the Duke of Newcastle and I have wrote to you, how nearly affected the King is with this proceeding in the business of Mecklenburg', a reference to a mandatory letter by Charles VI ordering the enforcement of a decree by the Imperial law court that entailed the removal of Hanoverian administration and troops from its neighbour Mecklenburg, whose Duke, Charles Leopold, had been driven into exile as a result of a serious dispute with the nobility, some of whom were influential in Hanover. Mecklenburg, indeed, was a matter of great sensitivity to George II, as it had been to George I. The issue led to British diplomatic efforts on behalf of Hanoverian interests. There was British pressure for help on her then ally, France, with the British ministry claiming that, should any power seek to drive the Hanoverians from Mecklenburg, George II would have the same right to the assistance of his allies, by the defensive clauses in the Hanover treaty, as if there was an attack on any part of his dominions (a claim the French understandably contested). In addition, the Wittelsbachs were pressed to include satisfactory promises of assistance over Mecklenburg in any agreement with George II.[17]

The current of Hanoverian concerns during the reigns of George I and George II was constant, as British ministers were only well aware. Evidence of the importance of Hanoverian interests can be taken forward by noting that in 1729, when an alliance between Britain and France on the one hand and the Wittelsbachs on the other was again under negotiation, Clemens August demanded that George settle his grievances over Hanoverian policy affecting the bishoprics of Hildesheim, Osnabrück and Münster, particularly the municipal rights of Hildesheim and the issue of the will of George's uncle, Ernst August, the previous ruler of Osnabrück, while, in turn, George was dissatisfied with the provisions for Wittelsbach support over Mecklenburg. At the end of 1730, a major quarrel over Hildesheim's municipal rights came close to conflict, and led to Wittelsbach anger with Hanover, which Townshend tried to assuage,[18] while, in turn, George was angry about a failure by the Wittelsbachs to support his interests at the Imperial Diet.[19]

Again, in 1729–30, as in 1725–6, Hanoverian factors can be seen as playing the crucial role in the failure of negotiations with the Wittelsbachs. Indeed, the trajectory of these negotiations can be related to Hanoverian goals. Initially, there was a wish for Wittelsbach military support, as well as backing in the Imperial Diet, especially over Mecklenburg, and the granting, by Clemens August, of permission for the French to move troops to Hanover's assistance. This led to a subordination of British interests, in the shape of proposals for British subsidies for the Wittelsbachs and a guarantee of the Jülich-Berg succession by Britain. However, in the winter of 1729–30 and the following spring, Hanoverian motives for the alliance diminished, due to signs of a reconciliation between George II and Frederick William I of Prussia, while the Hildesheim dispute and the absence of support at the

Diet were major irritants in relations between George, as Elector, and the Wittelsbachs.

At the same time, it is appropriate to adopt a wider perspective. Over Hildesheim, Stephen Poyntz, British envoy in Paris, expressed to his Bavarian counterpart, Louis-Joseph, Count Albert, his hope that 'the good understanding between His Majesty and the Elector of Cologne would not depend on such little incidents, since he could not but know that complaints of this kind were mutual'.[20] Irritants, indeed, were important, but less so than fundamental differences over Clemens August's demand for a peacetime subsidy.[21] This was a key issue in dispute, hindering alliances, not only between Britain and German powers that might have supported Hanover, but also, more generally, in Britain's negotiations with other European states throughout the century.

In addition, the Jülich-Berg issue was important because of the possibilities it offered, by failing to satisfy the Wittelsbachs, for an improvement in Anglo-Prussian relations. The range of benefits that might stem from such an improvement, the goal of the mission of Sir Charles Hotham to Berlin in 1730, indicates the difficulty of distinguishing British, Hanoverian and royal interests: an alliance with Prussia would isolate Austria in the Empire, helping Hanover, facilitate British negotiations with Russia, reduce British dependence upon France and the Hanoverian need for Wittelsbach support, lessen tension over Mecklenburg, and solve some of the matchmaking problems presented by George's numerous progeny.

It is useful to plunge early on into the detail of specific negotiations, because they serve as a reminder that the building blocks of events used for purposes of analysis and debate were in practice far more complex than is generally appreciated. This serves not to suggest that the course of events can never be recovered, and that all interpretations are of equal validity; but, rather, that great caution is required in trying to establish what happened, and, even more, why. In short, the significance of what is often treated as mono-causal evidence needs to be rendered more problematic. In part, this returns it to the contemporary context of contention and debate.

There were indeed reasons for such contention. Some were political in the widest sense in that they rested on ambiguous or contested constitutional points. The Act of Settlement of 1701, under which the Hanoverians succeeded, had stated that no war should be fought for the defence of interests that were not British without parliamentary consent, and that this consent should also be required before the monarch could leave Britain. The latter clause was repealed before George I's accession, and he visited Hanover on five occasions during his reigns – in 1716, 1719, 1720, 1723 and 1725 – without having to seek approval from Parliament, or from his British ministers, many of whom were unhappy about his long absences, and sought to limit them. In 1727, George I died on his way to Hanover. George II, who had left Hanover in 1714 and stayed in Britain while Prince of Wales, revisited the Electorate frequently once he became King: in 1729, 1732,

1735, 1736, 1740, 1741, 1743, 1748, 1750, 1752 and 1755. No other British monarch, however, went there until George IV did so in 1821, the last visit by a ruler of both Britain and Hanover.

These visits served as the basis not only for the reinvigoration of Hanoverian diplomacy, but also for the development and implementation of interventionist British schemes, as indeed also was to happen in 1821. During these trips, British ministers, as well as the monarch, met high-ranking Continental statesmen whom they were unlikely ever to see in London. Negotiations were facilitated, and time was gained, which was vital in any discussions involving more than two powers. In 1719, there was pressure for James Earl Stanhope, Secretary of State for the Northern Department, to make a trip from Hanover to Berlin in order to consolidate Anglo-Prussian links:

> Monsieur Ilgen wishes of all things you would make a turn hither, though it was only to dine with the King [Frederick William I] at his country house, go back immediately . . . he is sure it would have an extraordinary effect for the future, and considering what impressions little circumstances make on the temper of the Prince, and how hard it has been to remove by the most solid reasons and interest the prejudice of a few hours conversation with the Czar, I must really join with Monsieur Ilgen in his solicitations.[22]

While British ministers were in Hanover, it was also natural for them both to think of an active Continental diplomacy, in part in terms of Hanoverian interests, and to be aware of Hanoverian vulnerability. This was the case with Townshend in 1725 and 1729, Carteret in 1743, and Newcastle in 1748.

The provision in the Act of Settlement that no war could be fought for non-British interests without parliamentary approval was not reversed, and was, in theory, a major restriction on royal powers, greatly limiting any attempt to use British foreign policy for the support of Hanover. However, the terms of the Act of Settlement proved very ambiguous and unhelpful in practice. The relationship between royal rights as King, and obligations as Elector, constituted a new area for debate over the prerogative, one that was defined only after much disagreement.

The views of Georges I and II were most contentious politically in the late 1710s, with regard to Sweden and Russia, and in 1740–55, especially 1740–8, with regard to the Prussia of Frederick II, the Great (r. 1740–86). In both cases, this led to political disputes in Britain, as some ministers contested the royal interpretation of British interests. These criticisms have received insufficient attention, as the non-interventionist tradition of ministerial thought has generally been considered in terms of the financial concerns expressed by Walpole and Henry Pelham, who were the key First Lords of the Treasury under the first two Georges: for 1721–42 and 1743–54 respectively.

There were also, in fact, other intelligent reasons for doubting the wisdom of diplomatic initiatives and commitments arising essentially from the Hanoverian connection. Thus, with regard to opposition to Peter the Great in 1719–21, the Russian conquest from Sweden of Estonia, Ingria and Livonia could be presented as a challenge to British commercial interests in the Baltic. In practice, Russian economic growth was to be a fruitful basis for expanding British trade which was regularised with a trade treaty in 1734. Furthermore, whatever the supposed threat from Russia, it was not in Britain's interest to play the leading role in creating or sustaining an anti-Russian alliance of weak and divided powers. As a result of hostility to Russia from the late 1710s to the early 1730s, Britain was drawn into support of Denmark and meddling in Swedish politics, but securing the alliance of both faced serious problems, and neither power could contribute greatly to Britain's international situation, and certainly not to the extent of Russia.

While George I was most concerned about Russia, not least because of the marriage of relatives of Peter the Great to the Dukes of Holstein-Gottorp and Mecklenburg, both of whom had disputes with him, George II was more worried about Prussia. Under Frederick William I (r. 1713–40), the Prussian army appreciably increased in size. Furthermore, whereas Frederick William's relations with his uncle and father-in-law, George I, although not always close, were generally respectful, those with his cousin and brother-in-law, George II, began poor, rapidly worsened, and never really improved.

This gave a new direction to the legacy of confrontation left by George I. At his death in 1727, Britain, in alliance with France and the Dutch, was opposed to Spain, with which Britain had serious points in dispute over trade and Gibraltar, as well as to Austria, Prussia and Russia. None of the latter had serious points of dispute with Britain, but all of them were hostile until 1731, in large part as a consequence of the Hanoverian connection. Hesse-Cassel was paid a subsidy from 1726 until 1732 to hold 12,000 troops ready for the protection of Hanover and, in the face of domestic criticism and references to the Act of Settlement, ministers were obliged to argue that Hanoverian security needs arose from her dynastic link with Britain.[23] Hanover indeed posed in an acute form the problems of tension over commitments and terms common to all alliances. In 1757, at a time of Austrian attempts to ensure that George II as Elector was neutral, Holdernesse, then British Secretary of State for the Northern Department, commented 'the Court of Vienna have an affectation of treating with the King in his Electoral capacity only, and at the same time propose conditions directly repugnant to some of his engagements as King'.[24]

Aside from the issue of relations with Hanover, there was also the question of what the monarch could do with other aspects of British foreign policy, especially the legality and/or acceptability of peacetime subsidies for foreign powers, whether or not these were intended for the benefit of Hanover. The unfixed nature of the Revolution Settlement had been clear from the outset, and indeed the changes in 1694–1707, especially, but not only, the Triennial Act, the establishment of the Bank of England, the lapsing of the Licensing Act, and the passage of the Acts of Settlement and Union, were, in some respects, more significant than the constitutional changes in 1689. This situation did not cease in 1707, or 1714; and relations with Hanover in part should be considered in this context. The changes introduced, or attempted, in 1716–19, including the replacement of the Triennial by the Septennial Act, the repeal of legislation against Non-conformists passed by Queen Anne's Tory ministers, and the Peerage Bill, indicated the continuing willingness of Whig ministers to make substantial revisions.

From the perspective of George I, it was reasonable to expect the same men to provide support for his Baltic policy. This issue, which split the ministry in 1717, indicated, however, the problems of defining acceptable parameters. It was particularly difficult, in a period of rapid constitutional change, for ministers to argue that a given policy was unacceptable on constitutional grounds, not least when doing so risked serious royal displeasure. Instead, it was more appropriate to fall back on the arguments of political acceptability and prudent policy-making.

This indeed was the position of Robert Walpole, a minister from 1714 to 1717, and first minister from 1720 until 1742, who promised the monarch parliamentary management (and thus money), but, at the same time, used the exigencies of such management to urge restraint in governmental initiatives and demands. This was a far from easy process, but Walpole's defeat of his major political rivals within the ministry in 1720–2, a defeat further strengthened by additional ministerial changes in 1724–5, rested on the crucial governmental need for parliamentary support and, in turn, made his position easier. This led to a shift in the position of Hanover in British politics. The opportunities George I had sought, with the support of James, Earl Stanhope and Charles, 3rd Earl of Sunderland, the key ministers in 1717–20, were replaced, in his later years, by caution. This owed much to George's age, and to the lesser opportunities for expansion stemming from the international situation, especially, the end of the Great Northern War in 1721, but Walpolean politics also played a role. The restraint urged by Walpole over potential Baltic commitments in 1723 demonstrated this.

More generally, throughout the period, British ministers and commentators who depended on a conception of international relations, national interests and foreign policy as fixed were all challenged by the extent, pace and unpredictability of change. Culprits were sought for both the resulting uncertainty and for the problems arising from international developments. In Britain, as it was easy to attribute difficulties to what was new, so there was a temptation to attribute blame to the Hanoverian connection. In part, this was justified, as, at the very least, the connection created serious difficulties for British foreign policy, but, at this point, that is not the topic at issue. Instead, there is the question of the construction of blame. In many respects,

Hanover acted as the equivalent opposite to another geographical locator of blame, Utrecht.

The latter, a reference to the peace settlement of 1713, was used, from the Hanoverian accession in 1714, by pro-government spokesmen in order to query the loyalty and probity of the Tories, as a Tory government had brought Britain's participation in the War of the Spanish Succession to a close by negotiating the Peace of Utrecht, and, it was alleged, had jeopardised the Hanoverian Succession by abandoning Britain's allies, including Austria, the Dutch and Hanover. In 1741, in response to reiterated government references, the *Champion*, an opposition newspaper, asked 'Should the Treaty of Utrecht be eternally railed at?' In 1755, however, a pamphleteer repeated the argument that the breach of wartime alliances that the negotiation of the treaty had entailed was designed to help a Stuart *revanche*.[25] The emphasis on Utrecht also served to suggest that Whig critics of the government who co-operated with the Tories from the 1717 had abandoned crucial principles. Hanover served as a mirror-image, enabling opposition spokesmen to berate the ministry for failing to understand and/or defend national interests, and thus for being unfit to govern. This offered a valuable, and more 'modern', alternative to the notion of dynastic legitimacy as the *leit-motif* of political debate. Instead of focusing on the rights to the British throne of the Hanoverians (an issue that left little space for political debate, other than of a treasonable character), it was possible to ask whether the ministry was legitimate in the sense of sustaining the national interest.

This was an aspect of a more widespread European political development during the eighteenth century: the separation of ruler from nation, not least in terms of an automatic assumption that the identity and interest of the latter were submerged in the former. The causes of this separation were varied, including a lesser stress on the themes and idioms of sacral monarchy. In the case of Britain, the legacy of seventeenth-century constitutional struggles was a distinctive degree of dissociation of ruler from nation that was expressed in particular in the position and rights of Parliament. This dissociation was taken further with the accession of George I. His personality was limited, his charisma minimal, and his quest for popularity perfunctory. The journeys of both George and his successor, George II, to Hanover also represented a particularly clear dissociation of monarch from nation, and were highly controversial as a consequence.

That the Georges had responsibilities as Electors that were served by these journeys did not mean that their espousal of Hanoverian interests was not also free from serious criticism within the Electorate. This was an aspect of a more general question about the extent to which the dynasty, both as Electors and as Kings, were following goals that posed problems for their German subjects. In particular, the territorial expansionism they pursued as Electors, and the power politics they were involved in as Kings, as well as the implications for Hanover of the link to Britain, led to disquiet among the Hanoverian ministers, particularly over the Electorate's vulnerability. This was part of a more general tension between Elector and ministers that matched those of Crown and ministers, and that was neglected by contemporary British commentators. At the same time, it is important to note tensions within the Hanoverian ministry. While some aspects of this have been ably studied,[26] much still requires attention, especially for the 1730s.

To note a distinction between Electorate and Elector, and, also to explain the need for the Electors to consider the Electorate, does not, however, diminish the issue created for British politics and politicians by the Hanoverian link. Although a parallel was offered by the disquiet among the Hanoverian ministers, this disquiet was far more pronounced, however, in the case of Britain, not least because of the role of Parliament and the press there. The problem for the ruler of the balancing act among commitments required from the key figure in a personal union affected in particular George I and George II, and as both King and Elector, and, in both capacities, it strained political assumptions. At the same time, European rulers did not always make a distinction between Britain and Hanover. Instead, they could think of George I and George II as acting in one capacity, rather than two;[27] and British ministers and diplomats were well aware of the difficulties that arose as a consequence.

Indeed, a dynamic for the personal union was provided by the repeated difficulties confronted by the Electors. The affirmation or negotiation of peace, as in 1721, 1727, 1731, 1748, 1763 and, to a lesser extent, 1783, brought relief from difficulties or the prospect of them, but, for much of the period, Hanover was under threat, and there was a dangerous 'structural' factor in the international system: the rise of Russia and Prussia. These, especially the last, posed greater challenges to Hanover than the earlier 'great powers' that had intervened in north Germany in the seventeenth century: Austria, Denmark, Sweden and France. The rise of Prussia more than anything else defined Hanover's international situation, especially from 1740; and that is why attempts to blame the Electorate's difficulties on Britain, and therefore to argue that Britain owed support, are unconvincing. Tension was accentuated by George II's poor relations with his uncle by marriage, Frederick William I, and with his cousin, Frederick II. In turn, both Frederick William and his son were regarded as personally hostile to George. This was greater than the animus shown George III by Frederick II.

An instructive example of Hanoverian vulnerability is provided by the major crisis in the last years of George I's reign that stemmed from the confrontation between the Alliances of Hanover and Vienna which began in 1725 and lasted until shortly before his death in 1727. Government apologists argued that Hanover was exposed because of Austrian and Spanish grievances towards Britain, specifically respectively over British opposition to the Ostend Company, and over Gibraltar and trading interests in the New World. This claim ignored the extent to which the pursuit of Imperial authority under Charles VI brought George I into confrontation with Hanover, while the more specific defiance by George as Elector, an Imperial prince, aroused Imperial outrage. Through their postal interception and deciphering network, British ministers were aware that foreign ministers and diplomats were concerned about the relationship between Britain and Hanover, and also believed that, through the King, Hanoverian and, therefore Continental, commitment was pushed hard. In 1725, Karl Josef von Palm, the Austrian envoy, reported that British ministers had sought to present the Treaty of Hanover as a commitment by George I as both King and Elector. Palm was told by these ministers that George had entered the Treaty not as Elector but as 'a King of England who at the same time is an Elector and Prince of the Empire', and that 'no King of England, on account of his being a Prince of the Empire, can ever resolve to forbear taking the best care he is able of his English subjects, or neglect to make such leagues and alliances as may tend to be safety and welfare of the whole English nation'. Palm's account of the British ministers captured a fluidity in the presentation of the Anglo-Hanoverian relationship (and therefore to a degree in the relationship itself), as political requirements in Britain led to varied statements about the flow of commitment, about mutual obligations, and about the responsibilities of ministers: 'though they would take it very ill if in other cases one should make the distinction between the King and the Elector of the Empire, yet now their chief refuge and excuse depends upon the said distinction'. Giuseppe Riva, the Modenese envoy, who claimed to be close to Mehemet, George's confidential Turkish body servant, reported 'the King is overjoyed at the Parliament having engaged for his dominions in Germany'.[28]

The first crisis of Hanoverian vulnerability during George II's reign, that in 1729, owed nothing to Anglo-Prussian differences, but stemmed directly from Electoral differences with Prussia. George retaliated for vigorous Prussian recruiting policies, which infringed his rights as Elector, by arresting Prussian soldiers then in Hanover. Charles VI argued this was unreasonable as the soldiers had valid passports and were on the public way, but George claimed that the Prussian methods were a breach of the peace.[29] The two crises with France – in 1741 when invasion threatened, and in 1757 when it occurred – were responses to George II's policies as a German prince, rather than blows against Britain: in 1741 he was backing Maria Theresa of Austria, and in 1756, in pursuit of Hanoverian security, had allied with Frederick II. In contrast, when, in 1756, the French, in response to British policies in North America, wished to attack Britain in Europe, they invaded Minorca, not Hanover. Earlier, in 1740, in the first stages of the War of Jenkins' Ear with Spain, France had responded to the prospect of British gains from Spain not by threatening to invade Hanover, but by sending a fleet for dispatch to the Caribbean.

In both 1741 and 1756–57, in the very difficult circumstances of European power politics, George II found it impossible to control the consequences for Hanover of his policies in Germany. George's ability to push Maria Theresa toward compromise helped end the First Silesian War between Austria and Prussia in 1742, but this was a course greatly encouraged by Prussia's military success and by Austria's need to focus on other issues. In contrast, the context was far less conducive for settling Maria Theresa's differences with Charles Albert of Bavaria, and thus ending Franco-Bavarian co-operation. This did not cease until 1745 when Charles Albert died and his successor ended the conflict with Austria.

Both context and George II's ability to influence developments were also found wanting at the start of the Seven Years' War. Allied to Frederick in 1756, George found that he could not prevent Prussia from precipitating war in Europe, and thus exposing Hanover to attack and Britain to the collapse of its Continental alliance system.

That Frederick II was George II's first cousin added particular piquancy to the difficulties in their relationship. This dimension has been underrated of late because of the tendency to focus on structural factors and systemic elements when discussing international relations, but that analysis under-rates the extent to which the views of individuals still played a crucial role in policy. Aware of the rivalry, the opposition London newspaper *Old England*, in its issue of 1 August 1752, was being mischievous when it suggested that, as a Protestant, George should support Frederick (and not the Habsburg heir, the future Joseph II) as the King of the Romans, i.e. next Emperor.

In both the 1740s and the 1750s, once war had begun, Hanover had little to offer allies. It was vulnerable to invasion, and its army was small (a maximum in the 1740s of 26,471). The fate of Bavaria in 1742 and Saxony in 1745 during the War of the Austrian Succession, and of Saxony in 1756 in the opening campaign of the Seven Years' War, indicated that all second-rank German principalities could be readily overrun. An awareness of vulnerability also affected peacetime diplomacy by, and on behalf of, Hanover. It was reasonable therefore to see the Hanoverian connection as an incubus for Britain, and one made more serious by shifts in the international situation.

This, however, by no means exhausted the debate because, alongside the public sphere, was a private sphere of debate, one indeed that is generally neglected. This private sphere was the world of ministers and diplomats, and bar for public breaches, as with the Whig Split of 1717–20, or Pitt the Elder's movement into opposition in 1754–5, this debate left little trace in the public world. Its focus was also different. Instead of an emphasis on obvious differences of interest, and a language of clarity and outrage, came a stress on detail and a concern about the content of policy.

Although these strategies and spheres of debate can be segregated for purposes of analysis, they, in reality, overlapped, and part of their political importance rested on this overlap. For example, the consequences of the public debate could serve to accentuate divisions within the ministry, while an awareness of the latter could play a role in this debate. Further-more, the far from fixed nature and consequences of any overlap made it more important politically. This was also true of the confusion of means and ends. For example, Continental interventionism tended to involve both subsidy treaties and, in wartime, an emphasis on the British army, both of which were unpopular, while, in contrast, naval armaments were popular,[30] indeed seen as British, and this affected discussion of the goals for which they were intended.

In office (1714–17), in opposition (1717–20), and, returned to office (1720–42), the career of Robert Walpole illustrated these tensions within the government. As so often in the period, however, it is important to note the character of, and lacunae in, the sources. Much Walpole correspondence survives, but most of it is on patronage matters, and we only glimpse his views on foreign policy episodically and, frequently, at second-hand. The particular episode that commands attention, because it bulks large in the surviving sources, is Walpole's role in preserving British neutrality in the War of the Polish Succession (1733–5). Aside, however, from the one-sided nature of the sources (we know very little directly of George II's views),[31] it is unclear how far we can use this episode to provide a more wide-ranging analysis. This is a reminder of the more general need for specificity in discussion and analysis, and of the related hazard of arguing from particular instances to a general account, and then back from that general account to explain both those and most/all other instances.

Allowing for these caveats, it seems the case that Walpole had a clear-cut assessment of national interest in which the Hanoverian commitment appeared as an add-on. This, however, was an add-on made necessary by the monarch, not only due to the monarch's role in the operation of the political system, but also because Walpole was a committed Whig, and Hanoverian rule guaranteed the Protestant constitutional settlement that the Whigs sought to maintain. This conception of the interests involved in the Hanoverian connection separated it from any general discussion of the virtues and disadvantages of Continental interventionism and, indeed, they were different to Walpole. Despite this great value derived from Hanoverian rule, Walpole like other ministers, even an enthusiast for interventionism such as Thomas, Duke of Newcastle, a Secretary of State from 1724 until 1754, and then First Lord of the Treasury until 1756 and from 1757 to 1762, treated the add-on of Hanoverian commitments[32] both as not terribly welcome necessities, and as undertakings that could, and should, be judged in terms of prudential considerations of benefit and cost. The general discussion of policy attracts more interest from scholars concerned with public debates, but Walpole's more narrow conception, both of British interests and of the diplomatic strategies to be employed in pursuit of them, is one that needs to be recovered in order to appreciate the range of responses possible to the Hanoverian connection.[33]

A recovery of the range of responses challenges the somewhat Manichean presentation of the debate over the pernicious, or other, implications of the Hanoverian connection. This is generally in terms of a dichotomy between Whig ministries committed to the connection pursuing a foreign policy based on a sound assessment of needs and benefiting from the connection, and, on the other hand, retrograde Tory xenophobes apparently unable to understand wider national interests or to respond sensibly to international developments. Such a presentation is a travesty of the Tory view, not least because it crudely simplifies the latter and underrates the degree of Tory knowledge of international relations, but also fails to appreciate the extent of critical Whig views. The travesty of Tory views is serious as it reflects and sustains an inability to understand the character of the public debate. More seriously, treating critics of the Hanoverian impact as Tories, and therefore *ipso facto* foolish, and presenting modern scholars who assess this view sympathetically in the same light, is seriously distorting.[34] It is adopting the perspective of a particular Whig tradition of interventionism, and also failing to understand the degree to which Stanhope, Townshend, Carteret and Newcastle saw the support of Hanover as an integral aspect of this interventionism largely because they regarded threats to the Electorate as a challenge to the policy and not because they saw Hanoverian goals as benign. More generally, as a consequence of failing to appreciate the debate, it is difficult to grasp the context within which British ministers responded to options.

Adopting another approach, it is possible to probe the archives in both Britain and Germany in order to throw extensive light on contemporary criticism of the impact of the connection. This is valuable at a functional level, but fails to address adequately the ideological character of the link. The Hanoverian Succession was a direct consequence of the application of political anti-Catholicism to dynastic ends in a monarchical society. From that perspective, functional problems that arose as a consequence were very much secondary. However, political anti-Catholicism was far more acceptable (and definable) in the defensive context of preventing a Stuart *revanche*, rather than in providing a rationale for pro-active policies; and this created a problem in defending policies that arose from the Hanoverian connection, and therefore, to a degree, the connection itself. This was overridden to an extent during the reign of George I, when the unattractive public implications of the alliance with France from 1716 were, to an extent, shadowed by the rhetoric of anti-Catholicism and the reality of Jacobite attempts: the '15, the '19, and the Atterbury Plot.[35] Such a rhetoric was particularly seen in the early 1720s, in response to Catholic zealotry, for example in the Palatinate and Poland, and, even more, during the confrontation between the Alliances of Hanover and Vienna from 1725, in which Britain, allied to France and, initially, Prussia, was opposed to Austria and Spain.

Yet, on the whole the Hanoverian connection was not followed by a Protestant foreign policy. Far from it: Hanover's major rival, especially from 1726, was Prussia, a Protestant power that made much of its animosity to Austria, and often identified this with the Protestant cause. Indeed, Hanover depended for its security on the support of France until 1731,[36] and thereafter, albeit to a very varied extent, George II, as both King and Elector, sought to protect Austrian interests, or, at least, his conception of these interests, until 1756.

This was a prudent policy, but, although the defence of the Hanoverian Succession in Britain made it possible to present policy as Protestant, it scarcely conformed to a confessional ideology. In the absence of a Protestant foreign policy, there were few available defences for foreign policy. The most common, that of the balance of power, joined an ideological justification of policy to that of prudence. Defences of British foreign policy in terms of the balance of power, however, invited criticism both on the prudential terms of the difficulty of applying the theory in policy terms, and in specific conjunctures. Furthermore, the relationship between the Hanoverian connection and the balance was sufficiently vague to invite the rejoinder that it was not relevant,[37] indeed that neither contributed to the other.

It is also important to address the role of subjective considerations in contemporary and modern judgements. These are related, because it is unclear how sensible it is to abstract the intellectual response that 'should' have been made from the political context. If criticism of the consequences of the Hanoverian commitment are presented as xenophobic, even paranoid, and as arising from a failure to understand the major developments in Europe and of Britain's role in them, then many eighteenth-century speakers and writers, and much of the ambience and ethos of public (and private) discussion of foreign policy will be seen as unsatisfactory.

In contrast, restoring attention to contemporary debates entails considering attitudes as well as interests and goals, as these attitudes were directly relevant to issues of best policy and practice. In simple terms, and again allowing for a failure to conform to party political alignments (which reflected multiple factors, not least religious views), there was a tension between 'Whig' and 'Tory' attitudes towards the international system. The Whig attitude lent itself much more readily to the pragmatic, functional defence of the Hanoverian alignment, although there was also an idealistic component, in which 'Glorious Revolution' principles, anti-French views and anti-Catholicism co-existed, frequently uneasily. Richard Rolt wrote of the British forces under George II that entered Germany in 1743: 'brought there, as the sons of liberty, to oppose the arbitrary views of France in Germany'.[38]

Assuming that, through rational human analysis and action, it was possible to create a more benign international system, most Whig commentators, however, offered a mechanistic viewpoint, in many respects in thrall to Newtonian physics. An additional intellectual background was that of political economy. In the Whig view, there were clear-cut national interests (both British and foreign) that could be readily assessed and balanced, and it was therefore possible to devise collective security systems that encompassed Hanover. These views made sense of, and demanded, interventionism. This was the approach of many, but by no means all, British diplomats, of some Secretaries of State, most obviously Stanhope, Carteret and Newcastle, and of several influential scholars of the last half-century.

This approach required criticism of the opposite viewpoint, but this 'Tory' attitude, which enjoyed considerable sway, including among many who were not Tory in party politics, in fact drew on a coherent intellectual and moral philosophy. It was inherently pessimistic about the possibilities of creating trust and workable collective systems, and inclined to assume that any settlement of differences would be precarious, if not short-term. This attitude was lapsarian, rather than Newtonian, and with a stress on the human volition of rulers and ministers, not the mechanics of the balance of power. Uncertainty and, therefore, risk, were central to this analysis. In appreciating the limitations of the schematic understanding of national interests and international relations, this approach offered a powerful critique of interventionism, and thus challenged the value of collective systems of guarantee, and of commitments stemming from the Hanoverian connection.

Alongside reasoned criticism came vitriol. Its character can be gauged from *A Sixth Letter to the People of England, on the Progress of National Ruin; in which it is shown that the present grandeur of France, and calamities of this nation are owing to the influence of Hanover on the councils of England* (1757). The front page bore a pointed quote from Revelations about the white horse of Hanover: 'And I looked, and beheld a pale horse: and his name that sat on him was Death, and Hell followed with him.' Aside from condemning William III, there was a vigorous attack on the idea of supporting the 'liberties of Germany' that broadened out into contempt for German rules: 'to afford the liberty to needy Electors and little despotic Princes around whose sterile territories an English race horse may gallop in an hour, a sovereignty scarce large enough for pygmies, to sell the blood of their enslaved fellow creatures to all the nations of the Earth, the venal and avowed foes of human nature'.[39]

Whatever the vigorous spleen of public debate, the uncertainty of parliamentary responses to foreign policy and of tensions within the ministry helped ensure that the clarity of diplomatic conception, and the schematic model-building of the language of the balance of power, did not describe adequately the nature of the British domestic context for foreign policy. The potential political challenge posed by the latter overlapped with, and gave point to, the tension between 'Whig' and 'Tory' attitudes already referred to. In both, the Hanoverian connection was troublesome, but the potential problems posed by royal demands on behalf of the Electorate were restrained during the 1720s and 1730s, not only by Robert Walpole's skill, but also because threats to Hanover, for example by Russia in the early 1720s, Austria and her allies in 1726–7, Prussia in 1729 and 1738, or a French advance east of the Rhine in 1734 or 1735, were not realised.

Crucially, there was no war involving Hanover in 1725–7, while, in 1733–5, in the War of the Polish Succession, Hanover was not seriously endangered. This was important because, whatever the cause of the conflict, and however defended in public debate, the dynamic of events in such a conflict would have cruelly exposed ministerial and political differences over

Hanover. In the 1740s, however, the situation seriously deteriorated on both heads, and this led to the major agitation over Hanoverian interests that caused such political problems in Parliament in 1742–4. International events thus created a specific context in which disagreements that already existed acquired a sharp political point; and this, in turn, influenced general discussion of both the Hanoverian connection and interventionism.

From this perspective, Newcastle's post-War-of-the-Austrian-Succession attempt to arrange a strong collective security system designed to prevent war had a strong grounding. The policy was misguided in diplomatic terms, and, partly as a result, unsuccessful, but it rested on the political insight that, in terms of relations with the King, it would not be easy for a ministry to refuse Hanover support in a conflict, yet that the provision of such support might cause serious political problems in Britain.[40] In the event, even William Pitt the Elder, repeatedly a scourge of what he presented as Hanoverian measures, had to accept the dispatch of British troops to Germany in 1758. He was able, however, to present it both in terms of assistance to Prussia, a reasonable claim, at least in so far as keeping Frederick II in the war was concerned, and also, far more problematically, as a means to conquer America (i.e. Canada) in Germany.

Like Newcastle's approach, Pitt's policy was risky, because more exposed to the uncertainties of international developments, than that of Walpole. The latter's attitudes had, instead, been carried forward by his protégé (and Newcastle's brother) Henry Pelham, First Lord of the Treasury from 1743 until his unexpected death in 1754. Newcastle and Pitt were very different in their political methods and resonance, but, in office, they shared a commitment to action, necessarily so if they were to co-operate. In 1746–54 this involved support for the 'Old System' followed during and after the War of the Austrian Succession – Britain's alliance with Austria and the Dutch, which served royal and Hanoverian ends, by essentially acting as a military deterrent to Prussia, while appearing also as an anti-French step (which it indeed was), and thus matching the assumptions of British politicians. The clash in policy and priority between hostility to France and opposition to Prussia had led to significant political and diplomatic difficulties over goals and means during the War of the Austrian Succession, but the coming of peace in 1748 permitted the shelving of the apparent differences between the two objectives.

However, securing the peace by restraining France and Prussia through a collective security system made Britain dependent on her partners and also left it unclear whether France or Prussia were the major challenge. Furthermore, Newcastle's system left uncertain whether, in the event of war, intervention could surmount the strategic problems of Hanoverian vulnerability and the policy issues of British political ambivalence toward the Electorate, and achieve success. These problems of vulnerability were to take Hanover in a different direction to Britain, indeed to a coerced neutrality in 1757. As a consequence, British ministers, such as Robert, 4th Earl of Holdernesse,

Secretary of State from 1751 to 1761, and Newcastle, were to be very free in their criticism of their Hanoverian counterparts.

The British commitment to action carried with it serious risks. Confrontation with Russia failed in 1720–1 and in 1790. In the 1750s, Newcastle's diplomatic schemes fell foul of the difficulties posed by obdurate allies, and of the Duke's failure to appreciate the direction of international relations. Furthermore, in 1758, when troops were sent to the Continent, they were committed to the weaker of the two alliance systems in Europe, and the pessimistic tone of much British diplomatic and ministerial correspondence reflected this awareness. The joy that greeted Frederick II's victories was, in part, relief that the consequences of Britain's alliance system could be avoided.

Both Newcastle and Pitt felt constrained by George II and his Hanoverian concerns. Newcastle was greatly influenced by his visit to Hanover in 1748, not least by meeting the leading Hanoverian minister, Gerlach Adolf von Münchhausen; and his ministerial allies in Britain drew attention to the Duke's new-found clarity. Newcastle's wish to rout his ministerial rival, John, 4th Duke of Bedford, Secretary of State for the Southern Department, as indeed happened in 1751, was also important, as he needed royal support to this end. A sense of dependence on, indeed anxiety about, George's opinions, continued, thereafter, to characterise Newcastle's views. In his turn, Pitt was obliged to back help to Hanover if George II was to be persuaded to disavow the Hanoverian neutrality of 1757, which threatened the diplomatic and strategic coherence of a foreign policy that then rested on alliance with Prussia alone.

Ironically, it was the future George III who most powerfully represented the ambivalence toward Hanover in the late 1750s, as well as once he came to the throne in 1760. He took up the critical attitudes of Robert Walpole toward an active foreign policy, and, in doing so, linked royal authority to non-interventionism. As Prince of Wales, and influenced by the problems of the Seven Years' War, George criticised the partiality of his grandfather, George II, for Hanover, and, as King, he was determined to disengage from the 'German war', the German part of the Seven Years' War, and to avoid loading Britain with subsidies.

To discuss the attitudes and policies of George III, which are covered in Chapters 8 and 9, is to look far ahead from the opportunities and problems that became so rapidly apparent from the Hanoverian accession. While comparisons over such a period are instructive, they also risk neglecting the specificities of debate and discussion in particular contexts. In considering the latter in the following chapters, it is important to reiterate that the differences of contemporaries should not be slighted or misrepresented by reference to factious opposition. Given modern scholarly disagreements over theories of international relations, as well as the clarity with which, in modern democracies, politicians and publics contest definitions of national interest, and disagree vigorously over how best to pursue them, it is surprising that debate over foreign policy in the past is not taken more seriously.

The need for caution is strengthened by a consideration of the archival situation. The position is discouraging in so far as work being carried out by scholars is concerned, but encouraging with respect to the partly untapped archival riches that exist. Alongside the major holdings of State Papers in the National Archives, not, at least so far, decimated by the travails of history, such as war, there is a richness in private papers held in public archives. To take, for example, the 1740s and 1750s, the British Library holds the Newcastle papers, as well as those of another Secretary of State, Holder-nesse, of the Lord Chancellor, Philip, Earl of Hardwicke, of his diplomat son, Joseph Yorke, and of another prominent diplomat, Andrew Mitchell. Furthermore, foreign capitals provide the papers of diplomats accredited to the British court.

These holdings indicate the wealth of material that survives and that requires attention, but while that poses one problem, a more serious one arises from the understandable tendency, faced by such holdings, to look no further. This is unfortunate as it can lead both to the oversight of material and also to a failure to give due consideration to what does not survive, or which survives in only a patchy state. In the former case, there are for example important holdings that throw light on the politics of foreign policy in a number of collections, such as the Tweeddale papers in the National Library of Scotland. As far as the latter is concerned, the effects of destruction, both peacetime, especially at the end of the Anglo-Hanoverian union in 1837, and also arising from World War Two bombing, on the holdings in Hanover are serious, as they hinder a full understanding of the impact of the Hanoverian link. This is more serious because of the use of Hanoverian channels by the King, not only for German matters but also in order to maintain secrecy.[41]

There are also major gaps in the assessment of British policy arising from the absence of surviving papers, most obviously for William, Lord Harrington, Secretary of State for the Northern Department in 1730–42 and 1744–6; while the patchy nature of the papers of Carteret, who held that post in 1742–4, are a problem, especially for his subsequent period in office from 1751 to 1763 as Lord President of the Council, when he remained influential. The value to be gained from a study of the papers of Edward Weston, an Under Secretary from 1729 until 1746, and 1761 until 1764, which survive in the British Library, the Lewis Walpole Library in Farmington, Connecticut, and in the care of his descendant, John Weston-Underwood,[42] highlight the lack of similar extensive holdings on the part of others who occupied the office, such as William Chetwynd (1744–8), John Potter (1746–9), Richard Leveson Gower (1749–51) and James Rivers (1754–65).[43] The same is true later in the century, with the valuable holdings of James Bland Burges in the Bodleian Library drawing attention to the lack of material of the same extent for other Under Secretaries.

A 'supply-side' account – here be archival holdings – is of value as it clarifies material worthy of new, or fresh, examination. A 'demand-led' account is also appropriate. It draws attention to the topics currently of concern, but, in doing so, also highlights what is receiving insufficient attention. While literature, opinion, and extra-parliamentary action all had an impact on high politics,[44] the focus on them can be disproportionate, and, indeed, is so in much of the literature.

The interconnectedness of policy issues, and the often obscure nature of policy formulation, make it difficult to delineate the contours of political debate fully, and it is here that problems with the sources become a major issue. In particular, it would be desirable to trace debates within the ministry, and how they changed, as well as the process by which individual ministers took part in a wider discussion of policy. The state of the sources, however, only highlights aspects of both questions. For example, the papers of Newcastle and Hardwicke in the British Library and of Pelham in the Clumber collection in Nottingham University Library, throw much light on tension between Newcastle and Pelham.[45] This focused on money, especially peacetime subsidies and, therefore, the costs of interventionism, with Pelham, who was critical of such subsidies and worried about the costs, offering a reprise of the views of his earlier patron, Robert Walpole. In contrast, the detailed views of the ministers opposed to the Pelhams in the early 1750s, especially of Bedford, are less clear, although the reports of foreign diplomats offer useful guidance.[46]

More than chance played a role in the survival of material. There was also concern about writing or keeping sensitive material on the part of some. Thus, Holdernesse complained from Hanover to Joseph Yorke in 1755 about the disagreeable nature of his situation in the face of the collapse of Britain's alliance strategy, adding 'I dare not explain myself upon paper so much as I could wish; when I have an opportunity of an hour's talk with you, you will find me very open and frank'.[47] Historians are left to speculate about such comments, and about their corollary: sensitive issues kept for conversations for which there are no hints on paper.

A Secretary of State from 1751 to 1761, Holdernesse is a minister who deserves greater attention. Unlike Newcastle and Pitt, he had a valuable background as a diplomat. Holdernesse could also write in a pithy fashion. In December 1755, he informed Yorke that he would have been being misleading 'to have given hopes that England could hereafter take that share in the affairs of the Continent, that she has done upon former occasions, that is a nail that will not drive in these times, and it is in vain to attempt it; we might spoil our tools, but should not advance in our work'.[48]

The issue of surviving papers becomes less important during the Pitt-Newcastle ministry of 1757–61, as the number of key ministerial players was reduced, essentially to Pitt and Newcastle; and their views can be readily clarified,[49] although a systematic survey of the opinions of the other ministers would be useful. Prior to then, however, the situation is less clear and, as

Britain was at peace from 1748, formally until 1756, there was a greater number of policy options to consider. A focus on archival issues thus supports that on party attitudes in underlining the need for caution in assessing the causes, course, and consequences of the debate about policy.

3 Securing the new dynasty, 1714–21

The merit of having settled a universal peace in Europe . . . will make him [George I] so popular that I can not but think he may have what Parliament he pleases.

(A foolishly optimistic Duke of Newcastle, 1719)[1]

It is clear that Hanoverian interests remained of great concern to George I after he moved to Britain in 1714, and that this was accentuated by the opportunities for expansion created by the weakness of the Swedish empire after Charles XII's defeat at Poltava in 1709, and also by the anxieties stemming from the rise of Russian power. It is also readily apparent that the King's concerns affected his ministers for two related reasons: first, a wish to find favour and to work with the monarch, and, second, an awareness that threats to Hanover might serve the interests of hostile foreign powers, and thus need to be countered. The relative and respective impact of these factors varied by minister, and according to circumstances. As a result, it is inappropriate to offer a linear account of the subject. For example, despite earlier concern about the possibility of invasion, most seriously by Russia in 1716–17, by Austria, Prussia and Russia in 1726–7, and by Prussia in 1729 and 1738, the first actual advance on Hanover in this period was by French troops, and not until 1741.

Hanover was vulnerable, and regarded as such by Hanoverian, British and foreign commentators. The Electorate lacked strong natural defences: as with most German principalities, most obviously Prussia, its frontiers were established by feudal, not geographical, considerations. Most of the Electorate was between the Elbe and the Weser rivers, the North Sea and the Harz mountains, but there were also important sectors between the Elbe, Mecklenburg, Holstein and the Baltic, and also west of the Weser. Moreover, the frontiers had not been supplemented by any system of fortifications. As a consequence, the defence of the Electorate was dependent on its army and its allies. The army, established in 1665, was, like that of most German principalities, modest in size. It was increased with the Dutch War (1672–8) and thereafter averaged 10–16,000 men, rising to 22,000 during the War of the

Spanish Succession, in which Hanover was involved from 1701 until 1715. The establishment, however, was reduced in 1715 to a size of 14,500–15,000, and did not rise again to about 19,000 until after 1727.[2] This army offered no real protection against attack by powerful rulers, especially that of neighbouring Prussia, whose effective size was 66,861 by June 1729.[3]

Hanover's geographical and international position made it particularly liable to threats. The trans-Elbean territory, the Duchy of Saxe-Lauenburg, occupied in 1689, made Hanover especially sensitive to developments around the Baltic, especially in Mecklenburg and the Sleswig-Holstein isthmus, while its western possessions made it concerned about events in the Westphalian Circle to the west and also by the control over Rhine crossings such as Rheinfels. Hanover also lay astride any Russian advance into northern Germany, a major threat during the reign of Peter the Great (1689–1725), under whom, and against George I's wishes, Russian troops wintered in neighbouring Mecklenburg in 1716–17. Hanover also lay astride any Danish moves south into Lower Saxony, any French advance toward the western frontier of Brandenburg (the central area of the Prussian dominions), and any attempt by the rulers of Prussia to amalgamate, or otherwise link up, their widely separated territories in Westphalia and the Lower Rhineland with Brandenburg. There were Prussian territories to the east and west of Hanover, just as there were Danish possessions to the north and west.

Hanoverian security therefore dictated a search for allies and supporters, of which Britain was the most prominent, and Hesse-Cassel, its aid purchased with British subsidies, the most immediately useful. During the course of the Anglo-French alliance from 1716 to 1731, the prospect of French assistance was also important. Indeed, the negotiation of the alliance had been pushed hard for Hanoverian ends.[4]

Such an alliance had not been anticipated when George I came to the throne, and it reflected the unpredictable and contingent nature of international relations, and therefore of the parameters within which British policy had to be defined. The modern concept of strategic culture cannot be readily applied to policy in the 1710s, except by noting that the quest for security led to major changes in the alliance system. George's accession was followed by the replacement of the Tory government by the Whigs, who had bitterly opposed the Utrecht settlement the previous year. Indeed, initially the Whigs sought to recreate the alliance that had fought France in the War of the Spanish Succession, which, in the circumstances, could only be seen as a bellicose Continental policy. The Hanoverian link, however, appeared to make this necessary, as, in Britain, French action in support of the Jacobites was believed imminent.

Louis XIV, however, died in 1715 to be succeeded by his great-grandson, Louis XV, born in 1710. The Regent, Philip, Duke of Orléans, was more cautious than Louis XIV had been, and readier to abandon the Jacobite option, and this helped clear the path towards better relations with George I. So also, on the other side, did Austro-Dutch differences over the Austrian

Netherlands: repeatedly, the dependence of British Continental interventionism on allies was made problematic not only because the latter often
failed to accept British assumptions, but also because of clashing interests
and priorities between the real or desired allies. The Anglo-French treaty,
signed on 28 November 1716, guaranteed Hanover and the Protestant
succession in Britain, and undertook to ensure that 'James III', the Stuart
Pretender, left Avignon for Italy. This alliance transformed the situation,
providing not only for the security of Hanoverian rule in Britain, but also for
the Electorate. In 1717, when close to war with George as Elector, Peter the
Great of Russia visited Paris, the French rejected his offer of an alliance in
return for subsidies. The following year, the thanks of George I for the
readiness of France to send help in case of an attack on Hanover were clearly
expressed,[5] and the King continued to express his view that the alliance was
mutually beneficial.[6]

It was to be claimed, however, that Hanoverian interests made the British
government overly pro-French.[7] It was certainly felt necessary to ensure that
guarantees of assistance encompassed Hanoverian acquisitions. Thus, the
gain of the duchies of Bremen and Verden, occupied in 1712 and ceded by
Sweden in 1719, accentuated the problems already posed for Britain by the
diplomacy of Hanoverian vulnerability.[8] The attitude of a British official
was captured by George Tilson, Under Secretary in the Northern Department, in his reference to 'our silly investitures . . . I am not quite reconciled
to the seeking them with earnestness'.[9]

Critics claimed that threats to Hanover arose from its expansionist aspirations, and George's success in gaining Bremen and Verden lay like a trail
through subsequent criticism. 'Safety and Tranquility – An excellent new
ballad' of 1722, included a verse beginning:

> For Bremen then he made a league
> And else for Verden too.[10]

The *True Briton* of 7 June (os) 1723 in a facetious remark claimed:

> It is a vile and false insinuation that the disaffected party amongst us
> would make, that the obtaining and securing those additions to the
> Electorate of Hanover, have been the secret springs that have governed
> and directed our behaviour in all foreign affairs.

This conformed to the notion of secret cabinets and plans that played such a
large role in critical accounts of foreign policy. The view that, via George's
leading minister, Andreas Gottlieb von Bernstorff, the particular interests of
the exiled Mecklenburg nobility, who were opposed to their Russian-backed
Duke, influenced Hanoverian policy, acted as an ironic counterpoint to the
idea that Hanover did the same for Britain. Attempts, in response, to justify
Britain's Baltic policy, specifically the dispatch of fleets there, in particular

by emphasising the need to secure Baltic naval supplies, appear to have had little impact, although this is difficult to gauge.

Initially, George I's reign had seemed to offer bright prospects for the advance of Hanover in the ranks of German powers. This was an important aspect of the Hanoverian optimum of 1714–18. The new dynasty in Britain rapidly overcame the attempt at a Stuart *revanche* in the '15. Its ministers established an effective alliance with France that, while pushed hard for Hanoverian reasons, greatly lessened British vulnerability. The ministers also formulated a peace plan for the Mediterranean that led to a spectacular naval victory over Spain off Cape Passaro in Sicily in 1718. The dispatch of the fleet to the Mediterranean had been pressed for by both Charles VI and Orléans, and was a testimony to the perception of British capability.[11] Furthermore, Hanover looked set to benefit territorially from the partition of Sweden's trans-Baltic empire, a benefit seen not only in the gain of territory, but also in denying territories to other powers, especially Denmark.

Hanoverian opportunities and importunities, however, helped to divide the Whigs, with ministers separating over George's expectation of support for his Baltic policy; although, in addition, differences over power in Britain, and between George and his heir, the future George II, contributed greatly to the Whig Split. In turn, the British ministry had to be concerned about the foreign perception of this dispute.[12] There was particular tension over the use of British warships in the Baltic. In order to protect the important trade with the Baltic from Swedish privateering, a joint force of British and Dutch warships was sent there in 1715. It ended the Swedish blockade of St Petersburg and Riga, but was then affected by contrary political pressures. The Dutch sought to maintain a strict neutrality, but Admiral Norris was pressed by Hanoverian advisors of George I to block maritime supply lines to the besieged Swedish fortress at Stralsund. Due to the Dutch stance, Norris did not do so, but the request anyway was illegal: under the Act of Settlement, George was not permitted, without parliamentary approval, to involve his British forces in war on behalf of Hanover, and Britain anyway was then an ally of Sweden. In 1716, there was tension over whether British warships would act against Russia in the Baltic, and Norris took pains to emphasise his support for British as opposed to Hanoverian objectives.[13]

These disputes contributed to the ministerial division, as Edward, 1st Earl of Orford, the First Lord of the Admiralty, was close to Walpole. In April 1717, the ministry sought to secure a definite commitment from Parliament to support George's anti-Swedish policy. A large money supply was to be voted, and trade with Sweden to be prohibited. In turn, the opposition argued that British money was being used to serve Hanoverian ends in Bremen and Verden. This was the occasion for the dismissal of Townshend, which was followed by the resignation of most of Walpole's followers.[14]

More than Whig divisions, however, was involved. In opposition, and shorn of the commitments of office, which had led, in the early 1710s, to Bolingbroke's active diplomacy, and of what he termed 'the men of business',[15] the Tories had reverted to the 'Country' policy of opposing an interventionist role in European politics; or what Charles, 3rd Earl of Sunderland, the First Lord of the Treasury, called 'the old Tory notion that England can subsist by itself'.[16] However loyal or disloyal the Tories were to the House of Hanover, most were stridently anti-Hanoverian in proclaiming their support for a 'British' as opposed to a 'Hanoverian' foreign policy. This made a Tory–ministerial alliance in the late 1710s impossible. George I and James, Earl Stanhope, Secretary of State for the Northern Department, were determined to play a major role in Baltic and Mediterranean affairs, but naval expeditions, and, even more, war, would dictate higher taxation, and such a policy could not be supported by the Tories. The Austrian envoy reported sensitivity about the cost of naval preparations.[17] Thus, contention over foreign policy related not simply to the opportunism of political debate but also to serious divisions over domestic issues. The Jacobites sought to exploit the situation by seeking information about the activities of the fleet in the Baltic that could be useful in Parliament and the world of print.[18]

This Whig Split did not stop George and his advisors from continuing with their policies, but the Hanoverian optimum ended in 1719–21, as the Stanhope/Sunderland ministry proved unable to retain or regain control of Parliament, while the bursting of the South Sea Bubble in 1720 caused a political as well as a fiscal crisis. Furthermore, the attempt to intimidate Peter the Great of Russia into accepting the British peace plan for Northern Europe failed miserably.

The failure to maintain acceptable relations with Peter the Great had caused a marked deterioration in Hanover's position. Once Russian troops had advanced into Mecklenburg in 1716, there was the repeated fear that they would return, one that George I referred to in 1719 after Hanoverian troops had moved into the Duchy to enforce the Imperial judgement in favour of its aristocracy.[19] In 1715, Charles-Leopold, Duke of Mecklenburg-Schwerin had married Peter the Great's niece, Catherine.

Thus, the possibilities that had opened up in 1716, when George had encouraged a Russian invasion of Scania as a knock-out blow against Charles XII, were rudely replaced by fears and a degree of Russophobia that increased George's need for British diplomatic and military assistance. These fears were accentuated by the dangerous prospect of hostile co-operation between Peter the Great and Frederick William I of Prussia, who was concerned about Russian strength and felt intimidated as a result. Far from the 'balance of power' working to balance strength and expansion, threatened powers could be intimidated into support. Indeed rumours about this co-operation circulated widely in the late 1710s.[20] A resulting sense of Hanover as an incubus for Britain that had to be protected was captured in the remark of 1719 by Stanhope that, as soon as an alliance with Prussia had covered Hanover from Russian attack, it would be possible to work at saving Sweden from Russia.[21]

Diplomats were particularly sharp critics of the impact of Hanoverian considerations. They had to decide how best to adapt to the difficulties of their new role, and the resulting problems helped accentuate their unease about the Hanoverian link. In January 1720, Charles Whitworth wrote from Berlin:

> You will see by my relation how I am employed from Hanover. It would be much better to have a German Secretary or Resident here to solicit these points, whom I could second on occasion than to make me disagreeable by such commissions.[22]

Whitworth's problem at this period can be readily recovered because not only do his dispatches and private correspondence survive, but also his correspondence with Friedrich Wilhelm von Görtz, then effectively head of the government in Hanover. Whitworth received instructions from three different sources: Stanhope, the Secretary of State in London, the Hanoverian Chancery in London, and the ministers in Hanover. On behalf of George as Elector, he was instructed to deal with a rich variety of problems: forced enrolments of Hanoverian subjects by the Prussians; the cession of fiefs and presentations to churches situated in Wolfenbüttel and Bevern; a border territorial quarrel; works on the River Elbe; Prussian support for George's brother, Ernst August of Osnabrück, in his quarrel with papal procedure; Prussian policy in Hamburg; and the concerting of diplomatic strategy to obtain, from Charles VI, investitures for Frederick William I and George of territories obtained from Sweden.

With reason, Whitworth argued that these instructions harmed Anglo-Prussian relations, and his wider purpose of retaining Prussian support for a coalition aimed against Peter the Great. Writing to Görtz about the Hamburg affair, Whitworth bluntly suggested that the Hanoverian ministry was overly committing George I's credit in a dispute that did not merit it. Görtz was also informed that a border quarrel, complicated as it was by differing maps, should be settled by civil process in a court of justice, and not by negotiation. Whitworth argued that issues such as the Wolfenbüttel fiefs would make it difficult to establish good relations, and wrote, with respect to instructions from the German Chancery in London: 'I cannot comprehend the reasonings in the two orders directed to me . . . except they be designed to create jealousies at this court and overthrow all we have been doing.'[23]

Whitworth was also concerned about whether the orders he had received from the German Chancery had been concerted with the British ministers and noted that he would have preferred 'at least some hints from Mylord Stanhope, which is my proper channel'. Subsequently, Whitworth was to argue that Britain played too forward a role in religious disputes in Germany, then at a height,[24] again a role that could be attributed to George as Elector. Indeed, greater British governmental interest in Protestantism on the Continent, especially in Germany, was a consequence of the Hanoverian link. Whitworth was also ordered, via the German Chancery, to back the interests of the Polish Protestants in co-operation with Prussia. In 1721, Whitworth observed, in response to an enquiry that reflected governmental concern:

> Mylord Townshend may be sure I shall always be very cautious what part of my correspondence I communicate and to whom: to my Secretary of State I always act without reserve; to others I only impart just so much as I think necessary for carrying on his Majesty's service . . . and it is for that reason I sent you copies of what I have writ of late to Mr. Bernstorff and Mr. de St. Saphorin. If you reflect on what passed in my late Lord Stanhope's time you will easily believe that I have particular reason to have very little confidence in the first, but as His Majesty refused to employ any Hanover minister here, I am obliged to keep up a correspondence with that Regency from time to time: you may be sure that it was none of my seeking; for the commissions I generally receive from them being about private disputes are not often agreeable.[25]

There were also tensions about representation at Vienna.[26] It was not solely at the level of individual diplomats that the Hanoverian link created difficulties. In 1718–19, there was serious tension over British policy in Northern Europe. Stanhope was not fully informed of the anti-Prussian and anti-Russian slant of the alliance George, as Elector, signed on 5 January 1719 with Charles VI and Augustus II of Saxony-Poland, and the treaty left disquiet among the British ministers about Bernstorff's attitudes. This was not the full extent of the difficulties, as the French government, which had negotiated with George as both King and Elector, was angry not to have been consulted, and the resulting complaint played a role in the tensions arising from a failure to keep the British ministers informed. In response, Bernstorff told George that Stanhope and James Craggs, the Secretary of State for the Southern Department, were more French than German,[27] an instructive comment about the implications of interventionism: ministers were labelled in response to their alliance preferences.

The dispute helped make George appear an unreliable ally, as the French ministry was made aware of bitter rivalries around George, and was also unable to obtain reassurances as to whether the treaty contained secret clauses. Guillaume Dubois, the French foreign minister, was informed by his British counterpart not only that this was a treaty simply involving George as Elector, and restricted to defensive clauses, but also that the British ministers were not always kept informed.[28] The French retorted, that, whatever differences there might be between the British and Hanoverian ministers, agreements entered into by the latter invariably led to British intervention. Stressing the role of the Crown in British foreign policy, the French were well aware of the influence of Hanoverian interests, and emphasised their willingness to support guarantees for Hanoverian security. As an added twist, the sophistication of the Hanoverian postal interception and deciphering system ensured that the Hanoverians were able to read about British complains to French diplomats concerning their influence.[29]

The resulting crisis in credibility was not restricted to the French. Sunderland told the Prussian envoy, Friedrich Bonet, that the British ministers were neither responsible for, nor supported, policy towards Prussia. Bonet soon after made a suggestion about Prussian approaches that threw light on the workings of George I's court when he suggested that, if more was expected from British ministers than from Hanoverians, it could be useful if letters sent from Frederick William I to George were written in French, rather than German, as responses to the former went via the British minister and to the latter via the Hanoverians.[30] In the event, Bernstorff was to a considerable degree marginalised as George changed emphasis. In October 1719, Sunderland felt able to report back from the Hanoverian hunting palace at Göhrde that George 'will not suffer any foreigner to meddle in our affairs, this you may depend upon'.[31]

Aside from political disputes, attempts under George I to develop commercial links between Britain and Hanover were unsuccessful, although George made an effort to respond to British interests, for example satisfying complaints by merchants about difficulties in importing tobacco into the Duchy of Bremen. There were, moreover, problems stemming from the Hanoverian link, not least direct pressures on British ministers to provide benefits for the Hanoverian élite, including favours at Customs and profits from government patronage, while Hanoverian courtiers sought to benefit from the disposal of offices and peerages. Angry British ministers were concerned about the political implications of the spoils system, James Craggs, Secretary of State for the Southern Department, complaining in 1719, 'I have been one objection to Gortz's coming, which is the filling of a new purse. It is incredible what prejudice all these sales of offices and other underhand dealings occasion to the King's service.'[32] Aspects of this pressure indeed entered the public domain.[33]

In 1719, Craggs also directed attention on another aspect of sensitivity, that of the comparison of benefits between Britain and Hanover. He warned Stanhope,

> As to the request made to the King by the magistrates of Frankfurt, that His Majesty would give them leave to make a collection in Great Britain towards repairing their losses by fire, the Lords Justices are of opinion, that the encouragement of such a design might be a bad precedent, and occasion a great clamour in England, where misfortunes of the like nature are so frequent, that the Crown is sometimes obliged to discourage applications made on behalf of its own subjects. Your Lordship who best knows the humour of the people here, will be best able to represent this matter to His Majesty.[34]

The South Sea Company, of which George I became Governor in 1718, proved a highpoint of opportunism and corruption. Shares were provided for George and for relatives, such as Melusine von der Schulenburg, who was sufficiently close to lead to reports that she was his morganatic wife, and who became Duchess of Kendal in 1719. She, herself, had a correspondence with the Empress that encompassed international affairs.[35] In addition, there was a rush by Hanoverian ministers to benefit from the South Sea Company, one writing in July 1720 that those who had been with George in England had returned much enriched by the money they had made from the Crown's share. Later in the year, it was suggested that the Hanoverians' stake in the Company's affairs would encourage them to press for George's speedy return to England when the Bubble burst.[36]

Another scandal engulfed the Harburg Company, founded, with high hopes in Hanover,[37] to carry on trade between Britain and Hanover, and granted a charter in 1720. The Company's attempt to launch a fraudulent lottery in London was rejected by British ministers and when, nevertheless, it was launched in December 1722, the House of Commons intervened, declaring the lottery fraudulent and illegal. The failure among modern scholars to note or understand the impact of such controversies leads to an inability to grasp a real basis to hostility to the Hanoverian connection. John Barrington, MP for Berwick, the Sub-Governor of the Company, was expelled from the Commons for his role in promoting and carrying on a fraudulent undertaking. His support for Hanoverian goals had earlier led Barrington to speak in the Commons in 1721 for a subsidy to Sweden, and he gained an Irish peerage in 1720.[38] The royal family was directly involved: George I was a keen supporter of the development of Harburg[39] and his eldest grandson, Frederick, was Governor of the Company.

International difficulties proved a backdrop to domestic disputes. The death of the hostile Charles XII of Sweden in 1718 had provided George with an opportunity for a major recasting of northern Europe. The accession first of Charles's younger sister, Ulrika Eleonora, and then of her husband Frederick I, the heir to Hesse-Cassel, ensured a far more favourable position within Sweden. With French support, George was able to negotiate the cession of Bremen and Verden to Hanover, and, in return, Sweden obtained peace and a guarded promise of British support against Russia. In order to impose a Russo-Swedish peace that would return most of Peter's conquests, George sought to create an alliance of Sweden's former enemies plus France, Austria and Britain. This would have been a highwater mark for British interventionism, both diplomatic and military and a marked demonstration of the impact of the Hanoverian link. In 1723, Frederick William I was to argue that there was no doubt that a close alliance of France, George I and himself could have a major impact on European affairs.[40] George's plan, however, proved unrealistic, anticipating the failure of the attempt to intimidate Russia in 1791 (see pp. 165–6). Charles VI and Frederick William I proved unwilling to attack Peter, the financial crises that affected Britain and

France sapped their determination, Peter refused to be intimidated, and in 1721 Sweden prudently accepted the Treaty of Nystad, under which Peter kept most of his conquests.

This striking failure for the Continental commitment is not given sufficient weight because, with the exception of against Poland, Peter and his successors did not pursue the aggressive schemes that were feared. For example, Peter's naval demonstrations against Denmark on behalf of Charles Frederick of Holstein-Gottorp in the early 1720s went no further, and in 1726 Peter's widow and successor, Catherine I, rejected a request from the Duke of Mecklenburg for the assistance of Russian troops. Furthermore, Russian relations with Britain improved from the early 1730s, and thus the impact of the failure to limit Russia was not appreciated. This was underlined because opposition to Russian gains in 1772 and 1791 was not taken to the point of action. Thus, the major weakness of Britain's Continental aspirations revealed in 1720–1, its unrealistic dependence on a weak alliance system, did, and does, not play a sufficiently large role in the analysis of British policy.

Maritime links with the Electorate could also appear important from the perspective of British security. Hanoverian troops were available to help repel action in support of the Jacobites. In 1715, Stair responded to French interest in whether Hanoverian troops would be sent to overcome Jacobite action by declaring 'there were 10,000 or 12,000 men on the Elbe, in case the King of Sweden or any other foreign power thought fit to support the rebellion, and that Staden and Hamburg were at least as near Scotland as Karlscrona, or any other port, from whence the rebels could be supported'.[41] Yet, Hanoverian assistance was only an aspect of the possibility of foreign support, which could also be obtained from the Dutch and from Hesse. More generally, the presence of the Hanoverian dynasty did not introduce the problem of protecting Britain from foreign intervention on behalf of the Jacobite claimant, as it had been a factor since 1689. Furthermore, the period since the 'Glorious Revolution' indicated that, whether for geopolitical, strategic or commercial reasons, Hanover was certainly not necessary to the cause of British interventionism on the Continent. Instead, if anything, it was a constraint as well as an encouragement because of the need to consider the defence of the Electorate and the territorial ambition of the Kings as Electors.

At the same time, a defence was made of interventionism on grounds that bore little reference to Hanover and, instead, focused on issues of national interest. A memorandum drawn up for the government toward the close of George I's reign presented a series of treaties with Continental rulers as the means by which both this interest and the Hanoverian succession had been secured. It asserted:

> That the security, trade and religion of Great Britain makes defensive alliances with foreign powers absolutely necessary, not only for the

preservation of the peace betwixt us and our neighbours; but also for keeping the other considerable powers from a rupture, by which we may in consequence be involved etc.

That His Majesty, from having pursued this rule, ever since his accession, has hitherto preserved the common peace, and procured to us the tranquility and happiness we now enjoy.

This theme was then traced through Britain's treaties:

the suspicious behaviour of France, with regard to the Pretender and the rebellion induced His Majesty to make a defensive alliance with the Emperor, May 25th 1716.

This alliance had such an effect, that the Regent [of France] thought fit to change his measures, and to enter into a defensive alliance with His Majesty and the States; by virtue of which the most essential points of the Treaty of Utrecht, with regard to the successions to the Crowns of Great Britain, and France, and the demolition of Dunkirk were executed, and the behaviour of France with regard to His Majesty took another turn.[42]

The value of this approach, however, was gravely compromised in political terms by the charges of Hanoverianism. Thus, at the same time that, in terms of policy (as well as Court politics) the Hanoverian link encouraged interventionism, as far as public politics were concerned, the link helped to make it problematic. This contrast threw attention on the politics by which this tension had to be adjusted.

4 Cold wars on the Continent, 1721–31

Historians accustomed to the sensational conflicts of the previous two centuries, have largely ignored the frenetic diplomacy of the 1720s, dismissing it as an uneventful interlude of 'sterile congresses and alliances'.

(Charles Ingrao, 2002[1])

it is certain you can have nothing solid with France, sooner or later she will return to her old maxims as the dog to his vomit.

(Charles Whitworth, envoy in Berlin, 1721[2])

This chapter takes a period commonly ignored and shows how it has much to offer not only in the consideration of eighteenth-century British foreign policy, but, more specifically, in the assessment of the context and consequences of interventionism. In the last fifteen years, the 1720s have received insufficient attention,[3] and it is easy to see why. From the perspective of the dominant meta-narrative of British policy, namely the rise to imperial hegemony,[4] the 1720s appear far less important than the mid-century years, especially the Seven Years' War. Furthermore, from the perspective of growing problems in the imperial relationship, and the potent fracturing of the trans-Atlantic link, they appear far less important than the 1760s and 1770s. In addition, compared to the conflict of the preceding and following decades the European diplomacy of the 1720s appears inconsequential, deterring scholars from devoting sufficient attention to a period that also suffers from the more general shadowing in European history of the decades prior to mid-century.[5]

Yet the 1720s is worthy of attention for a number of reasons, although the documentary basis that might permit an understanding of their respective importance for contemporaries is absent. First, the decade indicated the deficiencies of the interventionist ethos and practices of the 1710s,[6] indeed saw the revenge of particularities and events on the discourse of international order, culminating with the failure, first, of the international peace congress of Soissons in 1728–9 and, second, that of the Anglo-French alliance in 1730–1. Secondly, the 1720s saw a response to the major powers of Central and Eastern Europe – Austria, Russia and, to a lesser extent, Prussia – that was instructive not only for future problems in relations with them, but also for the more general problem of interventionism. Thirdly, the effort shown in protecting Britain's overseas position, not least in deploying naval strength, particularly in 1726 and 1729, was significant. Lastly, the 1720s provides an opportunity for probing the contours of British public debate on foreign policy as it adjusted not simply to these developments but also to the problems of the Hanoverian connection.[7]

The point of departure is a long letter sent in August 1725 by Charles, 2nd Viscount Townshend, Secretary of State for the Northern Department from 1721 until 1730, and the dominant figure in British foreign policy, to Horatio Walpole, envoy in Paris, and not therefore in Townshend's department, but a key diplomat and one of Townshend's brothers-in-law. The background was the need felt by the government of George I to respond to the crisis created by the recent and unexpected alliance between Philip V of Spain and the Emperor Charles VI, the ruler of Austria and the other Habsburg territories.[8] Townshend was then with the King, George I, in his native Hanover, removed from the cautious restraints of British domestic politics, and he gave full rein to the tendency for international rearrangement that was such a major feature of the diplomatic thought and negotiation of the period. This tendency is neglected when, as is usually the case, attention is devoted to the language of the balance of power and the related assumption by many that goals were limited.[9]

Townshend, however, saw both need and opportunity for a major change in the international system, one that would have entailed a significant reversal of the policies pursued by Britain during and after the War of the Spanish Succession (1702–13). He argued that, if a new conflict broke out, Charles VI must be deprived of the Austrian Netherlands (the basis of modern Belgium), which he had received from the Spanish Habsburg inheritance as a result of the War of the Spanish Succession:

> My Lord Stanhope[10] who talked with me frequently upon this subject sometimes before his death,[11] was of opinion they should be given to [Leopold I] the Duke of Lorraine, and in order to obviate an objection which arose at first sight, viz. that the said Duke would not be able to support them, he proposed that the Electorates of Cologne and Trier, and the Bishopric of Liège should be secularised, some equivalents found for the present possessors, and all those countries put together under the government of the Duke of Lorraine or some other prince. But this scheme, however reasonable it might have been, could it have been put in practice, did so abound with difficulties, that it was the vainest of imaginations to think it could ever be brought to bear; neither can I see any reason why England or Holland should be looking out for a third prince to give these dominions to, after the experience they have had for many years, that when they are in weak hands, the excessive burden of

defending them lies wholly upon those two powers, and when they are in hands in some degree strong enough to defend them, they are made use of against them.

As a result, Townshend, who in 1709 had played a major role in negotiating a treaty under which the Dutch garrisoned a number of 'barrier fortresses' in the Austrian Netherlands as a defence against France, now proposed a partition of the territory between Britain, the Dutch and France. Britain was to gain Bruges, Newport, Ostend and Plassendahl, 'with a territory annexed to them sufficient to maintain the garrisons in those places' and a joint garrisoning of Ghent. He also sought to counter possible objections, one of his remarks indicating the caveats of an experienced diplomat about the ready use of the concept of the balance of power as a justification of policy:

> The first would be, that the taking the Low Countries from the Emperor would be weakening him too much, and consequently overturning the balance of power in Europe. In answer to this, it may be truly asserted, that it will not in reality weaken the Emperor, for he does not draw one shilling of money from those countries, neither can he call away one regiment from thence to the assistance of any other part of his dominions; so that it cannot be truly said to weaken the Emperor in any sense, except one, and that I own is a very material one viz that it will free His Majesty as King and as Elector, the Nation and the States General from the hardest of bondage which they do and must labour under, as long as the Emperor continues in possession of those countries. He will then indeed have it no longer in his power to engage us in a war, whenever he thinks fit, upon terms never so unreasonable (as whilst those countries are in his hands he really may) nor to treat us ill, and force us into all the unreasonable measures he thinks fit to prescribe; but we, on our part, shall not be less in a condition, for having those countries put into our hands, to help him, whenever the Balance of Europe requires it.[12]

This letter illustrates the accretional nature of source-based diplomatic history as it comes from a volume that had not been deposited in the British Library when James Chance wrote his *The Alliance of Hanover* (1923), the major study of British foreign policy in the mid-1720s. The letter also indicates the problem posed by the fate of Townshend's diplomatic papers. There were major dispersals of material from the family seat at Raynham in 1911 and 1924, and other losses to collectors,[13] and Townshend diplomatic material is now held at a number of repositories including the Beinecke Library, the Norfolk Record Office, the British Library, the National Library of Australia and Raynham.

The impact of the lack of a consolidated holding has been accentuated by the failure to study the papers before they were dispersed. In 1754, Horatio Walpole wrote to Townshend's son (Walpole's nephew by marriage),

Charles, 3rd Viscount Townshend, to remind him that he had asked to borrow the 2nd Viscount's letters and papers as ambassador and Secretary of State, 'being employed in spending my leisure hours, to vindicate the administration in which his Lordship was concerned, from the false, and injurious calumny of the late Lord Bolingbroke's posthumous works'; only to meet with the reply that the 2nd Viscount had decided to 'write a history of his own times', had died before he could complete it, 'yet as he had resolved rather to take the trouble on himself of drawing up this historical account than to leave it to any other', it was clear that his wish was that his papers not be read by anyone else.[14] As a consequence, Walpole was not granted access to them, and there was no systematic study of the collection.

The net effect of the neglect of Townshend is that the interventionist strand in British policy in the 1720s has not been studied from the 'inside', from the perspective of a detailed examination of the papers of its progenitors, as with Ragnhild Hatton's work on the late 1710s, particularly on Stanhope's peace plans, and the studies, by Reed Browning and others, of Newcastle's policies in 1748–56.[15] The nearest equivalent to the situation with reference to Townshend is the patchy nature of work on Carteret, the effective director of foreign policy in 1742–4, a patchy nature that again, in part, reflects the paucity of the sources.[16] As a mirror-image, the views on foreign policy of ministers who were critics of interventionism, such as Henry Pelham, have also received insufficient attention. Recent work on Pelham shows how knowledge of the sources can also be accretional.[17]

Townshend's interest in territorial acquisition may seem out of line with British foreign policy after 1713, but there was a sense that Britain's territorial position in Europe had not been fixed with the Utrecht settlement. Territorial interest focused on the Mediterranean, where Gibraltar and Minorca had been gained from the War of the Spanish Succession, and with interest expressed in the acquisition of Majorca,[18] and later in the century in Corsica and Sardinia. Townshend's focus, in contrast, was on the Low Countries, an area that could not be covered by the navy, but one that traditionally was of key strategic interest to Britain. From the British point of view, the Dutch were seen as surrogates for the defence of the Low Countries. In order to protect the latter from French incursion, treaties were negotiated in 1709, 1713 and 1715, creating a barrier of Dutch-garrisoned fortifications. Frustration, however, with the international situation led to occasional speculation about the establishment of a British presence, and Townshend's suggestion prefigured interest in the idea of a British garrison in Ostend expressed during negotiations in 1748.[19] The strategic sensitivity of the region was enhanced by the possibility that it, especially the port of Ostend, could be used as the base for an amphibious attack on Britain and, indeed, the Jacobites sought to interest the Austrian government in such an idea during the mid-1720s.[20]

Townshend's letter indicates that Continental interventionism amounted not simply to a focus, re-active or pro-active, on maintaining existing arrangements, with the rationale of preserving the balance of power, but, also, to a more pro-active and pointed willingness to use force to re-order the European system; indeed, almost a pre-emptive attitude. This is an aspect of British foreign policy that tends to be neglected, or is presented in a positive light as an enabler to policies designed to ensure peace.[21] Indeed, such a strand can be seen from the diplomacy of the Partition Treaties in 1698–1700 designed to prevent war over the Spanish Succession to that of the Congress of Vienna in 1814–15. As such, the proposed redistribution of territory appears different in character to the more selfish policies of the powers that partitioned Poland in 1772–95,[22] or, indeed, those who sought to despoil the Swedish empire in 1700–21, a group that, eventually, from 1715, included George I as Elector of Hanover.

It is scarcely surprising, however, that others did not see British interventionist aspirations in that light, just as there was also concern about Britain's maritime hegemony. Horatio Walpole, indeed, rejected Townshend's proposal as impracticable in terms of domestic politics, specifically the assumptions of the political nation,[23] indicating that the dual role of many diplomats, also as parliamentarians (in Horatio's case then as MP for Great Yarmouth), affected the judgement of at least some. Townshend himself did not persist with the plan. Another leading diplomat, later also an MP, Charles Whitworth, referred to the problem of Britain being 'the Knight Errant of Europe'.[24]

The doubts about Continental interventionism expressed by diplomats indicate that those also voiced publicly by opposition speakers and writers were not without merit. In 1723, doubts were also expressed by Robert Walpole, the First Lord of the Treasury, then acting as Secretary of State during the absence of the two Secretaries (Townshend and Carteret) in Hanover. In response to pressure from George I for a promise of assistance for Sweden if it was attacked by Peter the Great, Walpole expressed his concern that competition among the ministers for royal favour would lead to rash engagements when it would be better for Britain to remain neutral.[25]

Concern about the details of interventionism was linked to a wider anxiety about the uncertainty of relations with the Continent. The most problematic were those with the interests of the King as Elector of Hanover. At times separate, and, at times contributing to domestic concerns, it was also the case that interventionism aroused a hostile response from foreign powers. Indeed, the more ambitious the interventionism, the greater the chance that the permutations involved would help bury it in problems, especially as alliances were sought. This was a point understood by Townshend when, in 1726, at a time that Britain was seeking allies against Austria, he opposed giving Bavaria assurances over the future of the Habsburg succession when Charles VI, who had no sons, died.[26] Indeed, by the time Charles died in 1740, there had been several abrupt changes in the international system.

The diplomacy of the 1720s indicated clearly the difficulty of creating an effective interventionist system, as attempts, by the British ministry, at the same time, to retain the French alliance, settle Austro-Spanish disputes and restrain Russia proved too much, not for the fertile imagination of ministers, but for the practical execution of policy. This, in part, was an aspect of the degree of naivety in government assumptions. In 1722, for example, Townshend responded to Austrian concerns about the Anglo-French alliance by claiming that it was notorious that it was founded on a plan to establish and conserve the peace of all of Europe, and that this represented no threat to Charles VI, who should indeed co-operate with the allies,[27] an approach that reflected a failure to understand Austrian concerns and hopes, especially about the Habsburg succession and the position in Italy.[28]

Part of the problem for policy-makers was that they needed too often to rely on the threat of force, but that this was a limited asset not only in terms of the likely response of opponents, but also in terms of the strain placed on Britain's alliances. Thus, in the spring of 1720, Baron Karl Gustaf Sparre, the Swedish envoy in London, was able to report that the British were rapidly preparing a fleet of twenty ships of the line designed to assist in forcing Peter the Great to return his conquests from Sweden. Aside, however, from the problem of so doing, the pressure that Stanhope hoped to bring on Britain's main ally, France, to provide support for the policy[29] reflected the mismatch of goals and alliance system that so often characterised the attempt by interventionists to give a dynamic character to the latter. In an instructive comment on the, by then dead, minister the following year, Jean de Robethon, a Huguenot who acted as private secretary to George I and was an influential member of the Deutsche Kanzlei in London responsible for George's administration of Hanover, contrasted a new British envoy favourably with the vivacity and vast views of Stanhope.[30]

It was not only Stanhope who was no longer in control. In 1719, when the British government had moved towards speedy confrontation with Russia, Henry, 1st Duke of Kent, the Lord Privy Seal, was hopeful that naval action would help settle the problem:

> I only wish Sir John Norris may act as well and as readily on his part, as Sir George Byng did last year on his, and I question not but we shall have as good success; for our fleet in conjunction with the Swedes are able to beat anything.

James Craggs, Stanhope's co-Secretary, was disappointed by Admiral Norris's cautious response to Stanhope's policy:

> Sir John Norris has in a manner protested against it . . . he has surprised me, besides other reasons, I thought his personal pique to the Czar and his envy to Byng would have spurred him, but truly he comes out like all your blusterers a very little man.[31]

Kent, however, was replaced as Lord Privy Seal in June 1720, and Craggs died of smallpox in February 1721.

Another aspect of Stanhope's interventionism was provided by the war goal he enunciated during the conflict with Spain in 1718–20, what would now be termed 'regime change'. This goal was advanced in order to strengthen the international system, as understood by Stanhope, and also for prudential reasons. As he explained to Guillaume Dubois, the French foreign minister, he wanted the removal of Cardinal Giulio Alberoni, the most influential Spanish minister, in order to discourage other rash ministers from breaking treaties and seeking to overthrow rulers. Any peace with Alberoni, he claimed, would only be an armistice on his part.[32] Alberoni did indeed fall in December 1719, as the Spanish royal couple realised that his hold on office was an impediment to peace, but, once the latter was negotiated, their policies continued to be focused on Italian ambitions.

After his death, Stanhope's legacy was seen as problematic, but his example was difficult to resist, and each international crisis in the 1720s led to interventionist schemes. Most were overly ambitious. Thus, the hope in 1726 that the dispatch of a fleet to the Baltic would lead the Turks to attack Russia[33] rested on both wishful thinking and a misunderstanding of agency in the sense of the connections in international relations. The Turks were not going to be swayed by such action. Four years earlier, Carteret, then Secretary of State for the Southern Department, had told the Sardinian envoy that Victor Amadeus II, King of Sardinia, the ruler of Savoy-Piedmont, was in a position to be the counter-weight that Britain needed against the Habsburgs and the Bourbons, and that his forces, backed by British funds and a squadron in the Mediterranean, were strong enough to make him and Britain the arbiter of Italy.[34] This assessment ignored the military situation in northern Italy and the lessons of the War of the Quadruple Alliance with Spain: the defeat of the Spanish navy in 1718 by the British had not determined the struggle on land in Sicily between Savoyard and Spanish forces, an instructive instance of the weakness of an interventionism based on naval strength, but one lost to popular view in Britain due to the focus on success in battle. Allied to Austria and Britain during the War of the Spanish Succession,[35] Victor Amadeus had eventually been able to prevail against France in 1706, but this was no guide to what could be achieved without the support of a major land power.

To look at the cultural dimension, there were parallels between interventionist aspirations, the Whiggish interest in new constitutional and governmental arrangements, the apparent ability of Newtonian physics to reveal measurable and predictable relationships in the solar system, and the sense of optimism that focused on the South Sea Company, and led John, Lord Perceval to observe in 1720, 'there never was a more projecting year than this'.[36] Yet the British habit of defending their policy in terms of the support of the balance of power as the way to maintain peace,[37] or, to employ a modern concept, their stress on this as a normative basis for international order, was so disconnected from the attitude of other rulers that it is necessary to ask whether there was not some deep-seated intellectual flaw in the conceptualisation of interventionism. This is of significance for more than the 1720s, for it raises a fundamental question about British engagement with the Continent. It also relates to the deficiencies of structural interpretations.

This engagement with the Continent was presented at the time, and has been presented since, as stemming from a coherent and sensible response to Britain's geopolitical needs, in short an appropriate strategic culture.[38] The contours of the European world with which Britain engaged could be defined in terms of the interlinked ideas of balance of power and natural interests, and these could provide a clear guide both to how Britain should act, and to how other powers would, or, at least, should respond. Townshend presented the Anglo-French-Prussian Alliance of Hanover of 1725 as 'for the good of Europe' and as a means to end its troubles. Ever one for absolutes, he saw the goals of the rival Austro-Spanish Alliance of Vienna as 'with the utmost danger of destroying the peace, and subverting the liberties of Europe'.[39]

Thus, interventionism was the logical, the rational, position, countered only by the miserable prejudices of those who did not understand international relations and had no rational guide to define and explain best practice in policy, Tories in short. Five years earlier, the pro-government *London Journal*, a leading newspaper, in its issue of 1 October (os) 1720, claimed that

> The peace of the North and the establishment of the Protestant religion in the Empire, seem both very near at hand; neither of which, it is now very manifest, could ever have been effected without an universal war and desolation in that part of the world, if the court of Great Britain had not seasonably exerted themselves in a very extraordinary manner in both these affairs.

The domestic debate over foreign policy in the 1720s, particularly in the early and middle years of the decade, is an obscure subject that repays examination, but, first, it is necessary to consider the 'would', or, at least, 'should' approach to the policies of other states. This act-of-faith assumption helped explain the contrast between an apparently rational and consistent formulation of Britain's place in the international system and the somewhat incoherent nature of British policies, as *ad hoc* responses to situations in which other states did not act as anticipated led to a politics of frustration, despair and anger. For example, in the 1720s, it is striking how frequently the government, in peacetime, prepared (1720, 1726, 1727, 1729), or threatened to prepare, fleets, or, at least, squadrons, in order to give effect to diplomatic demands. In each case, the resort to the display of force represented an attempt to intimidate other powers into accepting British views, but, at the same time, tested the patience of Britain's allies, especially France. Particularly under Cardinal Fleury, the first minister from 1726, the French government was more reluctant to abandon the nuances of diplomacy for military preparations and brinkmanship. In 1729, proposals, from the British ministers left in charge of the government in London while George II went to Hanover, for the settlement of differences with Spain by the presentation of an ultimatum supported by the threat of naval action, specifically the blockade of Spain and of Spanish America, led to French protests.[40]

The British government found French reluctance frustrating, but the peacetime threat of force, while seen as a reasonable and acceptable response to the uncertainties and provocations of the policies of Russia, a state that was regarded, especially under Peter the Great, but also under his successors, as barely house-trained, did not seem acceptable in the case of Austria and Spain: although Spain itself mounted threatening naval preparations, for example in 1722, which exacerbated the general sense of uncertainty, as it was unclear for what they were intended. Furthermore, the British government's desire for settlement and certainty represented a different tactic to that sometimes suggested by envoys of welcoming continued disputes between other powers as possibly creating opportunities for Britain:[41] the ministry generally did not seek the need for managing uncertainty offered by the last.

On 27 November (os) 1722, the *Whitehall Journal*, a pro-government London newspaper, boasted that George I was 'stronger in his alliances and friendships abroad, than any king of England ever was before'. In many senses, the peace settlements of 1720–1, which ended both the war in the Mediterranean involving Britain, France, Spain, Austria and Savoy-Piedmont, and that in the Baltic – the Great Northern War – should have provided a propitious background for British foreign policy, as peace had been restored and the wars had sufficiently established the strength of the powers to permit a rational resolving of surviving disputes. In fact, the opposite proved the case. The wars left a range of disputes unresolved, including Spanish expansionist interests in Italy and Russian support for Charles Frederick, Duke of Holstein-Gottörp, a support that clashed with the concerns of Denmark and of George as Elector of Hanover, as well as a threatening Russian commitment to the Mecklenburg question.[42] In addition, it was readily apparent that rulers were not prepared to accept the British assessment of the course of the recent conflicts and confrontations, and thus of the relative distribution of power.

Philip V, indeed, saw peace as an opportunity to resume his Italian ambitions without the constraints of the war with France and Britain that he had not sought. When, in 1722, the British envoy noted that the Spanish minister José, Marquis of Grimaldo, was 'preaching to me every day against the exorbitant power of the Emperor and the necessity of lessening it to preserve the balance of Europe',[43] a frequent theme on the part of those concerned about Austria, for example Victor Amadeus II, the context was that of Spanish bellicosity, and not of the balance of power as a device for maintaining peace.

In the case of Peter the Great, there was no comparable sense that he had been checked in the recent war, while, for other powers, there was the same anxiety of unknowableness: the policies of neither Philip nor Peter could be readily explained in terms of the language of the balance of power. Instead, they appeared irrational, and thus unknowable. Coping with the consequences created both intellectual and policy problems. First, it was necessary to consider whether the goals and methods of these rulers could be understood and explained, other than as inchoate eruptions of a world of disorder that challenged the rationality of the international system. This, secondly, had related policy implications, for, if the latter was the case, then it was unclear whether there was any response other than to imagine that Britain was in a state of continuous war, and that the price of liberty was not only eternal vigilance but also a degree of preparedness that entailed both a high level of costly military preparedness and the shaping of Britain's alliance systems accordingly as part of an active interventionism. The former challenged domestic political assumptions about the nature and strength of the state, and about taxation, while the latter had serious implications, as it reduced Britain's options in alliance diplomacy.

The latter focused on France, and the state of the alliance can be variously emphasised. On one hand, it is appropriate to point out that it remained the basis of the foreign policies of the two states, and that they avoided supporting the interests of the other power when they threatened the vital concerns of their partner. On the other, it is possible to point to a lack of satisfaction with the conduct of the other,[44] and to stress the extent to which both powers unilaterally developed good relations with third parties, for example Britain with Prussia in 1723, and France with Spain in 1721–4 and 1727,[45] and often sought to persuade their alliance partner to yield in disputes with other powers. France, for example, backed Russian claims against George I in 1724, while British ministers expressed frequent concern about relations between France and Spain, although, in response, their French counterparts argued that they would strengthen the alliance.[46]

The question of where best to put the emphasis affected not only diplomatic consideration, but also the public debate. Both then, and on other occasions, government spokesmen, in Parliament and the press, found it difficult to introduce their audiences to the exigencies of alliance politics and the compromises that arose. This created difficulties in discussing the Hanoverian link, but was particularly problematic in the 1720s because of the strong element of distrust in British relations toward France, and because of the legacy of hostility between the two powers. Public support for an aggressive foreign policy was not constrained by the parameters of government policy-making. Instead, much of it conformed to an ideological, if not emotional, framework that was more comfortable with the Duke of Marlborough's campaigns against France in the 1700s than to any accommodation with the Bourbons. It would always have been hard for ministers and commentators to defend the difficulties of alliance politics, but it proved particularly so in the case of France. This was accentuated by the strength of the Whiggish conviction that Britain was the better-governed state and the more virtuous society: moral superiority was not the best basis from which to consider compromise.

Doubt about France was accentuated by concern over Franco-Spanish links, for Spain also triggered this sense of moral superiority. France had little support for the commercial privileges Britain had gained in the Spanish empire at the Peace of Utrecht in 1713, privileges that challenged French attempts to gain commercial concessions in this empire, limited French profits and led to persistent complaints from French mercantile circles, while France and Britain competed over colonial trade, for example in the West Indies and West Africa, and had clashing interests in North America.[47] Furthermore, France supported Spanish demands for the return of Gibraltar, captured by Britain in 1704, and ceded to her in the Utrecht settlement. In 1721, George I had promised to ask Parliament to return Gibraltar, but he evaded doing so, as Parliament would have rejected the approach.[48]

At a different level, French support for Spain also reflected wider conceptions of the international system. Although some French politicians supported an alliance with Austria, and this approach had been probed in 1715 and was to be attempted in 1728,[49] the dominant theme in French international policy was opposition to Austria. In so far as the notion of the balance of power had any real meaning, it was Austria that had gained the most in Europe since 1683, acquiring Hungary, northern Serbia and southwestern Romania from the Turks, and Naples, Lombardy, Sicily and modern Belgium from the Spanish Habsburg inheritance. Keen to weaken Austria, some French ministers looked with favour on Spanish schemes to regain her Italian possessions lost in the War of the Spanish Succession or, at least, to establish cadet branches of the Spanish Bourbons in Italy: but, to most British commentators, it was difficult to think of Austria as a challenge, because Britain had actively co-operated with Austria in the Nine Years' War and the War of the Spanish Succession.

Instead, for pro-government Whigs, it was easier to see Austrian strength as a valuable building block in the European order, but one that had been made actively disruptive by the particular interests of Charles VI. Indeed Horatio Walpole claimed that British public opinion regarded Austrian conduct and goals as comparable to that of France under Louis XIV, and similarly requiring a major effort to thwart.[50] That did not, however, have to entail a permanent lessening of Austrian power, and here Townshend's suggestion cited above was distinctly bold for a Whig minister. Tories, in contrast, had a potentially different response to Charles VI, as a Tory ministry had abandoned Austria in negotiating a unilateral end to the War of the Spanish Succession, and, as a prelude to doing so, Tory publicists depicted Charles's ambitions as excessive. This legacy of the Utrecht debate indeed played a role in the public discussion of policy in the 1720s, as politicians and writers sought to defend the present through the past, and vice versa. Alliance with France tested both approaches.

The British government was most suspicious of France in the case of Franco-Spanish relations, fearing, correctly, that France would seek commercial concessions and support aggressive Spanish policies in Italy. There was also serious tension over Baltic policy. Conscious of the decline of her traditional ally, Sweden, and of Russia's growing importance, France cultivated Russia in the early 1720s. This was at variance with the Hanoverian-influenced British policy which, from 1717 until 1730, was concerned to construct a Baltic alliance system that would restrain Russian power and, in particular, prevent Russian military intervention against Hanover on behalf of the Dukes of Holstein-Gottörp and Mecklenburg. Under George I, this policy was followed with scant consultation of France; and, indeed, with a reluctance to communicate details to the French government.[51]

Different policies in the Baltic produced strain, and led diplomats who were heavily involved in Baltic affairs, such as Whitworth, to be very suspicious of the French alliance and of French policies, and ready to advocate alternatives, in his case the concept of a Protestant league anchored on an Anglo-Prussian alliance.[52] Interest in co-operation with Victor Amadeus II[53] was an instructive, albeit less prominent, equivalent of this desire to reduce dependence on France. Whitworth did not see slight differences between Britain and France, but rather perceived France's Baltic strategy as an aspect of a more wide-ranging attempt to create a contrasting diplomatic system.[54] Like François, Seigneur de St Saphorin, who represented George I in Vienna, Whitworth thought that Austria should co-operate with George against Russia, and was angry that Austrian ministers did not heed what should be their interests.[55] In response to the concern of neighbouring powers about Russia, and thus their reluctance to co-operate against it, some British diplomats sought to offer a reassurance that relied on future contingencies, ironically comparable to the attitude that irritated the British government when shown by foreign ministers. Thus, in 1722, Whitworth wrote:

> The Czar may be a bug-bear to his neighbours; but neither his power, nor designs can immediately affect Great Britain, nor indeed be of any great importance to us, but in case of a general war, and by the diversion he might then make in the Empire. But I hope the prudence of his Majesty's councils, will be able to remove so disagreeable an incident, at least for some years; and in that time Providence may change the state of affairs to our advantage.[56]

The importance to George I of the apparent Russian threat in the early 1720s helped to put the Anglo-French alliance under strain. In 1717–20, there had been keen differences between Britain and France over Baltic policies, but these were subordinated to the common threat apparently posed by Philip V's aggression. The improvement of Anglo-French relations with Spain in the early 1720s – Spain acceded to the Quadruple Alliance in February 1720, signed a treaty with Britain and France in June 1721, and maintained generally favourable relations with both powers until the spring of 1725 – led, however, to a greater focus on Anglo-French differences over Russia, which included the French attempt to negotiate an Anglo-Russian reconciliation on terms judged unacceptable by George I. At the same time, French concern about the possibility of a *rapprochement* between Charles VI and Philip V, the very scenario that was indeed to occur in 1725 with the First Treaty of Vienna, caused French pressure on Britain for a settlement of Anglo-Spanish differences.[57]

Meanwhile, the death in 1723 of Dubois, French foreign minister from 1718 and, then, of Orléans, Regent for the young Louis XV from 1715, increased British anxiety about the intentions and stability of the French ministry.[58] This remained acute until the fall, in 1726, of Louis, Duke of Bourbon, the leading minister from 1723, led to a ministry under Fleury in whom the British had more confidence.[59]

Separately to this, the dynamics of Anglo-French relations altered in 1725, as the resumption of Franco-Spanish and Franco-Austrian hostility led to stronger French interest in the British alliance. This resulted in a return to the defensive rationale of the alliance, and it was then that it worked best, in both domestic and international terms. Both powers realised their mutual need, and the unilateral policy-making that had characterised the early 1720s was replaced by co-operation. Again, it is possible to present relations in different lights. The stress can be on an alliance strengthened by outside threat, or it can be argued that strains grew as the attempt to co-operate led to quarrels that had been mostly avoided whilst each power was largely going her separate way in the early 1720s. Thus, in August 1725, Horatio Walpole complained bitterly about 'the ignorance and incapacity in business' of France's leaders, and told Fleury, with whom he had close links, although not as close as he thought,

> What an ill impression the general opinion of their weakness, of their want of vigour and resolution in their councils and measures had upon the minds of all sorts of people to the disadvantage of France, that the timidity and concern they showed for fear of a war, would if care was not taken plunge them inevitably into a war.

There was still considerable British ministerial concern in early 1727 over what appeared to be French hesitation about going to war with the Vienna alliance.[60]

The search for co-operation was at once a facilitator and a barrier between, on the one hand, the means for the pursuit of foreign policy, both diplomatic and more forceful, at the government's disposal, and, on the other, the hopes of creating a coherent international settlement. The latter was eagerly sought: Horatio Walpole, in 1723, referred to 'a glorious prospect . . . of bringing the Congress at Cambrai to a happy conclusion, and, as the situation of affairs are at present in Europe, of settling the peace upon a solid foundation'; while to Newcastle the hope was of 'South and North being so settled, England will make the greatest figure that ever lived in any age, and our King be feared by his enemies and loved by his friends', and indeed 'make a greater figure in Europe than any of his predecessors'.[61]

This was a traditional theme of royal *gloire* that sits somewhat surprisingly alongside the usual emphasis on the balance of power, an emphasis that matched a commitment to the latter in British domestic politics.[62] The two ideas were partly reconciled in the concept of having, or holding, 'the balance in our hands', [63] but royal glory was indeed an important theme that is generally underplayed in modern treatments. Thus, in 1724, Horatio Walpole wrote to his brother Robert: 'Providence has by most surprising events, flung it into his Majesty's power to make the most glorious figure that ever was made by a British monarch, if the present opportunity be rightly understood and accordingly improved.'[64]

Alongside royal glory was the sense that a complete peace was attainable, and thanks to British efforts. In 1721, Temple Stanyan, Under Secretary in the Southern Department, wrote of 'the present interests of Europe, which we have now reason to hope will soon be settled upon a lasting foot'.[65] The previous December, George I's speech to Parliament had referred to the success of Britain's 'endeavours to establish a peace throughout Europe'.

Reality was far more difficult. The problems facing contemporaries in judging policy during the early 1720s was accentuated by the apparent importance of factionalism within the British and the French governments, and by the linkage of this factionalism to policy options. In the case of Britain, tension between the Sunderland and the Walpole–Townshend group dominated foreign perception, as the government was aware through postal interception.[66] This tension continued until 1724 when Carteret, formerly a protégé of Sunderland (who had died suddenly in 1722), was replaced as Secretary of State for the Southern Department by Newcastle who was then regarded as pliant by Walpole. Earlier, the deaths of Stanhope in 1721 and of Sunderland in 1722 had suggested a shift in British policy. Sunderland had guaranteed to the French government the pro-French views of Stanhope's successor, Townshend,[67] an interesting vignette on the character of both government and the alliance, but then he had died. It was scarcely surprising that the French government was keen to find out about political changes in Britain,[68] and, indeed, Carteret assured Dubois that Townshend was not pro-Austrian.[69] The possibility of a total change in the British government was suggested by French knowledge of links between Sunderland and the Jacobites, and the suspicion that this might lead to a Stuart return.[70] That did not happen, but intercepted diplomatic traffic ensured that British ministers were aware of subsequent French concern about a possible change of ministry.[71]

In turn, the British government associated its interests in France with those of Orléans, and saw the alliance in terms of his position and then of the Court politics that followed his death in 1723.[72] This underlined distrust of particular French diplomats, such as Louis-François-Armand, Duke of Richelieu, envoy in Vienna.[73] As a reminder of this related theme of dynasties and Courts, and of the extent to which an emphasis on the structural interests of states and on a states-system can be misleading, it is instructive to note a letter from Carteret of 1721:

> We begin to be very easy about the late matches in France and Spain. The Regent has sustained himself by them, and will still stand in need of the King, if he thinks of preserving his succession to the Crown of France. The Regent and the Cardinal [Dubois] continue their assurances to His Majesty, and Lord Sunderland and I are both of the King's opinion that these matches will be of great use to us for the present,[74]

the last an interesting caveat about the proposed marriages between the royal families of France and Spain. Looked at differently, French support for the alliance appeared based on a very small group that might be overthrown by death, by other changes in the royal family, or by the fall of the leading minister. This was understandably the hope of the generally over-optimistic Jacobites, 'James III and VIII' claiming in 1721 that he had only one enemy in France, Dubois,[75] but other commentators also shared this view. George Tilson, Townshend's Under Secretary, regretted Dubois' death in 1723 as he had 'a strong inclination towards England',[76] which he had indeed visited. Dubois was certainly disinclined to regard signs of domestic opposition in Britain as proof of instability,[77] and the French government provided its British counterpart with valuable information about Jacobite schemes in 1722.[78]

The instability of French politics challenged the possibilities of British interventionism and was certainly a factor in the shaping of the Anglo-French alliance.[79] The Austrians sought to play upon this instability, suggesting that Britain and Austria ought to plan the measures necessary in the event of France changing policy.[80] Uncertainty about the future views of France ensured that, unlike with the Dutch, Britain's most prominent ally after France, any strengthening of France was also a cause of concern to British policy-makers. This was a view that in part was underlined by the extent to which the notion of the balance of power encouraged a quantification of power. In 1722, Whitworth noted,

> It is impossible not to be satisfied with the Cardinal's [Dubois'] way of acting; and as all his views are certainly turned at present for maintaining peace, there is no reason to suspect his civilities; But at the same time his aim is to put the kingdom and the funds of the government in such a condition by degrees as will make them a very dangerous neighbour, if

ever their intentions should change, except we make the same use of this
interval on our side, and set ourselves in a posture to be respected, by
appeasing the discontents of the people, and taking just measures of our
affairs at home and abroad.[81]

The sense of needing to be on guard was captured by the pro-government
St. James' Journal of 23 February (os) 1723: it condemned the Tories for
negotiating the Treaty of Utrecht, declared that the Whig oversight of the
alliance had benefited Britain, and added 'as to France, it being naturally the
greatest and most powerful Crown of Europe, notwithstanding its circumstances or any lesser disadvantages; it is the interest of Great Britain to
watch its designs, and always to arm against any further acquisitions'. At the
same time, French diplomats thought that domestic trouble in Britain could
be of value for France.[82]

   Although more pragmatic and willing to mould interventionism to events
than Stanhope, Townshend did not share his brother-in-law Robert Walpole's more cautious approach to diplomatic commitments. Instead, the
willingness to respond to international developments and to consider different territorial arrangements, indicated by his letter of 1725 quoted above,
had been apparent prior to the crisis created by the negotiation of the Alliance of Vienna that year. Indeed, in accordance with the then anti-Imperial
direction of policy by George I as Elector, Townshend was regarded as
particularly keen to humiliate and restrain the Habsburgs.[83]

   This, however, entailed a pro-active policy that also required the prospect
of military support in order to overcome the small size of the British army
and the vulnerability of Hanover. In the late 1710s, this support had been
provided initially by alliance with the Dutch, who were willing in 1715–16
to send troops to Britain to help against the Jacobites, then, from 1716, by
alliance with France, and, finally, as additional strength was sought against
Russia, by the creation of a coalition that included Austria, Prussia, Denmark
and Sweden, with Prussia playing the key role in covering Hanover.[84] This
coalition, however, had fallen apart under the pressure of translating hopes
into action, and this left George I and his ministers in a difficult position in
the early 1720s. The Dutch were asked for troops in 1722 when Jacobite
action was anticipated against Britain,[85] but, aside from an initial lack of
unity on that occasion, they were not in a position to protect Hanover.[86]

   The British response, an alliance with Prussia in 1723, could be defended
by a ragbag of reasons, including religious affinity, opposition to the despotic jurisdictional aspirations of Charles VI,[87] or the pursuit of balance
within the Empire. Indeed, as the alliance conformed to traditional ideas
that religion should play a role in foreign policy, the pragmatism that motivated it was less apparent in the public sphere. In fact, the crucial reason for
ministers was the availability of Prussian troops. As Tilson noted, 'near
80,000 men, such well disciplined troops, are a very formidable body'.[88]
Townshend stressed the value of the troops, presenting them as a force

multiplier that gave Britain independence, but underplaying Frederick William I of Prussia's ability to determine his own priorities. Townshend also emphasised the domestic attraction of the alliance:

> the great advantage of the treaty we have made there; which in effect puts into the scale with His Majesty the whole force and strength of Prussia, at least three score thousand men, excellent troops. Before this the power of Great Britain lay only in its fleet, which though strong, and of great command in maritime cases; yet as every body saw how low the States General were, with the jealousies and distrusts that were fomented between the King and his Prussian Majesty and that we had no land forces to spare, the respect our fleet carried could not spread its influence so far as was necessary. But now this strict union is made with the King of Prussia, and his Majesty is become master as it were of so mighty a land force, he will not only be more secure, but also more respected both in the North and the South, and have it in his power to act more independently from the Houses both of Austria and Bourbon, and preserve the peace of Europe with less submission to the terms of either. This union so established must be lasting because the King of Prussia cannot but have the same views and interests with his Majesty in those respects . . . besides, this will sound well in England, nothing more than what we were engaged in before, and a renewal of an alliance only that have been long subsisting . . . and consequently impossible to raise any cavils and misconstructions there being no mention nor the least notice taken in this treaty of the late treaties made with the King of Prussia upon the account of the Northern War,[89]

in other words nothing with reference to Hanover's gains from Sweden.

The hope that Prussia would serve Britain's purposes fell victim, in 1726, to Frederick William's concern about Austria and Russia, for the rise of Russian power under Peter the Great had altered the international system even more than that of Prussia had done. Even without this, Townshend failed to allow for Frederick William's ability to define his own path. What was as interesting in Townshend's letter was the combination of the determination to act an important role and the wish to do so in an independent fashion. In some respects, this was an admission of the drawback of interventionism: its reliance on co-operation. One of the major attractions of 'Blue Water' policies, those that focused on maritime and trans-oceanic interests, in contrast, was that no such compromise in goals or methods was necessary. In modern terms, they were unilateral.

Another drawback of interventionism was the open-ended nature of the commitment stemming from the desire to settle problems. The host of challenges to British interests, included anxiety about Catholic intentions[90] (which was stronger than the concerns of Catholic powers, which, instead, focused on the position of co-religionists under British rule, for example in

Majorca,[91] Britain and Ireland); as well as fears over Jacobitism, worries about trade and Gibraltar, and the interests of the King as Elector. These varied concerns lent added weight to the desire to satisfy, or at least settle, the interests of others, for fear that, otherwise, they would act against Britain. There was also for British policy-makers the problem of means and goals, which focused in particular on Charles VI: the idea of preserving Habsburg power while, at the same time, restraining its actions, and of acting with vigour 'without coming to extremities',[92] posed problems that British ministers were unsure how to address,[93] and this was to be a dilemma in other alliances as well.

Whatever the goals of ministers, the regular need to face Parliament[94] created problems of its own. If, in 1726, George I could conclude 'that a steady and resolute behaviour on the part of the king and his allies, will soon reduce the Court of Spain to a necessity of abandoning their wild projects, and making up with those powers',[95] a problem was set by timing: the exigencies of domestic politics, not least the annual meeting of Parliament, ensured that 'soon' had to be sooner than for other governments. This helped account for the often frenetic character of British policy, especially late in each year, and the resulting strains in Britain's alliances as the British government made demands for clarification and support.

Modern scholars face the problem of how best to evaluate the response of ministers and diplomats to these dilemmas when the insights offered by the documents are very limited. George I's visits to Hanover in 1720, 1723 and 1725 ensured that there was both official and private correspondence between the ministers who accompanied the King and those who remained in Britain, and this has been cited in this chapter, but because George remained in England in 1721, 1722, 1724, 1726, and died *en route* to Hanover in 1727, there were no comparable sources for those years. Furthermore, George II did not visit Hanover until the summer of 1729. As a result, there is an episodic quality to the surviving material. Furthermore, the extent to which coherent accounts, as opposed to brief reflections, were offered is limited. There are also significant gaps in the private papers of ministers and diplomats, for example those of Carteret. The survival of letters in his hand marked 'burn this' and 'particuliere a bruler'[96] raises the prospect that he took steps to try to ensure the destruction of sensitive papers, and there is no reason to imagine that other ministers did not do likewise. Many of Robert Walpole's papers were burnt when he fell from office in 1742.

The Hanoverian stance in the international crisis of 1725–7 is particularly obscure. Bernstorff, who attended George I at Hanover on his visit in 1725, was unhappy with the estrangement from Austria seen with the negotiation of the Treaty of Hanover. George I's Chamberlain, Friedrich von Fabrice, sought to dissuade George I from anti-Austrian steps and was secretly in touch with Berlin, which turned to Austria in 1726, but it is unclear how far other Hanoverian ministers shared his views. George II's initial plan to send

Fabrice as envoy to Dresden, a possible base for negotiating a reconciliation with Austria (the Saxon envoy in London was secretly used to this end in early 1728) would have been unwelcome to Townshend, the relevant Secretary of State, who had unsuccessfully tried to get him dismissed in 1726, but one instance of the often acute suspicion felt by British ministers and diplomats toward their Hanoverian counterparts. In addition, although the Austrian envoy in London thought him too fearful of the British ministers, Hans, Count Bothmer was regarded as pro-Austrian, and was also believed to have been employed by George I to investigate a complaint by the Hanoverian Council of Ministers that Townshend had neglected the opportunity to win the support of Brunswick-Wolfenbüttel.[97]

More generally, relations between Brunswick-Wolfenbüttel and Hanover have been neglected as a way to approach Hanoverian policy, as have been the diplomatic archives for Brunswick-Wolfenbüttel which, for example, include material not only for August Wilhelm, Duke from 1714 to 1731, and his brother Ludwig Rudolf, Duke from 1731 to 1735, but also for the latter's son-in-law, Ferdinand Albrecht of Brunswick-Bevern, who was eventually to succeed to Brunswick-Wolfenbüttel in 1735 and who was a staunch supporter of Austria and a regular correspondent of Prince Eugene's. Aside from providing information on potential threats to Hanover, the Brunswick-Wolfenbüttel perspective is also of value because of suggestions that it could serve to manage a reconciliation between Georges I and II and Charles VI and/or Peter II of Russia.[98] This perspective can be supplemented from other sources, such as the correspondence between the French government and Baron Johann Christoph von Schleinitz, one of the leading Brunswick-Wolfenbüttel diplomats, who was in receipt of a French pension. Much of this correspondence focused on attempts not only to ensure good relations but also to provide a possible route for improved relations with Austria.[99] The correspondence includes hints that particular disputes between Hanover and Brunswick-Wolfenbüttel challenged the prospect of using this route,[100] but there was also comments on the negative role of Townshend and the inaction of Horatio Walpole.[101] Schleinitz saw Bothmer as a crucial intermediary for links between George I and Brunswick-Wolfenbüttel, although he also had Görtz in mind and claimed to be close to Münchhausen.[102] In 1727, Schleinitz emphasised the continued prospects for better relations between Hanover and Brunswick-Wolfenbüttel.[103]

The neglect of the Brunswick-Wolfenbüttel dimension for this and other crises underlines the extent to which much of the work on north German diplomatic relations for this period has not been done; the same, for example, is also true of Hanoverian-Saxon relations, an aspect of the general neglect of Saxony in recent work. Furthermore, Schleinitz, who was to play a partly unclear role in the troubled Anglo-Wittelsbach relations that helped to precipitate the crisis in relations between Walpole and Townshend in 1729–30,[104] is an instance of the large number of members of the diplomatic cast whose position is obscure and whose reports are therefore difficult to evaluate. The absence of much of the necessary work on links with Hanover's neighbours and near-neighbours underlines the stress, at the outset of this chapter, on the need for caution in making judgements.

The same conclusion emerges from the difficulty of assessing the views of both George I and George II. Informed observers, such as Friedrich Thöm, the envoy of Brunswick-Wolfenbüttel, reported differences between one or other monarch and the Hanoverian ministers,[105] but, irrespective of these differences, the paucity of consistently reliable accounts of royal views ensures only episodic vignettes, and it is difficult to assess how far these represented sustained views. Hanoverian initiatives certainly compromised British policy. In 1725, Charles Du Bourgay reported from Berlin that the Regency of Hanover had informed the Prussians that, if they continued forcible recruiting in Hanover, action would be taken to force them to respect Imperial law on the matter: this initiative had not gone through Du Bourgay's hands.[106]

Prior to the debate, from 1725, over the Alliance of Hanover, the 1720s were years in which the public discussion of foreign policy was relatively limited. Indeed, the lack of news was a matter of note, Tilson commenting on the Writer of the *Gazette*, 'Poor Samuel Buckley will murmur at peace and quietness; since it quite starves his consumptive gazette, but an Irish Parliament, and a Swedish Diet may now and then afford a morsel'.[107] In the event, the sessions of the Westminster Parliament in 1724 and 1725 were particularly quiet, and were perceived, both domestically and internationally, as a success for the government.[108]

In the meanwhile, the reduction of international tension outwith the Baltic, as problems over Italy between France and Spain were addressed to the international Congress at Cambrai which was formally opened in 1724 (discussions had been held there from 1722),[109] further helped dampen domestic interest in foreign policy. The complexity of the issues at stake – should the garrisons in Tuscany that would secure the eventual succession of Philip V's son, Don Carlos, be Spanish or neutral, and so on[110] – did not lend themselves to domestic discussion, and it was also difficult to work up a sense of urgency about them.

This was an apparently safe degree of commitment to European power politics, but it was also deceptive because the congress swiftly stalemated, which helped to underline the fragile basis of British optimism. This fragility was to be repeated in 1728–9, when the Congress of Soissons neither solved international disputes nor settled Anglo-Hanoverian concerns. Instead, the failure of the Congress was followed, in the summer of 1729, by preparations for war with Spain and by a panic about the prospect of a Prussian attack on Hanover.[111] In short, British policy alternated between a misplaced confidence in diplomacy and a reliance on the threat of force. Neither sufficed in the 1720s, but alliance with France helped cover these deficiencies, although it exposed the ministry to domestic attack and was also distrusted within the government, not least by diplomats,[112] a sentiment shared by French counterparts.[113]

In terms of the domestic British debate, however, it is uncertain how far the failure of policy can be said to have helped encourage the move toward non-interventionism that was to be seen with the years of Robert Walpole's dominance in the 1730s, and to become increasingly pronounced again from the 1760s. Indeed, the process by which ideas on foreign policy developed is unclear. In particular, there is a lack of clarity over how far the exchange of ideas related largely to the particular political context of the moment, and were in large part therefore opportunistic,[114] and, in contrast, how far they can be seen to have an independent existence.[115] In practice, the former helped account for partisan bite and political sponsorship,[116] leading to the reformulation of existing ideas for particular contingencies. If there was a major development in ideas about Britain's imperial status, that can be largely dated to mid-century,[117] and earlier anticipations, although interesting, were limited in their impact on the debate on foreign policy.

In the 1720s, the stop-start character of diplomacy, particular the alteration of congresses with war-panics, created problems for commentators, not least because of a practice of secrecy that thwarted diplomats themselves,[118] juxtaposed with a wealth of rumour, that fed off the secretive nature of European personal monarchies. *Wye's Letter*, the most influential British newsletter, not least because of its role as a source for newspaper items, noted in its issue of 24 April (os) 1722:

> Our advices from abroad still amuse us with stories of fresh wars ready to break out in Europe, particularly that the Czar has in view some enterprises of very great consequence; but what they are can't yet be known, his subjects being forbid, under severe penalties, to give notice to anyone abroad of what is doing in his dominions ... it is apprehended that the Czar will bend his main force towards Poland and Germany.

Two days later, another newsletter, the *General Post-Office Letter*, noted reports that Britain was to send a fleet to the Baltic, and Spain to invade Tuscany, while, on 28 April (os), it added that the Turks were to invade Poland, and the Pretender ('James III and VIII') was to move to France. If that was not enough to spread concern, *Wye's Letter* of 1 May (os), reported that the French were to invade Italy and the Russians Norway. Newsletters and newspapers strove to shape the news and reduce it to order. Thus, the *Evening Journal* of 7 December (os) 1727 began an article by remarking 'The present revival of the dispute in France concerning the constitution of Pope Clement XI, makes it necessary to refresh the readers memory with a general account of the rise and progress of that affair'. On the whole, however, news arrived and was presented in an episodic and apparently chaotic fashion.

The apparently kaleidoscopic quality of international relations owed much to the willingness of diplomats and newspapers to report rumours, and was exacerbated by the number of diplomatic projectors, accredited or, more generally, not, who agitated the waters, men such as Charles, 3rd Earl of Peterborough, Jan Willem Ripperda, Giuseppe Riva, Bishop Strickland and Scaramuccia Visconti, whose intentions and impact were, and indeed still are, frequently unclear.[119] If the shifts in British diplomacy made it difficult to present policy as consistent, they encouraged an emphasis on the particular moment. This provided opportunities to criticise opponents for inconsistency. On 11 February (os) 1727, the *London Journal* attacked the opposition *Occasional Writer*:

> But as self-love naturally disposes men to like those best, next to them-selves, who resemble them most, I do not wonder at your showing for the Emperor, whom you formerly so much abhorred, so great a concern and friendship, since he has acted so ungrateful a part towards this nation.

Even so, writers struggled with the question of what it was feasible to suggest. Benjamin Hoadly, an episcopal and expert defender of government policy, in his pamphlet *Enquiry into the Reasons of the Conduct of Great Britain with Relation to the Present State of Affairs in Europe* (London, 1727), opened with 'The whole face of affairs in Europe is, within the space of the last year, so much altered; it is almost impossible for the most unconcerned spectator to prevent his thoughts from running out into ques-tions and suppositions about it'.[120] Hoadly was critical of the inconsistency of Britain's current enemies: 'is not this the King of Spain – of that country which has always felt the want of the friendship of Britain' and of Charles VI, 'is not this Prince, whom we once bore upon our shoulders, out of the reach of all his enemies'.[121] Subsequently, in *A Defence of the Enquiry into the Reasons of Great Britain* (London, 1729), Hoadly argued, with reference to the Preliminaries of Paris of 1727:

> The measures therefore entered into, did not produce so much good, nor so soon, as might reasonably have been expected: and all men must judge to whose account this is to be charged. But then, we must not forget, what their immediate good effects were. Their preventing the execution of the worst designs against ourselves; the protection and encouragement given by them to those powers abroad, whose preserva-tion nearly touches our own national interest: and the like. But at length, they operated farther; and produced what was the main thing aimed at by them, viz a sufficient basis for a general pacification; and what must and would in fact have proved so before this time, had not the conduct of Spain, which could not be foreseen, prevented the natural and effectual operation of things.[122]

By 1729, Hoadly was an experienced writer on foreign policy, but he still found it difficult to cope with the problem of shaping the uncertainty of developments. It was simpler to focus on specific points. Thus, in 1730, *The Treaty of Seville and the Measures that have been taken for the Four Last Years, Impartially Considered*, an anonymous pamphlet, was able to explain the problems posed by Charles VI's establishment of the Ostend Company in 1722:

> the great objection I have to the Ostend Trade, is not merely as it is trade; but, what I think of much greater concern to England, as it is setting up a new naval power in Europe, and that at our door, as it were, and in our Channel. We suffered enough by the Dunkirk squadrons in the last wars, not to be sensible what a prejudice it would be to the British commerce to have the like squadrons always lying in wait for us at Ostend. But if Ostend were not so near, it is infinitely our concern not to suffer a new naval power to be set up, if we can possibly hinder it. If our fleet is our glory and our strength, as we are perpetually told it is, especially by the gentlemen of the other side, I would ask, how it comes to be so? Is it not because we are superior at sea to any other power? But how long shall we be able to maintain our superiority, if new naval powers are suffered to arise? Is not all strength comparative, and will not the greatest power of any nation become mere weakness, if it becomes easy for the neighbouring powers, by an union of their fleets, to be greatly superior to it? The British fleet can no longer be considerable, than while it is greater than any that can easily be combined against it; but that it is impossible it should long be, if the Emperor can ever have a naval strength.

This threat was substantiated by a sensible consideration of how Russian naval power had developed under Peter the Great, and with what consequences.[123]

Such a discussion was all too rare from pro-government writers or speakers, because most of the specific points at issue as far as the public debate was concerned were opposition issues or lent themselves to presentation in these terms. This was true of the retention of Gibraltar, Hessian subsidies, Spanish depredations, and illicit French repairs to the harbour of Dunkirk in breach of the provisions of the Treaty of Utrecht. The last was but the most prominent of a series of issues that served to undermine the alliance with France. Opposition spokesmen tended to argue from the particular to the general, using these individual cases to claim that the government had no sense of the national interest, and was therefore unable to defend it, and also to argue that Britain's alliance partners followed selfish and/or dangerous policies, and that government claims about the allegedly threatening intentions and moves of powers deemed hostile were exaggerated. For example, the Tory *Weekly Journal* was sceptical, in its issue of 11 February (os) 1721, about French statements that they would reduce the army, while, in January 1727, William Pulteney, the leading opposition Whig spokesman in the House of Commons, told the House that he had seen the terms of the Treaty of Vienna, and that they were only defensive.[124] Five years earlier, another leading opposition Whig, William, 2nd Earl Cowper, had complained in the House of Lords about the building of ships in British shipyards for France, offering a host of reasons, including the danger that the French government would change, the risk that the public would become fearful, 'Would the Romans have done this for the Carthaginians or vice versa?', and that 'it would not be permitted to build forts on a frontier, and sell them to a neighbour – ships are our forts'.[125]

In contrast, pro-government spokesmen tended to argue from the general to the particular, asserting principles of conduct which they then applied to points at dispute. More than this, however, was at stake. Pro-government spokesmen also advocated a conception of the international order in which they presented British national interests as expressed and defended. This approach encompassed alliance with France, commitments to Hanover and a holistic sense of the international order that required effort in order to thwart the impact of selfish particular interests. Thus, the pro-government understanding of international relations, a perspective that has not been probed adequately, matched that of the domestic situation: there opposition was treated as factionalism, and therefore denied legitimacy. In international terms, this attitude made it hard to respond to revisionist powers, while, in Britain, such an approach made it difficult to manage a transition of power between political powers. As a consequence, the proscription of the Tories that followed the accession of George I in 1714 helped lead to a Jacobite rebellion in 1715.

In the conceptualisation of international relations in the 1720s by British commentators, there was a comparable unwillingness to accept ambivalence. Although there were exceptions, the *London Journal* of 26 March (os) 1726 pointing out that it would be difficult to settle differences amicably, pro-government and opposition spokesmen both did all too little to encourage a sense that there were serious limits to what could be achieved. The relationship between this and policy can be suggested by the contrast with the 1730s, when the politics of prudence and the diplomacy of restraint was both pursued by the Walpole ministry and advocated by its spokesmen.[126]

In part, both a reluctance to accept ambivalence and, eventually, a politics of prudence were also responses to the uncertainty created by the astonishing sense of flux that characterised international relations in the period, and that is underrated when scholars focus on schematic analyses of international relations and the allegedly structural interests of states. Drawing on the presentation of particular monarchs and ministers as wilful mavericks, and resting on an awareness of the close relationship between foreign policy and the volatile world of domestic, especially Court, politics, this sense of flux led to a willingness to consider a range of options that is totally ignored by the ordered presentation of policy in the period. As an instance of the views of a well-informed contemporary, John, Viscount Perceval observed in 1726:

> France and the Emperor have no ground of quarrel neither has Spain any claim on France, only a resentment for sending home the Lady,[127] which surely ought not to be an occasion to raise Mars out of his sleep, but there is a spirit of Don Quixotism remaining there which joined with Italian revenge[128] provokes them to insist that Monsr le Duc[129] be removed from the management of affairs, if Frejus[130] have credit enough it may be brought about, and that may produce a new scene. France may grow cool in her alliance with us having no farther use of it, and we together with Prussia be left to renew our friendship with the Emperor and Spain as well as we can. If the Dutch accede to our alliance as tis everyday expected, it will be of service, poor and unprepared as they are, and then we may talk big in the ensuing Parliament against the Ostend trade, but otherwise I cannot think we shall take violent resolutions in that affair, especially if it be that there is so great spirit raised against this French treaty, that it will require all the ministrys attention to allay it without permitting them to look to things abroad. But I have been so used to see these sort of violent gusts end in a calm, that I don't think these quarrelsome gentlemen will carry their point, which they tell us is to unhinge the ministry. This requires a great deal more firmness and fidelity to each other to go that length than we have observed of late years, and there must go with it a secret co-operation of the Crown.[131]

This was very much the world of newspaper reports and of the far-flung speculations of anxious coffee-house politicians satirised by Henry Fielding in his play *Rape Upon Rape* (1730); but it was not separate from the debate over interventionism, nor from the world of diplomatic consideration. Indeed, diplomats read newspapers and newsletters,[132] and their correspondence, both then and throughout the century, was full of the unpredictable, the unexpected and the unknowable, frequently combining in the same report very contrasting items.[133] The sense of uncertainty created problems for ministers, with the public character of politics ensuring that British ministers were more exposed to scrutiny than Continental counterparts.

Aside from the difficulty of knowing how best to respond, there was also the question of how to understand and conceptualise this very volatile international world. The optimistic interventionist schemes of the 1710s, the congresses of the 1720s, and the politics of prudence of the 1730s were, at one level, strategies for an intellectual response. Whichever strategy was followed, however, the unpredictabilities that stemmed from the role of monarchs were a problem – would for example, Louis XV's reaching his majority 'dispose the present system of Europe to change',[134] or would his marriage have this effect, or, indeed, would he live any longer than his cousin, Philip V's son, Luis I, who was only briefly king of Spain in 1724? Indeed, in 1728, Louis had an attack of smallpox that led to an intense, albeit brief, period of international concern and speculation. In 1722, there was speculation that the death of Augustus II of Saxony-Poland 'would soon have the world in an uproar',[135] as it was indeed to do, but not until 1733; while, also that year, Townshend felt it necessary to ask the Sardinian envoy about a league of France, Spain and Russia intended to force Charles VI to provide a territory for 'James III and VIII'.[136] As an instance of the range of contemporary rumour, the papers of Louis-François-Armand, Duke of Richelieu, French envoy in Vienna, refer to an (in fact inaccurate) report at Brussels in March 1726 that Austria, France and Spain were secretly planning a Catholic league to restore Spanish control over the United Provinces and Stuart rule in Britain.[137]

The belief that governments in states with representative assemblies could readily be subverted or overthrown by domestic action or foreign bribery was an equivalent to uncertainty about dynastic outcomes. Thus, in 1726, Karl Josef von Palm, the Austrian envoy in London, reported that the British were using bribes to win Dutch and French support.[138] Some foreign envoys sought to co-operate with the parliamentary opposition in Britain, while the implications of any Jacobite action were also considered by diplomats. The instructions to the new French envoy in 1726 noted that opponents of the Anglo-French alliance made no secret of their hope that the death of George I would bring change.[139] Whatever the type of government, the extent to which policy was a response to specific conjunctures (a course urged by the French diplomat Anne-Théodore Chevignard de Chavigny in 1720 when he criticised closeness to Britain[140]) created problems for those seeking predictable order, as did what was perceived as a willingness to wait, if not procrastinate, in order to see if more favourable circumstances arose.[141]

Not only was it necessary for commentators to confront a challenging sense of flux, and to link the specific to the general (and vice versa); it was also necessary for them to match popular expectations that international relations should be clearly expressed. Philip Perceval struck the tone of desirable ready comprehension when he wrote to his brother in 1727, 'I can't but think our intermeddling between the Emperor and Spain has ended not much unlike some who have busily interposed to prevent mischief between a man and wife engaged in strife, who in the end got no other thanks but injuries from both';[142] while the sarcastic style of some of the printed polemic, such as the pamphlet *A Modest Apology for Parson Alberoni* (4th edn, London, 1719), contributed to the same end.

Aside from indicating the deficiencies of an interventionist ethos and practice, British foreign policy in the 1720s also suggests that an apparently inconsequential period could play a role in the development of this policy. This was particularly so because of the weight of memory seen in the public debate over policy and also, albeit less clearly, in the deliberations of ministers. The Peace of Utrecht proved particularly controversial, not least because it served as a lodestar for judgements of the War of the Spanish Succession and of Tory views on foreign policy. *A Letter from a Gentleman at Edinburgh to his Friend in London* (London, 1719), a pro-government pamphlet, claimed that Utrecht had failed to offer sufficient protection against the consequences of the Bourbon accession, referring, in contrast, to 'the Quadruple Alliance [of 1718], which supplies the defects of these treaties as to the separation of the two crowns [France and Spain], and the securing the Protestant succession in Great Britain'.[143] On 12 March (os) 1726, *Mist's Weekly Journal*, the leading Tory newspaper, and one written by an active Jacobite, pointed out that the Whigs had changed their position on Utrecht:

> those who formerly clamoured against the Peace [of Utrecht], are the people who now murmur more than any others at the too great power of the Emperor [Charles VI], though they have not gratitude enough to give their thanks to those[144] who were wise enough to put a stop to it before it grew more dangerous.

If nothing from the 1720s matched the impact of Utrecht, the decade, nevertheless, left a legacy of events and issues to debate and consider. Aside from the continuation of the French alliance, these included the crisis over Spanish depredations in 1729, one that helped guide responses in a similar crisis a decade later, as well, more generally, as the confrontation between the Hanover and Vienna alliances, and the apparent futility of the international congresses at Cambrai and Soissons. There was to be no such enthusiasm for congresses in the 1730s. These responses were as much aspects of the learning curve of post-Glorious Revolution British foreign policy as the major conflicts of 1689–97 and 1702–13. As already indicated, however, care is required in considering the interaction of experience and ideas. A reaction against the 1720s can be seen in the 1730s, but Newcastle, a Secretary of State from 1724 until 1754, was to be the central figure in the interventionism that followed 1748.

The 1720s are not alone in suffering relative scholarly neglect. The same is true for example of Britain's Continental policy from the failure of The Hague negotiations in 1735 to settle the War of the Polish Succession, until the accession of Frederick the Great in Prussia in 1740, and, again, albeit to a lesser extent, recently of Carteret's foreign policy during the 1740s, and of that of the Fox–North ministry in 1783. Given the importance of foreign policy and war in British political and governmental history of the period, this neglect of the factors shaping the state's international goals is unfortunate. As significant, it is necessary to judge these factors in terms of the assumptions of contemporaries and the pressures moulding their consideration. To downplay these in favour of modish modern conceptions is unhelpful.

5   Opposition to
interventionism, 1731–40

Proportionate coverage of foreign policy in the 1730s has suffered from the general focus, for the century as a whole, on periods of war, not least the moves towards war, as well as wartime alliance dynamics, both of which appear very important as a result of interest in the expansion of empire. This Atlanticist focus on British policy has been further enhanced by a stress on relations with France and Spain. In contrast, there has been a relative neglect, especially over the last decade, of relations with Northern, Eastern and Central Europe, particularly so for periods of peace. Thus, relations with Prussia appear of great consequence during the Seven Years' War (1756–63), but far less so for the 1730s. The latter indeed can claim to be one of the most obscure periods in British foreign policy. The negotiation of the Second Treaty of Vienna in 1731, an agreement between Britain and Austria that brought the Anglo-French alliance to a close, has attracted attention, as has British neutrality in the War of the Polish Succession (1733–5),[1] and the outbreak of the War of Jenkins' Ear with Spain in 1739,[2] but the intervening periods have been largely neglected.[3] This is particularly the case from the failure of the attempt to mediate in the War of the Polish Succession[4] until the end of the decade, with the important exception of deteriorating relations with Spain.

This is unhelpful, as the late 1730s provided an important case study of the consequences of what, in some eyes, was a policy of failure: it can be seen as indicating both the drawbacks of isolationism and, on the contrary, the failure of interventionism. In the late 1720s and early 1730s, in contrast, there had been a determined interventionism, and an engagement with the problems of the Continent. This had led not only to the negotiation of the Second Treaty of Vienna in 1731, but also to a determined effort thereafter to solve outstanding problems, especially disputes in Italy involving Austria, Sardinia and Spain.[5]

Setting this against the background of the Hanoverian link is difficult, as the role of Hanover in British foreign policy in the 1730s is unclear, not least because the views and position of Johann Philipp von Hattorf, head of the Hanoverian Chancery in London until 1737, and of his successor Ernst, Freiherr von Steinberg, are obscure. The view that Hanoverian goals had too great an impact was held by experts. In the negotiation of the Second Treaty of Vienna, the Hanoverian demands were eventually shelved, having been, as Thomas Pelham, MP as well as diplomat, noted, 'the chief clog to this negotiation'. Indeed, Charles VI had referred to George's wish to have the Mecklenburg issue settled in accordance with his fantasies.[6] Thomas Robinson, envoy in Vienna from 1730 to 1748, was a knowledgeable critic of the impact of Hanoverian concerns. He wrote to Newcastle, significantly not the Secretary of State for his department, but a political patron, in 1732:

> almost all that has for two years past come out of the German Chancery, whether at Hanover, or at London, has done more hurt to the good understanding of the two Courts, than anything else . . . the Emperor is to be won by the King with mutual offices and mutual complaisance, and by the Elector, not even without deference in some things . . . the Emperor will always look upon himself as Emperor, as judge, and in some sense as superior.

Robinson even suggested that the Hanoverian ministers deliberately spun out disputes:

> The last difficulty about the affair of Mecklenburg had never existed, if what has been demanded since for some of the troops to remain in the country has been asked sooner. His Majesty laid his finger upon that very defect in the former instructions given to Mr. Diede, but his German ministers would not remedy it, for fear the affair of Mecklenburg should be finished too soon, and to my knowledge, their intention was to spin it out, for his Majesty's amusement as it were, during his stay in Germany; and, in truth, what would become of those busy gentlemen, if they had not some such affair in their hands to exercise their talents upon, and to make themselves meritorious. Would to God, they could do it without implicating the King, as King . . . I am persuaded his Majesty's pretensions to Oostfrize have not been so much revived for the sake of hindering that country from falling into the King of Prussia's hands, as for employing those of the good ministers at Hanover.

Newcastle also emphasised the importance of Electoral issues, and stressed their significance to George II:

> upon the whole, I must, as a sincere well-wisher, advise and hope, that the Emperor will do us justice upon the Hanover points, for a backwardness there would have an ill air . . . if once Mecklenburg, Sleswick, which seems in a pretty good way, and what relates to the King of Prussia was adjusted upon a right foot, I think you would never hear from hence but upon agreeable subjects.[7]

Slighting the problems posed by the issue, in 1733, Robinson was ordered by William, Lord Harrington, the relevant Secretary of State, to assist the Hanoverian envoy 'as usual whenever it maybe necessary'.[8] The following year, Horatio Walpole wrote to his brother about orders received from George II to correspond directly with Hattorf:

> this cannot go on for long without being perceived in the office, and consequently by Lord Harrington . . . as it will I suppose relate to His Majesty's demands concerning a negotiation about Bergh and Juliers; and as I am afraid these demands will be unreasonable and break off the negotiation; it may not be proper that the correspondence should appear in the office.[9]

In 1735, Cyril Wych wrote to Tilson:

> If the German ministers hear that there is a design of giving me credentials to the circle of Lower Saxony and employing me at some other courts they will oppose it with all their strength because they would never have an English minister employed in Germany but when they have brought themselves into some scrape to help them out again.[10]

The practice of policy by Hanover and Britain was frequently different, not least because of the commitments of the Elector as an imperial prince. During the mid-1730s, British diplomatic resources were employed for Hanoverian ends when, in 1733–4, Russia was used to pressurise Prussia during a Prusso-Hanoverian dispute over Mecklenburg. There was, however, a clear and obvious contrast between British and Hanoverian policy during the War of the Polish Succession (1733–5), and one that created problems for British ministers and diplomats, as well as disquiet in the government of Britain's leading ally, the United Provinces, which was concerned about George's forwardness.[11]

Despite her obligations to Austria under the Second Treaty of Vienna, Britain was neutral in the war, but, in contrast, George II, as Elector, was active in rejecting a Prussian approach to maintain peace in the Empire jointly, and, instead, in voicing support for the Emperor, Charles VI; while 5,600 Hanoverian troops served in the Imperial army on the Rhine.[12] George, it is true, delayed sending his troops in early 1734 when Austria pressed for assistance against France, but the threat, that spring, that Marshal Belle-Isle, who captured Trier and Trarbach in April, would move on to seize the Rhine crossing at Rheinfels and invade Hesse-Cassel, led George to dispatch them. He also pressed for the occupation of Rheinfels by Hessian troops, and used Robinson to exert influence upon Austria to condone such an occupation,[13] a clear use of the British diplomatic system for a Hanoverian goal, and one that ignored the spirit of British neutrality. Rheinfels was expected to fulfil very different objectives to that planned in 1726–7.

It is, however, too easy to see the war as an episode in which George's desire that Britain take part in the conflict was thwarted by Robert Walpole, so that, as pro-governmental spokesmen, such as the *London Journal* of 1 May (os) 1736, pointed out, Britain and Hanover did not act together in the war. The evidence offered to this end in John, Lord Hervey's oft-cited *Memoirs*[14] is insufficient. George certainly complained about his British ministers and the need to consider Parliament, but Hervey's view of George as a monarch readily manipulated by Queen Caroline and Walpole presented George in overly simplistic terms and underplayed the King's ability to further his own views. As much of the evidence throughout the period for clashes between monarch and ministers over foreign policy is fragmentary or elusive, it is not surprising that great weight has been placed on British neutrality during the War of the Polish Succession, but the evidence only extends so far.

It is also necessary to move from the theatrical starkness of Hervey's highly coloured palette, and to assess, alongside the Hanover–Britain–Austria question, the questions raised by George's anxiety about Prussia. Relations had deteriorated in 1733: aside from continued differences over East Friesland,[15] in which British diplomats, such as William Finch in The Hague, were instructed to stay in touch with the ministers in Hanover, promises of assistance to the Dutch from George, as both King and Elector, in the spring of 1733 in a dispute over Prussian recruiting led Frederick William I to threaten an invasion of Hanover. The entire episode throws light on the problems of treating every issue as either British or Hanoverian. Frederick William claimed that the dispute was not the business of Britain;[16] but both Britain and Hanover would have been affected had Prussia succeeded in intimidating the Dutch.

In addition, attempts to settle the Mecklenburg question had failed in 1731–3, and the resumption of civil war in the duchy in September 1733 led to Hanoverian, Prussian and Wolfenbüttel movements of troops into it. George used British diplomats to press Austria and Russia to persuade Frederick William to remove his forces, but Frederick William broke a promise to do so; and, in order to ensure Austrian pressure, George delayed the march of his troops to Rhine, which scarcely conforms to the attitude described by Hervey. In the event, Hanoverian troops remained in Mecklenburg until 1735, and Hanover remained in control of eight districts until a loan was redeemed in 1768, while Prussian units continued in the duchy until 1787.

The order to the Hanoverian forces to march at once to the Rhine was not dispatched from London until 20 April 1734, and, then, in response to two letters from Prince William of Hesse-Cassel of 8 and 12 April, about the risk of the French crossing the Rhine, a course, ironically, George I's ministers had favoured in very different circumstances seven years earlier, when Hanover had seemed threatened by Austrian attack. The delay had also owed something to a dispute with the Emperor over the conditions of service of the Hanoverian troops, while George, in addition, had refused to send his troops until reassured about Prussian troop moves.[17] At the same time, it was only on 9 April that the Reichstag had declared war on behalf of the Empire. The Hanoverian troops reached the Austrian army on 2 June, swiftly earning praise from its commander, Prince Eugene.[18]

The dispatch of the troops indicated how George's Electoral position provided him with opportunities for action he lacked as King. This was also grasped by foreign governments.[19] Thus, in October 1733, when Robinson told Count Sinzendorf, the Austrian Chancellor, that a political alliance with Russia was not an option, 'for the plain reason of its being absolutely impossible to hope that the Parliament would ever be induced to make good any demands that might be founded upon any stipulations of even a defensive nature, and much less for any guarantees', he met with the question 'if H.M. then as Elector could not enter into a more extensive alliance'.[20] The dispatch of the troops also underlines the theme of security in Hanoverian policy, as this was the crucial factor in prompting George to act in 1734.[21]

In 1734–5, Prussian threats to intervene in the bitter quarrel between Denmark and Hamburg raised George's concern anew, but, again, it is unclear how this affected his attitude to the War of the Polish Succession, and to British neutrality in it. Both then, and subsequently, British diplomats were to draw attention to the relationship between developments in north Germany and the ability to oppose France, in order to suggest that a satisfactory solution to the former, especially, but not only, to disputes between Hanover and Prussia, would permit stronger opposition to France.

The situation after the close of the War of the Polish Succession in 1735 was very different. Britain was excluded from the Austro-French negotiations that led to a new diplomatic settlement, and ultimately to the Third Treaty of Vienna of 1738. The British response to this is of great interest, as it provides a case study of the possibility, popularity, and consequences of non-interventionism. That, however, is to provide a clear-cut schema that was certainly not obvious to contemporaries. Instead, there was an emphasis on uncertainty, both as to affairs in general and with regard to specific developments. The latter reflected the extent to which the Austro-French preliminary treaty, signed on 5 October 1735, did not lead to a readily accepted new order.

Here we hit the prime problem that faces the diplomatic historian, that of scale. With space always at a premium, there is a tendency to move forward rapidly from the preliminary treaty to the Third Treaty of Vienna, and also to present the late 1730s as a block of time that was brought to a close by hubris, in the sense of Frederick the Great's ambitious invasion of Silesia in December 1740, which launched the next unit, the War of the Austrian Succession. This has the additional merit, that the space saved would otherwise have been devoted to threatening events that were not to occur, particularly a successful Spanish defiance of the new Austro-French agreement, if not alignment, and also the outbreak of war in the Holy Roman Empire over the Jülich-Berg inheritance, the latter an issue that struck even interested contemporaries as 'perplexed and voluminous'.[22]

Yet, developments that do not come to fruition are of significance to historians, not least because they were important in setting the apparent parameters within which contemporaries assessed the situation and considered options. This was even more the case because there was a strong sense that the governments of Europe were far from fixed. Indeed, this was particularly pronounced in the late 1730s. First, a number of rulers were close to death, or believed to be so. The Emperor Charles VI, Frederick William I of Prussia and the Tsarina Anna were all to die in 1740, and Karl Philipp, Elector Palatine, in 1742. It was widely believed that such deaths would lead to major changes in policy, if not to succession contests. This was particularly likely in the case of the Habsburg inheritance, as Charles's lack of a son would test his provision for an undivided succession by his elder daughter, Maria Theresa, but was also important in the case of Karl Philipp, as his death would force matters to a head over the Jülich-Berg inheritance.

Secondly, there was uncertainty over the stability of particular governments, although not particularly over that of Britain. Instead, Walpole's success in 1734 in overcoming the 'Country' alliance of opposition Whigs and Tories, that had earlier attracted considerable diplomatic attention, made subsequent opposition appear weak. Furthermore, having won the 1734 general election, the ministry did not need to face another until 1741. The principal challenge appeared to be the death of Queen Caroline in 1737, as she had been correctly seen as a major support to Walpole; but foreign governments speedily appreciated that, though now a widower, George II would stick with Walpole.[23]

The language in which concern over the stability of particular governments was expressed by British diplomats is indicative of their attitude toward the international system. Benjamin Keene, an experienced envoy with long service in Spain, reported from there in 1736 about the situation after the death of the long-established first minister, José Patino:

> we have the more to apprehend from the vivacity and flirts of the Queen [Elisabeth Farnese], in case they should seize her with respect to us now she is let loose to her own imagination, without having any one about her that has credit or weight enough to restrain it. Patino's maxims of force and power will stick by her for a long time. They, with her own temper, will be capable of pushing her forward, to any extremities; and, though in the execution of them she will find the want of the resources Patino was master of, yet as thus must be learnt from reflection and experience, it will not prevent her from beginning broils.[24]

Such a personalisation of policy is not in accord with modern presentations of international relations, but it captured the reality of political systems in which the impact of dynastic interests, and the weakness and small size of bureaucratic institutions, combined to give force to the inherent character of personal monarchy. Cardinal Fleury, the leading French minister from 1726 until his death in 1743, felt it important to assure the British envoy in 1736, about Louis XV, 'that thank God the King of France did not love war for the sake of war . . . and that he did not doubt but he had instilled these principles so thoroughly in the French King that he would always stand to them'.[25]

There was particular anxiety in Britain about the French ministry, as the octogenarian Fleury, born in 1653, was believed close to death. This indeed was the prime concern of British commentators, for the death, retirement or replacement of Fleury threatened to lead to a major change in Anglo-French relations. These had been greatly harmed by the British government's unilateral *rapprochement* with Austria in 1731, but, while seeking to thwart the British quest for allies and thereafter undermining the British diplomatic system, the Fleury government had taken care to avoid steps that might provoke war. This was particularly the case during the War of the Polish Succession.[26]

If Fleury fell, there was concern that his replacement would be the much younger Germain-Louis de Chauvelin (1685–1762), foreign minister since 1727, and the prime exponent in the French government of anti-Austrian policies. Chauvelin was regarded as being hostile to British interests, and indeed the British ministry was overly prone to see French policy in terms of a 'good cop, bad cop' routine, with different tendencies being personalised in the case of Fleury and Chauvelin. This was taken further because Chauvelin was correctly seen as closely linked to the Spanish government. Thus, the concern that the Whigs had felt, during the War of the Spanish Succession (1702–13), that a Bourbon succession in Spain would lead to a threatening degree of unity between France and Spain, now seemed to be brought close to fruition, and, indeed, throughout the period, British governments displayed great anxiety about the state of Franco-Spanish relations.

The War of the Spanish Succession might appear long distant from the events of the late 1730s, and, indeed, there is a tendency to sectionalise foreign policy, in this case by envisaging some sort of discontinuity in 1713–15 as a result of the Treaty of Utrecht (1713), the Hanoverian Succession (1714), and the death of Louis XIV of France (1715). This, however, is misleading; instead, it is important to note continuities in careers, issues and controversies. To a certain extent, these continuities can be seen in terms of the modern concept of strategic culture, but that is only appropriate if the extent to which ideas were debated and interests contested is appreciated.

This debate and contestation took on added meaning in light of the uncertainty about other countries. Ironically, this sign of fluidity in policy did not lead British commentators to doubt the notion of the clarity of British national interests. Instead, there was a conviction that the very uncertainty about foreign intentions made it more necessary to affirm British interests clearly.

The uncertainty about the views of foreign states had a further polemical purpose within Britain, in that it was used by opposition commentators to support the notion that the government did not understand the international situation, and could not therefore be trusted to defend national interests. This thesis moved seamlessly from criticism of British policy in the War of the Polish Succession – on the grounds both of failing to block the Bourbons and of the inability to negotiate a settlement to the conflict, a criticism that continued postwar[27] – to condemnation of subsequent policy in terms of a failure to influence Continental developments. The debate over foreign policy in this period is generally neglected. Partly this reflects the pressure of space and the desire to present a clear account, but there is also the issue of celebrity status. Criticism of government policy in the late 1720s and early 1730s is associated with the *Craftsman* newspaper and the writings of Henry, Viscount Bolingbroke, both of which have attracted great attention. The same is true of the 'Patriot' critique in 1738–9 of an alleged failure to defend national interests against Spain, a critique that encompassed the pen of Samuel Johnson and the parliamentary speeches of William Pitt the Elder. What came between is neglected. It appears inconsequential, and is certainly difficult to unravel. There is no scholarly study of the period akin to that of Bob Harris on the 1740s,[28] and Harris casts very limited light on earlier, particularly non-'Patriot', writing. This failure to engage with the debate is unfortunate, not least as it ensures that the question of how far dissension and opinion influenced government policy is neglected. Thus, the 'feedback' mechanism between debate and policy, the existence of which is asserted for the Jenkins' Ear agitation of 1738–9, appears as if from nowhere.

The theme of the opposition, and indeed of some government supporters such as William Hay (see p. 5), was the need for eternal vigilance, but the ministry faced a harder task in public debate. It was concerned, if not suspicious, about at least aspects of the direction of French policy, but this was not a line that could be readily taken in public. The ministry was also aware that it had to deal with the options available. At the beginning of 1736, the only real opposition to the new Franco-Austrian alignment came from the wartime allies abandoned by France in her unilateral negotiations in 1735: Charles Emmanuel III of Sardinia, the ruler of Savoy-Piedmont, and Philip V of Spain, both of whom had ignored British diplomatic pressure in joining with France against Austria in 1733.

Philip V was in a critical position as his dynastic interests in Italy on behalf of his sons by his second marriage were challenged by the new alignment, and he had troops in the peninsula that would have to be moved back to make way for the territorial provisions intended by Austria and France. In particular, although Philip's elder son by his second marriage, Don Carlos, was, under the peace agreement, to gain the kingdom of Naples, he was to lose the duchy of Parma and his claim to the succession to the grand duchy of Tuscany. Instead, the latter passed to Francis Stephen, Duke of Lorraine, who, in February 1736, married Maria Theresa: he was to succeed there in

1737. In turn, Lorraine was given to Stanislas Leszczynski, father-in-law of Louis XV, who was to leave it to his daughter and her heirs: it thus passed to the French Crown in 1766. Philip hoped for more from the peace, and it was not until February 1737 that the Spanish government ordered the evacuation of Spanish troops from disputed areas in Italy, and not until 15 April that Spain formally signed a peace agreement with Austria.

Alliance with Spain represented a way for Britain to try to balance the new Austro-French alignment, but, in an instructive comment on the supposed interest of the politicians of this period in balance of power politics, such an alliance, instead, was primarily seen in light of the distrusted Philip V and his largely justified reputation for disruptive policies and for unreliability. Rather than encouraging Philip to reject the new alignment, Horatio Walpole reported from The Hague that he had agreed with the Dutch leaders 'that our utmost efforts, and exhortations should be used to bring that court into the present system, and that a deviation from it would expose the whole to the most dilatory, and dangerous consequences'.[29] Horatio Walpole sought not balancing alliances but, instead, a system to encompass all: 'the system would be imperfect and precarious if all the powers concerned in the war did not become parties to the pacification'. To that end, he favoured the negotiation of a settlement that powers were invited to join, rather than the panacea of the 1720s, 'a congress, which of late years (as experience has shown us) are of no manner of service but to create delays, intrigues, and confusion'.[30]

In both Parliament and the press, the ministry's spokesmen presented the peace as in accordance with its wishes,[31] and indeed the close of hostilities in 1735 had ended pressure in Britain for an expensive and risky intervention in the war. What was less clear, however, was whether the settlement could be sustained and the peace won for British interests; and this focused attention on the topic that had dominated discussion of foreign policy in the 1720s, the extent to which France could be trusted. Yet, alongside this element of continuity, there had also been an important move toward a less interventionist line. In part, this was a matter, on the part of government spokesmen, of defending the failure to intervene in the War of the Polish Succession,[32] and thus signalling that a change in policy had occurred, not in 1735 or 1736, but earlier, when policies associated with Stanhope in the 1710s and Townshend in the 1720s had been abandoned. Chavigny, the French envoy, who was close to the opposition, detected a more general rejection of interventionism, and reported that 'la maxime d'aujourdhuy est de se mêler de peu'.[33]

As argued above, however, the apparent clarity that a structural account of the debate over policy offers has to be replaced by an awareness of uncertainty. This was not only true in Britain. For example, the police reports in Paris noted in January 1736 that it was being claimed that war between France and Spain was certain, while there was also talk there of a plan for the Elector of Bavaria to make gains in the Low Countries.[34]

Uncertainty, in turn, led to concern and also encouraged caution. Indeed, whereas one response was an attempt at fixity, seen with the language of the balance of power, another was an unwillingness to become overly committed to any particular international situation. Harrington wrote to Robinson in Vienna:

> The way of thinking which you have met with in your Court – as to the Maritime Powers being only to guarantee the new establishment of Europe, and not the execution of what is to be immediately done in pursuance of the present preliminary articles, agrees entirely with the King's own sentiments.[35]

Bold scenarios were on offer for something more. Aside from the implausible one of co-operation with Spain, there was the possibility of a return to the pre-1731 situation of a British alliance with France. This might appear surprising in light of the conflict between the two powers that was to follow in 1743–8 and 1754–63, but, in the late 1730s, the previous experience of war with France (in 1689–97 and 1702–13) was shadowed by the alliance between the two powers in 1716–31. Indeed, the Walpole ministry appeared to face the prospect of better relations, with Fleury and Chauvelin offering different routes to the same end. The importance of this to the government was indicated by the personal role of Robert Walpole. He had a confidential correspondence with James, Earl Waldegrave, envoy in Paris, about talks with both the French ministers, a correspondence that survives in Waldegrave's private papers at Chewton House. As they apparently did not lead to anything, they have been neglected, but, aside from the degree to which these talks did in fact contribute to a relaxation in British suspicion of French policy, and thus eased the passage toward the Third Treaty of Vienna, the discussions are instructive for the issues raised and the language employed. Fleury, who 'frequently' threw out hints of 'a stricter union and friendship between England and France', argued in November 1736 that an alliance was necessary in order to 'check the ambitious views he concluded the Emperor and Spain would have, when once the pacification should be settled'.[36]

This looked toward future French attempts to improve relations – by Puysieulx in the late 1740s, D'Aiguillon in 1772–3, and Vergennes in 1786 – and also reflected a sense of contrast between satisfied, or at least predictable, powers; and those that were unsatisfied and unwilling to be constrained by collective discipline, especially Spain. The following July, Waldegrave reported:

> The Cardinal touched a little upon the private treaty he proposed to make between England and France, for the maintenance of the balance of Europe, and for hindering any one power from encroaching on his neighbour or disturbing his possessions . . . upon the whole the Cardinal

did not seem very solicitous about it at this time. He is sensible that till the definitive treaty is brought to perfection, and until he has given His Majesty full satisfaction about the engagements France has or may have with other powers, nothing can be done, from whence your Grace will easily conclude that this matter is not likely to be brought soon upon the anvil.[37]

The discussions can be regarded in a number of ways. It is possible to see them in a negative light: as the French ministers gulling their British counterparts, a view that accords with a presentation of the Anglo-French negotiations during the War of the Polish Succession. This is a 'zero-sum' approach to international relations, in which one power can only benefit at the expense of another, but it was one frequently expressed in a public politics in which suspicion of France was readily re-echoed. For example, the *Craftsman*, in its issue of 6 January (os) 1739, launched an attack on diplomacy in general and, in a passage that was characteristic of much opposition writing, assumed British omniscience, specifically criticising French intervention in Corsica where there was opposition to Genoese rule:

> With what views France thrust her mediation and armed plenipotentiaries into Corsica, the poorest politicians we have can explain; but with what views such wise and honest ministers as we are blessed with at present, have suffered their progress in that island, is beyond the length of my penetration to fathom with any certainty . . . will inevitably affect the trade of Great Britain . . . it is high time to do something more than think . . . for really the manner in which France has carried on her mediation ought to irritate the Corsicans rather to die . . . than to submit to the terms offered to be imposed upon.[38]

In the face of such criticism, the probing of possibilities for improved relations, instead, was both important to the general reduction of tension, and also necessary if Britain and France were to be able to confront particular crises, such as the Jülich-Berg succession in 1738, and the outbreak of war between Britain and Spain in 1739.

As a reminder of the multiple contexts of diplomacy, Fleury and Waldegrave also on 19 November 1736 discussed the position of the Jacobite Pretender, 'James III and VIII'. Whatever the state of Anglo-French relations under other heads, it was necessary for the British to be confident that France would not support the Jacobite cause, as among foreign powers it was best placed to do so. Fleury indeed promised that there would be no help. Rumours to the contrary were one of the more implausible instances in this period of suggestions of imminent conflict. British sensitivity over the issue was shown in 1737 when relations were broken with Venice over the friendly public reception there of Charles Edward Stuart.[39]

The Jacobite challenge was in fact only a minor element in European diplomacy in the late 1730s. There was far more likelihood of war between Austria and Spain over Italy in 1736, a probability that drew on Spanish preparations in Catalonia, or over the Jülich-Berg succession in 1738, or of Spain escalating the dispute with Portugal that had began in 1735 into an invasion in 1736; and conflict indeed broke out in South-East Europe, with first Russia and then also Austria going to war with the Ottoman empire. As Robert Daniel, the British envoy, noted from Brussels in August 1736, 'The public affairs of Europe are looked upon as very much entangled yet, and the peace precarious. Amidst these probable notions, an infinite number of the most improbable and absurd daily succeed one another here.'[40] Troop moves, such as those of the French into French Flanders in the summer of 1737, were followed with great attention. Some of the reports were of immediate threats to British interests. The *Daily Advertiser* of 4 March (os) 1737 reported 'The armament at Barcelona was designed to be employed against Minorca [a British possession from 1708], whilst 30,000 men in the neighbourhood of Malaga were to advance towards Gibraltar, to oblige the English to divide their forces, which could not fail to render the undertaking successful.'

War and the prospect of war also threatened any sense of stability in the international order, which challenged British interests in so far as Europe was concerned. War also offered a more specific challenge, in that the real or possible consequences of conflict had knock-on results. However troubled British commentators might be by the alignment between France and Austria, they regarded Austria as a crucial balancer of France, and were worried by the war between Austria and the Ottomans (1737–9), particularly as Austria was unsuccessful in this conflict. Yet, as a reminder of the sense of unpredictability, it had initially seemed that the French would seek to stop Austria from attacking the Ottomans, as the latter were mistakenly seen as vulnerable.[41] Indeed, George Tilson, an experienced Under Secretary, noted that 'in England the politic heads are arguing how dangerous it would be to trade, to the Protestant religion, and to our civil interest to have the Turk driven out of Europe,'[42] anxieties that looked towards those expressed at the time of the Ochakov crisis in 1791, although then the focus was on geopolitics, and certainly not on the position of Protestantism.

The same concern about French intentions was aroused by signs of tension between Sweden, from 1738 a French ally, and Russia; although, despite earlier panics, war between them did not break out until 1741. In each case, there was a suspicion that France had instigated the crisis in order to weaken other powers, and to strengthen its position in Europe, and this concern was at least a background factor in the British evaluation of international relations, especially from 1737. Indeed, a French subsidy treaty of December 1738 prevented Sweden from concluding any other alliance without first notifying France, and led to fears of a French-financed Swedish naval build-up. The following year, a small French squadron appeared in the Baltic, while the Swedes sent troops to Finland. In March 1738, the British had intercepted a letter from Jean Jacques Amelot, the French foreign minister, in which he revealed that the French government would see what happened in the Balkan war before it tried to stir up the Swedes against Russia.[43] In the event, Fleury drew back from pressing Sweden to attack, but the British government lacked confidence about both French intentions and Baltic developments.

The prospect of war between Prussia and Karl Philipp, Elector Palatine, over the inheritance to the duchies of Jülich and Berg brought out another dimension to British foreign policy as it threatened to expose Hanover, either as Prussian forces advanced on the Rhineland or, even more, if George opposed Prussian moves. This was not only a specific concern but also brought to a head the more general anxiety about the consequences for British policy of the Hanoverian link. Here, there was a troubling intersection, both with the domestic debate over policy and with the prospect of developing an alliance system. In the first case, sensitivity over the position of the Crown was the issue, with, in addition, specific reference to the question of whether the government was doing sufficient to defend national interests. As far as the second was concerned, alliance with Prussia appeared to offer an alternative to the Austro-French alliance, and one that took on additional weight for some due to a common Protestantism.

Thus, rumours of war raised multiple issues about the direction of foreign policy. From the government's point of view, a tension can be detected under this heading in the late 1730s. From the perspective of domestic politics, the fact that war panics in 1736–8 did not lead Britain into conflict and, crucially, that there was no war over the Jülich-Berg question, was a major boon, not least as this helped retrain expenditure, and thus both indebtedness and taxation, in a difficult economic period. Land tax had risen from one to two shillings in the pound (five to ten new pence) in 1733, but, thereafter, was held at two shillings until 1740.

In contrast, there was a measure of anxiety among diplomats, especially on the part of the active Horatio Walpole, about the failure to construct a strong and effective diplomatic system. This contrast was far from new, but is noteworthy none the less. This is not least because the particular emphasis of the experts was on the bankruptcy of the diplomatic system that played the greatest role in British public discussion of foreign policy, and that in a way represented the diplomatic heritage: the Grand Alliance with Austria and the United Provinces that had been central in securing the Revolution Settlement in Britain and in resisting France in 1689–97 and 1702–13. The late 1730s therefore takes on added importance in the discussion of Britain's 'true' interests and 'natural' policy, concepts that were important to (and in) the understanding of the period.

The possibility of an alternative alliance was important in any discussion, but here there were major problems. Philip V was ruled out as quixotic, although the ability of the British government to settle, albeit only for a brief period, differences with Spain in 1738 without the intervention of France indicated what was possible. A better prospect seemed to be that of Prussia, especially if it could also lead to alliance with Russia. Indeed in January 1739, in an instruction intercepted and deciphered by the excellent British postal interception system, Charles Emmanuel III noted reports that George II and Frederick William I were to settle differences, and that Tsarina Anna was to join them in order to balance the French alliance system.[44] Four months later, Carteret, then in opposition, told the House of Lords that a treaty with Denmark was 'only a good beginning. Not of use on the Continent unless you gain Prussia.'[45]

At a schematic level, this appeared the obvious solution, and, from that perspective, the late 1730s takes on interest as a period that prefigured, at least in prospect, the alignments of the Seven Years' War (1756–63) when France was allied with Austria, and Britain, still under George II, with Prussia. Indeed, Robinson reported Austrian disquiet on that head.[46] The press echoed such thoughts. On 30 January (os) 1739, the *London Farthing Post* reported that France was pressing Spain hard to join the Franco-Austrian alignment in order to counter-balance a projected alliance of Britain, Prussia and the Dutch.

This, however, is to place the apparent logic of the international system above the particular views of contemporaries, a common course in a certain tradition of scholarship, but one that fails to offer adequate explanations for motive and event. In the case of Anglo-Prussian relations, it is necessary to focus on 1736, for the specific reason that George II went to Hanover that year, providing an opportunity for intensive negotiations on German matters, and was not to return there until 1740, while, more generally, as later with George's visit to Hanover in 1748 after the end of the War of the Austrian Succession, the immediate post-war period provided opportunities for a fresh start in diplomacy. As in 1748, the prospect of better Anglo-Prussian relations was thwarted by particular Hanoverian interests. The most important was the recruiting for the Prussian army in neighbouring territories carried out in defiance of the views of George II. This was not a new issue, and indeed had come close to causing war in 1729, but it revived in 1736, in part because it offended George's sense of sovereignty. His determination to have the recruiting stopped[47] exacerbated a situation already made difficult by mutual distrust. Horatio Walpole, who sought better relations, criticised Frederick William I for inconsistency, adding 'his own temper and conduct are the chief cause of this dislike and distrust the world has generally for him'.[48] Guy Dickens, the envoy in Prussia, was similarly critical, and added an interesting comparison with non-European states. He described Prussia as:

> a power whose politics and maxims of late years have shown that they are glad of any troubles that may arise, and even desire to foment them; in hopes to making their advantage of them by oppressing, without any regard to the public good, whosoever is the weakest and play the same

part on the Continent as certain states on the coast of Africa do on the water.[49]

The last, a reference to the Barbary powers of North Africa, provides an instructive instance of the value of the diplomatic texts for evidence of attitudes about how international relations operated in practice. The description of Frederick William I implied a correct or normative method of operation in international relations – the furtherance of the 'public good' – from which he was deviating. A similar scepticism about the appropriateness of the conduct of other powers, however, was expressed more widely. Thus, in 1739, Trevor wrote from The Hague 'the more we want friends, the dearer we must pay them; and that foreign courts like stockjobbers will raise their price and take their advantage of our straits or alarms'.[50]

In contrast, British ministers could urge the pursuit of a mixture of the balance of Europe, with additional factors more pertinent to states seen as 'fellow travellers': namely 'the preservation of the common libertys and the security of the Protestant religion'.[51] Alongside these goals came attitude. As representatives of a 'satisfied' power, with the crucial proviso of in Europe, British ministers were wary of ambition there, and this led to a preference for a 'pacific spirit'.[52]

The logic of interventionism varied with particular conjunctures. The need for co-operation with Prussia seemed very specific to the Jülich-Berg issue in early 1737, as then there was a general slackening of international tension outside the Balkans. This was further encouraged in February when Chauvelin was dismissed.[53] Edward Weston, one of the Under Secretaries, remarked:

> little time is employed upon foreign business, and indeed there is not much at this time of that sort, the state of Europe seeming to be at present in a sort of calm, by the execution of the Preliminaries [for Peace], the dismission of the Spanish embarkation [alleged for Italy], and the disgrace of Mr. Chauvelin.[54]

To the government, the fall of Chauvelin was a very welcome step, like that of Choiseul in 1770, as he had been seen not only as hostile to Britain but also as a bellicose minister determined to make gains for France. His fall also led to an approach from Fleury to Horatio Walpole for the renewal of a 'perfect confidence',[55] and to links between Fleury and Robert Walpole via Waldegrave, who, significantly, was awarded the Order of the Garter, a sign of royal favour.[56] Walpole was ready to write in fulsome terms:

> There is nothing that I have always desired more and do now most earnestly wish than to establish and cultivate a perfect good understanding and confidence with the Cardinal, if his Eminency will be pleased to explain himself to your Lordship upon what points, and in what manner

he proposes to settle and confirm a perfect friendship and union between our royal masters for their mutual honour and interest, he shall find on my part all the readiness and sincerity he can possibly desire.[57]

Fleury made it clear that he was worried about Austrian strength, specifically her power in Germany, and the need to prevent her from encroaching on the German princes, a point that could be expected to appeal to George II, as well as the danger that she would gain Tuscany, and thus become too powerful in Italy, and the threat that, on the failure of male issue, the duchy of Württemberg would become a Habsburg territory, as it had done briefly in the early sixteenth century.[58] Chauvelin's fall, however, could not lessen long-term British uncertainty over French policy, while, in the shorter term, Horatio Walpole was concerned about the continued influence of the former minister's ideas.[59]

Longstanding fears about the health of the elderly Fleury were exacerbated in early 1738 when he became particularly ill. From this perspective, anxiety about French views toward the Habsburg succession, the Balkans and the Baltic were reasonable, even if the timescale for their coming to fruition was a distant one. A build-up in British governmental concern on this point from 1738 was, in fact, to be cut short by the unexpected focus on trans-oceanic relations with Spain, but it is instructive to recover evidence about this fear, as it helps point the way toward the more marked anti-French character of foreign policy from 1741. Thus, in January 1739, Robert Trevor told the Dutch Pensionary that Fleury

> had succeeded but too easily in making the world believe what it has indeed so much reason to wish, namely, the moderation and disinterestedness of France ... I told him, I would not dispute at present how far the provocation given the French king in the person of his father in law may have been sufficient to reconcile the enterprise, and issue of even the last war[60] with those principles; but I would defy any body to account for upon the foot of that inoffensive system, the far-fetched, and expensive alliances, which France was now negotiating in the North, without any provocation, or visible occasion whatever ....

Trevor continued by throwing doubt on the motives 'for all those mediations, guarantees, and negotiations, however new and unnatural into which France has of late years so officiously thrust herself, in order to extend her sphere of action, and to create a more general dependence upon her'. He also linked diplomatic initiatives to the specifics of military strength, arguing that French schemes in the Baltic were intended 'to indispose, and divert the several Protestant powers in Lower Saxony from contributing their forces towards opposing any enterprise that France may come to make upon the Rhine, or on the side of Flanders': French policy was therefore linked to the threat to Hanover, a prominent member of the Lower Saxon Circle, and the latter seen as a potential, but vulnerable, resource in the anti-French camp. To Trevor, such a consequence under a bellicose successor of Fleury would simply represent the culmination of the Cardinal's plans.[61] Concern about French diplomacy was matched by a close eye on French colonial moves and naval preparations.[62] The same was also true of those of Spain.[63]

At the same time, contemporaries argued that if what were feared to be French schemes came to fruition, there was the prospect of a recovery in Britain's diplomatic position, as the breakdown of Franco-Austrian relations would leave the latter ready to return to Britain. Indeed, the British government was hopeful, if not confident, that French policy would lead to an Austrian change in policy,[64] a view that reflected a belief in the incompatible interests of the two powers that appears anachronistic from the perspective of 1756 but far less so from that of 1741, when France attacked Austria. An Austrian change of policy, in turn, it was thought would have consequences in relations with Russia and Prussia, encouraging the former to pursue good relations with George II, while dissuading the latter from harmful steps. Yet, because Fleury was careful not to encourage Austria's enemies, especially Bavaria and Spain, it was understandable that Charles VI did not turn to Britain. He had been let down by her in 1733–5, and France as an ally could be expected to restrain Bavaria and Spain, as indeed her policies did.

As a consequence, the situation appeared particularly tricky for the British government: for the sake of what were believed to be inherent national interests, it had to stop Austria from coming to harm even though it was allied to France. Sir Everard Fawkener suggested from Constantinople that if Britain and the Dutch, and not France, could mediate the conflict in the Balkans this would end 'a very unnatural' system, that between France and Austria: 'and I persuade myself it will be an acceptable service to His Majesty, if I can be instrumental in preventing so great a prejudice to the Empire and Russia, as they seem desirous of drawing upon themselves, by the course they are suffering their affairs here to take, and if the scheme takes place they will henceforward be at the discretion of France.'[65]

Relations with Frederick William I, meanwhile, continued to be greatly affected by the Jülich-Berg question. At one level, this is an instance of how specific problems assumed a disproportionate importance, but, in fact, the main lines of foreign policy were involved. Thus, Jülich-Berg posed the question of how far Britain should co-operate with other powers that were involved in the issue. Austria and France sought to involve Britain and the Dutch in their diplomatic moves, but these risked accentuating poor relations between the latter two and Prussia. In February 1738, as a result of the negotiations at The Hague, Austria, Britain, France and the United Provinces presented identical notes at Berlin and Mannheim, suggesting that the succession should be mediated, but that the Wittelsbach claimant should provisionally occupy Jülich-Berg after the Elector Palatine, Karl Philipp, died, until such time as the mediators could arrive at a settlement. Frederick

William rejected the idea and, as a result, the French approached the British again in 1738, only to be rebuffed.

In January 1739, France and Austria concluded a secret treaty providing that the Wittelsbach claimant should occupy Jülich-Berg for two years after the death of Karl Philipp, which, in fact, was not to occur until 1742. At the same time, however, a new twist was provided by secret Franco-Prussian negotiations which ended in a treaty signed in April 1739 in which France guaranteed a stipulated portion of the duchy of Berg to Prussia, and also promised to persuade Karl Philipp to agree. There was no chance of the latter.

These negotiations revealed the limitations of diplomacy in the face of determined rulers. Karl Philipp was a weak ruler, but his policy indicated the restricted influence that a powerful state had over its allies. As with negotiations for a Balkan peace, the Jülich-Berg issue thus revealed the problems of intervention. George II's concern about Hanover and his far-from-secret personal obstinacy toward Frederick William I[66] were faced not by a united British ministry determined to seek the support of Prussia, but by genuine uncertainty over how best to respond to Frederick William. In political terms, this was complicated, not clarified, by pressure from opposition spokesmen.

Aside from the issues of distrust and inconstancy, there was also the question of the prudence of alienating France by supporting Prussia. It was only after the commencement of Anglo-Spanish hostilities, in late 1739, when French support for Spain appeared imminent, that the British ministry revealed a willingness to support Prussia over Jülich-Berg as part of the price of an Anglo-Prussia alliance. By then, however, it was too late. Frederick II in the early 1740s sought British backing for gains in Silesia, not Jülich-Berg, and any support of Prussia on this count risked pitching Britain against Austria, rather than France; an unacceptable choice. To see Anglo-Prussian relations in the late 1730s in terms of lost opportunities, at least in part, is to assume that an agreement could have survived Frederick II's accession in 1740, but, in light of his ambitious goals, that would have been unlikely.

Equally, the idea of joining with France in order to impose a settlement of the Jülich-Berg dispute, as a key aspect of securing the peace, would have been to risk a continuation of the attitudes and policies of the late 1710s and 1720s. These had been rejected by Robert Walpole, and, with the death of Stanhope in 1721 and the resignation of Townshend in 1730, his attitude was now clearly dominant within the ministry. Aside from caution about interventionism, there was also a concern about France and a lack of confidence in the United Provinces, Britain's most consistent alliance partner since 1689, but, in 1739, referred to by the knowledgeable British envoy as 'this decrepit state'.[67] Concern about France related both to the diplomatic situation and to military specifics. As Trevor pointed out in 1737, 'it is France, whom we [Britain and the Dutch] wish to keep out of Dusseldorf [part of Berg] rather than the King of Prussia; and that if we can not keep her out, we will at least not engage and league ourselves to keep her in'.[68]

George II's concern for Hanover ensured that the issue of interventionism was not simply of importance to British taxpayers. In June 1738, Guy Dickens, the British envoy in Prussia, went to supper at the house of General Grumbkow, Frederick William's principal advisor. Field Marshal Kurt Christoph, Count Schwerin, who, as commander of the troops of Charles Leopold of Mecklenburg, had briefly fought the Hanoverians in 1719, was also present, and warned that the Prussians would attack Hanover if there were trouble over Jülich-Berg; he and Grumbkow claimed that they would easily overrun Hanover. Dickens himself was generally sceptical about Prussian threats and military preparations 'since such orders have been so often given and as we have found by the event without any meaning and design . . . Those rodomontados, by which this court have chiefly distinguished themselves of late years.'[69] George, however, was more concerned, at least, judged by the report of a discussion with the French envoy, Louis-Dominique, Count of Cambis, in March 1738, in which Cambis urged that George, as Elector, prevent Prussian forces from advancing from Brandenburg to their Rhenish base at Cleves, from which they could exert pressure on Jülich and Berg. George responded that he would not let the Prussians through, but was concerned about the strength of the Prussians and wanted Frederick William's anger to fall on France and Austria, and not on Hanover.[70]

George's need to rely on Austro-French diplomatic pressure at Berlin in 1738[71] revealed the consequences for Hanover, and therefore Britain, of poor relations with Prussia, and also looked toward the option presented by Hanoverian neutrality in 1757. In 1738 and in 1757, as in 1772–3, had the First Partition of Poland led to international conflict, Hanover was on the front-line in any clash between France and Prussia.[72]

Later in 1738, conflict involving Hanoverian troops did break out. Fortunately for George, his opponent was not Frederick William I, but Christian VI of Denmark with whom he was in dispute over the territory of Steinhorst on the frontier of Saxe-Lauenburg and Holstein. Rejecting George's suggestion of negotiations, the Danes sent troops to occupy Steinhorst in late 1738, but they were driven out by a larger Hanoverian force. Although there were further military moves, and talk of war, including Swedish hopes that a conflict might enable them to regain Bremen and Verden, a settlement was reached.

George was fortunate that Frederick William I did not exploit the crisis, in which he had compromised British foreign policy. George used Trevor to obtain Dutch pressure on Christian VI, Trevor being instructed by Harrington, who was given information on George's orders by Steinberg. Furthermore, as was pointed out in the press, the crisis threatened the attempt to renew the Anglo-Danish treaty of 1734, which was now of greater importance because of Sweden's recent move into the French camp.[73]

A focus on George's actions and views serves as a reminder of the need to match the discussion of ministerial differences in France (and elsewhere) by considering tensions within the government in Britain. In 1736, Horatio Walpole, who accompanied George to Hanover as acting Secretary of State, wrote to his protégé Trevor:

> I do not wonder at your embarrass in your negotiations; consultations and orders are carried on in England with such confusion, and in so undigested a manner; the affairs of Turkey are in the province of one Secretary [of State, Newcastle], the directions to be sent to the Hague belong to the department of another [Harrington], these two I believe see one another but little, and I perceive that one [Harrington] writing nothing at all and the other [Newcastle] will not suffer nobody but himself to think or write anything that may concern his province.[74]

Institutional difficulties were not, however, the sum total of division. There were also tensions over policy and position. The Walpole–Trevor correspondence indicates that Walpole was concerned to keep it secret from the King:

> When you write by the messenger give your private letter to me apart to him from the dispatch; for his Majesty to whom the messenger goes first, opens often the dispatches, and enquires what the private letter holds although he does not open it, and therefore the messenger should reserve what has private . . . wrote on the side to be delivered by himself to me.

This was not the full extent of the subterfuge. The following month, Horatio Walpole added: 'I think, as you hint, it may not be amiss, if, sometimes when you have time enough, you should besides your particular letter to me *apart*, add another under that name that may be shown to accompany the dispatch.'[75] Opposition critics were certain that George was kept in the dark,[76] while foreign diplomats suggested a system of placatory compromise in which ministers satisfied the King in some respects in order to be able to contradict him in others.[77]

George's attitude reflected the more general one among rulers and princes that their personal integrity, and that of their families, was at issue in international relations. This was captured in a report from Robinson in Vienna, in which he repeated the comments of Francis Stephen of Lorraine:

> Good God, where are you! Where are the Maritime Powers! As for my part, continued he, I rely upon the King singly: Not upon treaties: not upon formal promises but upon what His Majesty has told me over and over again of his goodness for me.[78]

Horatio Walpole was to fall foul of George, but there is less evidence for the views of Harrington. The absence of his papers is a grave problem, but his lack of interest in writing at length is a more serious one, because very little survives from Harrington in the collections that remain, which include those of Newcastle, Horatio Walpole and, far less fully, Robert Walpole. As a consequence, there is a lack of clarity over ministerial differences prior to those that arose in 1739 over policy toward Spain and which are more fully recorded due to the survival of the Newcastle papers. Harrington lacked a confidential correspondence with diplomats in his own department whose private papers survive: Chesterfield and Trevor at The Hague, Robinson at Vienna, and Titley at Copenhagen, or indeed with diplomats in other departments such as Keene and Waldegrave.

The role of such links must be set alongside the usual emphasis on official correspondence. Robert Walpole kept Newcastle in the dark about his correspondence with Fleury,[79] only changing his mind when it became absolutely necessary as the correspondence could not pass unobserved.[80] In 1737, Newcastle wrote to Horatio Walpole, 'Whilst I was at Houghton, Sir Robert received from the King your long letter to the Queen. It is very particular, and clear, as to Chauvelin's fall.'[81] Foreign diplomats were convinced that Harrington had little power,[82] and his likely replacement was frequently reported.[83] Gout[84] and taciturnity[85] were also noted, as was a greater closeness to the King, with whom he shared a military background, than that of Horatio Walpole.[86]

The lack of clarity about the views of Harrington is unfortunate, as issues that were to bulk large after 1740 were indeed already important. There was not yet the need for alliances that Frederick II's invasion of Silesia seemed to make urgent, but, already, there was discussion about the likely consequences of Charles VI's death. Thus, in 1736, Horatio Walpole urged caution in negotiations with Denmark and Sweden 'for we must take care of not disobliging Muscovy; I think that power, if the Emperor does not do something to put the Czarina out of humour will be the strongest support to the Pragmatic Sanction'.[87] It was taken for granted that Britain would support the Habsburgs. In 1738, Newcastle referred to Britain and the United Provinces as the 'natural allies' and 'true friends' of Austria; while a prominent opposition Whig and former diplomat, John, 2nd Earl of Stair, predicted that 'the unnatural conjunction that now appears between the House of Austria and France would soon be dissolved, and the Emperor would return back to his natural connection with us'.[88]

Thus, the late 1730s can be seen as of importance for debate about Britain's 'true' position and 'natural' alignments. It links the world of the 1740s – Carteret's revival of co-operation with Austria against France and, later, the 'Old System' of Newcastle[89] – with the earlier attempt in 1731 to revive the Grand Alliance of the War of the Spanish Succession. If the processes by which such ideas were discussed, debated and developed are still obscure, and some of the chronology is still to be recovered, the extent to which the debate over policy interacted with the developing international situation is an important issue.

6 The crisis of public support, 1740–8

There are, indeed, some who seem to imagine that for us, who are surrounded by the ocean, and therefore are in very little danger of sudden invasion, to engage in the disputes of the neighbouring powers, or to regulate the distribution of dominion on the Continent, is a sort of superfluous heroism.

(Carteret, 1744[1])

The potential problems posed by royal demands were restrained during the 1720s and 1730s, not only by Robert Walpole's skill, but also because threats to Hanover, for example by Russia in the early 1720s, Austria and her allies in 1726–7, Prussia in 1729, or a French advance east of the Rhine in 1734 or 1735, were not realised. In the 1740s, however, the situation deteriorated on both heads, and this led to the agitation over Hanoverian interests that caused such political problems in Parliament in 1742–4. In 1739, indeed, Anne-Théodore Chevignard de Chavigny, a French diplomat who had served in London, had suggested that British governmental policy in negotiations with Denmark were influenced by a wish to prevent contention that could arise in 'un Etat populaire'.[2] By the standards of other West European monarchies, such contention was to be particularly vigorous in the early 1740s.

The death of Frederick William I on 31 May 1740 appeared to offer George II an opportunity to escape from his isolation, and initially posed no threat to Hanover. At first, there was optimism about the chance of better relations, and in June 1740 Münchhausen went to Berlin in order to win the newly acceded Frederick II's support.[3] Difficulties, however, were soon anticipated on account of Electoral interests. In July, Harrington sent a private letter in his own hand to Newcastle from Hanover, whither he had accompanied George:

I will venture in great confidence to acquaint you there are certain disputes and pretensions subsisting betwixt the Houses of Hanover and Prussia, which though they may appear to the rest of the world not to deserve so immediate an attention as other matters of a more general nature I fear however that till those are adjusted, in which I foresee great difficulties likely to arise, the general matters will go on but lamely and this is one principal reason why I am not overfond of a journey to Berlin as yet.[4]

Four months later, Count Osterman, the Russian foreign minister, himself a German by birth, told Edward Finch, the British envoy, that 'there might be a difference of interest between the two Electorates [Hanover and Brandenburg] which might have some influence on the counsels of the two Kings [Britain and Prussia]'.[5] These comments echoed those already made by Horatio Walpole about East Friesland, and might suggest that a clear case could be made of Hanoverian concerns preventing alliance with Prussia, as another instance of the Electorate thwarting British attempts to win the support of the powers of Eastern and Central Europe.

The situation in fact was more complex, pointing the way to the need for caution in analysing both other case-studies and also the more general nature of the relationship. In 1740, there was little sign of pressure for aggrandisement from the Hanoverian government.[6] Furthermore, far from there being a simple question of arranging a reconciliation between George II and the Hohenzollerns, Frederick II was seeking the best terms for his alliance from both George and Louis XV. The crucial issue was the Jülich-Berg inheritance, towards which France was best placed to help Prussia, both diplomatically and militarily. In addition, instead of there being, as has been argued,[7] a clear contrast between British ministerial enthusiasm for winning Frederick by making concessions, and reluctance on the part of George, unless he won equal concessions, the British ministry was itself split. Fears were expressed that Frederick would expect too much and that supporting him over his claims on the succession to Jülich-Berg would lead to war with France in the interests of Prussia and Hanover.[8]

George II, like his ministers, hoped to win Frederick's support, but was concerned about the extent and implications of the latter's demands. Long-held, if vague, views about how Prussia could join in to support the balance and 'liberties' of Europe, repeated to Frederick in August 1740 by Guy Dickens, the British envoy, appeared redundant in light of Frederick's stress on his own interests. His demands for British support over Jülich-Berg, Mecklenburg and East Friesland[9] threatened not only Electoral interests, but also British relations with other powers, and thus the multi-layered nature of British diplomacy.

Nevertheless, as conflict with France in the West Indies appeared increasingly likely in September 1740, ministers in London became more interested in the idea of winning Frederick's alliance.[10] France had played no role in 1739 when the War of Jenkins' Ear between Britain and Spain broke out, essentially over British attempts to trade with Spanish America. Nevertheless, for dynastic, geopolitical and commercial reasons, France was close to Spain; indeed on 26 August 1739, Louis XV's eldest daughter married

Don Philip, the youngest son of Philip V, and French maritime intervention on behalf of Spain appeared a prospect. The French government did not want Britain to make colonial gains from Spain, and, to lend backing to its position, sent a fleet to the West Indies in August 1740. Nevertheless, the French did not attack, and an uneasy balance, short of war, was maintained.

Had good relations been obtained with Frederick, then it is probable that Hanover would have been both secure and not an issue in British public debate in the 1740s. Given Prussian expectations, however, this was unrealistic, and there was a degree of naivety, if not opportunism, in subsequent claims that more should have been done, one pamphleteer writing in 1744: 'How easily might the heart of the young monarch be engaged after the father's death! He was inclined by nature, he was so from interest, if his good intentions had been managed.'[11]

The situation anyway changed on 20 October 1740, with the death of Charles VI. George sought co-operation with Frederick on the basis of assuring the Habsburg succession,[12] but the Prussian invasion of Silesia on 16 December shattered these hopes. Horatio Walpole commented on the Hanoverian response to the invasion:

> our master is divided between resentment and fears; he cannot bear to think of augmenting the territories of his Electoral neighbour on one side, and he justly apprehends that his own dominions should fall first a sacrifice should he stir on the other. His servants I think are all here of one opinion, blame and abhor the extravagant step, but see no remedy but palliating and accommodating remedies.[13]

In response to the invasion, George took a major role as Elector in trying to create an anti-Prussian coalition, for, although he threatened the use of Hanoverian troops, such activity could only be convincing if widely supported. Indeed, in January 1741, George planned action by Austria, Saxony, Hanover, the United Provinces and Russia. Britain was also supposed to contribute, not only by paying for Danish and Hessian participation,[14] but also by diplomatic support. Trevor was instructed to stir up the Dutch against Prussia and to ascertain from their leading ministers whether, if George acted in support of Austria 'and his German dominions should be attacked, as they lie by their neighbourhood to those of Prussia, so much exposed, in resentment', the Dutch would provide assistance.[15]

George's failure to create an effective alliance that could prevent Frederick from gaining and holding Silesia left no doubt of his second-rank status in northern Germany, but, initially, Parliament offered support to Hanover, as part of a plan designed to help Charles VI's heir, Maria Theresa, against her Prussian assailant. This prefigured Pitt's support from 1758 for the despatch of British troops to Westphalia to support Frederick II in the Seven Years' War. As on the latter occasion, however much this policy was in fact focused on Frederick II, it was seen by British ministers also as a means to help Hanover without leading to serious controversy.

In April 1741, at a moment of enthusiasm about a positive role for Britain in Continental power politics,[16] Parliament provided a vote of credit to enable George as King to fulfil his obligations to Maria Theresa, and assured him of support in the event of an attack on Hanover. Moving the Address in the Commons, Thomas Clutterbuck, one of the Lords of the Admiralty, declared that 'we ought to pronounce that the territories of Hanover will be considered on this occasion as the dominions of Great Britain, and that any attack on one or the other will be equally resented'. William Pulteney, the leader of the opposition Whigs in the House of Commons, however, sought to separate the issues of Austria and Hanover in order to provide a focus for attacks on the government. He supported aid to Austria, but was opposed to giving any guarantee for Hanover. Pulteney referred to the Act of Settlement of 1701, the constitutional basis of the Hanoverian succession, which stipulated that the monarch should not enter into a war for the sake of foreign dominions not belonging to the British Crown.

Concern about the international situation became more acute in the summer of 1741 as other powers, including France, Bavaria and Saxony, joined in the assault on the Habsburgs: France signed the Treaty of Breslau with Frederick II on 5 June 1741. Later that month, George agreed to act against Prussia, but Harrington, the Secretary of State who again accompanied the King to Hanover, claimed that 'there is no manner of doubt but that the measures His Majesty shall pursue, as King, will be revenged upon him, as Elector, unless timely care be taken to prevent it'.[17] Indeed, in negotiations with its Spanish counterpart, the French ministry presented the dispatch of their army towards Hanover in 1741 as their contribution to Spanish war goals, and thus to Franco-Spanish relations.[18]

Exposure to possible French and Prussian attack in the summer of 1741 had a serious effect on Hanoverian self-confidence, leading to support for neutrality and its maintenance. Hanover indeed was vulnerable. Its army had a complement of only 19,422 in 1740, and the vulnerability to French attack was compounded by anxiety about Prussia. Frederick deployed nearly 30,000 troops on the Hanoverian frontier when he invaded Silesia. Furthermore, the major build-up of active British naval strength in the early 1740s could not be used to help Hanover.

The vulnerability of Hanover was made abruptly clear in 1741. An advance by 40,000 French troops into Westphalia led George II to abandon his attempts to create an anti-French coalition, and, as Elector, to accept, on 25 September, a neutrality convention supporting the French candidate for Holy Roman Emperor, Charles Albert, Elector of Bavaria.[19] This was a measure that undermined the British government, which was then anxious to support Austria, and to be seen to do so. Although the Declaration of Neustadt was entered into strictly in an Electoral capacity, it was disliked by George's British ministers, who correctly feared that Electoral measures would be interpreted as affecting British conduct, as indeed they were by the opposition.[20] The convention led to severe criticism of George as Elector for weakening Britain's commitment to Austria, and embittered discussion about foreign policy in Walpole's last parliamentary session as first minister. It was viewed as evidence of a ministerial failure to defend national interests, especially when, allegedly as a result of a secret clause that did not in fact exist, the British fleet failed to prevent Spanish forces designed to attack Austrian Italy from landing in Italy.

Anxious to preserve the security offered by the neutrality convention, Ernst, Freiherr von Steinberg, head of the Hanoverian Chancery in London from 1737 to 1748, spoke with regret of British efforts in the last days of the Walpole government to encourage the Austrians, and the consequent delay in negotiating a general peace.[21] The British ministry, however, was opposed to the neutrality, and this led to a clear clash of objectives. In the spring of 1742, Hardenberg, the Hanoverian envoy in Paris, continued to act in accordance with the Hanoverian neutrality until the new British ministry was able to persuade George II to abandon this stance.[22] Walpole resigned on 11 February and Carteret, who became Secretary of State for the Northern Department, drove British policy in a more bellicose and anti-French direction. British troops arrived in the Austrian Netherlands on 20 May. Fortunately for the Electorate, the conclusion, actively mediated by John, 3rd Earl of Hyndford, of the separate Peace of Breslau between Frederick II and Austria, on 11 June 1742, by which he abandoned the French, provided Hanover with vital security, as the French, now fully engaged with the Austrians further south, had moved their troops from Westphalia.

The resonance of the argument made by Pulteney in 1741 helps explain the sensitivity of the subsequent Hanoverian neutrality, which helped to set the tone for serious public attacks in 1742–4 on the real or alleged role of Hanover. As a result of the neutrality, Hanoverian security became of greater concern, with repercussions for much of British foreign policy, while the role of Hanover became a major issue in Parliament, the press, and within the ministry.[23] The Commons debate on 10 December (os) 1742, over hiring 16,000 Hanoverian troops for the army being assembled in the Low Countries to support Austria, witnessed not only a high turn out of MPs (which was, in turn, to be surpassed when the hire of Hanoverians was debated on 18 January (os) 1744), but also the publication of the division list.[24] George Bubb Doddington, an opposition Whig, warned the Commons in December 1743:

> If every man in this House were to be silent upon that head the people without doors would soon find out what tools they were made of; they would soon perceive their being sacrificed to the interests and views of Hanover, and this would render every honest man in the nation not only discontented with our public measures, but disaffected to the illustrious family now upon our throne; the necessary consequence of which would

be, that our present constitution must overturn our present establishment, or our present establishment must overturn our present constitution.

The following month, another opposition Whig speaker, John, 4th Earl of Sandwich, called upon the House of Lords to heed what he presented as the general voice:

> It may be hoped that these sentiments will be adopted, and these resolutions formed by every man who hears, what is echoed through the nation, that the British have been considered as subordinate to their own mercenaries, mercenaries whose service was never rated at so high a price before, and who never deserved even the petty price at which their lives used to be valued; that foreign slaves were exalted above the freemen of Great Britain, even by the King of Great Britain, and that on all occasions, on which one nation could be preferred to the other, the preference was given to the darling Hanoverians.[25]

In the same debate, Charles, 3rd Duke of Marlborough, who had resigned his commission after the battle of Dettingen in protest at what he saw as the favour shown the Hanoverian troops by George II, declared:

> It is not possible to mention Hanover, or its inhabitants, in any public place, without putting the whole house into a flame, and hearing on every hand expressions of resentment, threats of revenge, or clamours of detestation. Hanover is now become a name which cannot be mentioned without provoking rage and malignity, and interrupting the discourse by a digression of abhorrence.

Indeed, opposition spokesmen pressed hard for government to take note of public views.[26] A sixpenny opposition ballad of 1744 claimed:

> Abroad our gallant army fights
> In Austria's cause, for G-m-n rights
> By English treasure fed
> Hessians and Hano— too
> The gainful trade of war pursue
> With C——t [Carteret] at their head.

The cost of the Continental commitment was also an issue, repeatedly so. This was unsurprising given the economic recession of the period. On 27 November (os) 1744, the *York Courant* published a 'Chronicle of the Year 1744', a parody of the Bible, including 'The money of England was plenteous in Germany and in Flanders, and in Italy'. Money represented national interest in a concrete case.[27] *Old England*, in its issue of 17 November (os) 1744, referred to the British as:

a great, powerful, brave people, taxed, fleeced, and oppressed, for purposes foreign to their interests ... Of all causes which concur to the breaking a people's independency, none contribute so much as foreign wars, unnecessarily undertaken, expensively maintained, and ingloriously prosecuted.

The critique of Hanoverian influence related not only to subsidies,[28] but also to the supposed interests of the Electorate in Germany, not least territorial aggrandisement. As an example of the secret springs literature, one pamphlet of 1743 claimed:

> whenever peace is made, it will be at the expense of the Queen of Hungary, in Italy, as well as in Germany, provided any acquisitions of power or territory can be gained by France to Hanover. Here centres all the politics of the Court of London.[29]

The extent to which ministers were forced to defend the Hanoverian subsidies underlined the problems posed by the Hanoverian connection. The issue was the public expression of much wider disquiet about the influence of Hanover on British foreign policy, and the role of Hanover in British public life. This had been a major issue in the late 1710s, but rose to a peak in the early 1740s, before being largely extinguished by the upsurge of Whig loyalism (though not unity) linked to the Jacobite challenge in the '45.

In part, the critique was an aspect of a more general failure to accept the limits to the resources and capability of allies. Instead, it was easier to ascribe weaknesses or failure to a lack of will, or even to nefarious intentions. Combined with a tendency to assume that others should share Britain's diplomatic and military priorities – in other words, that, in British eyes, there was such a lack of will – this was an aspect of a systemic failure in public debate to understand Britain's allies, and therefore the parameters for Britain's diplomatic and military strategies. That British politics and government were frequently misunderstood by allies did not make this failure any better. At the same time, although the reasons for the disappointing results of Britain's alliances were not understood, the results were readily apparent, and this fuelled dissension.

The issues of the 1740s provided an opportunity to test in crisis and war the expectations engendered during the more pacific previous two decades. Events provided a series of shocks. If Hanover was politically the most sensitive issue in foreign policy, it was not the sole matter in contention as far as interventionism on the European Continent was concerned. The latter indeed proved a dismal failure, accentuating dissension over policy, and over how best to implement it.[30]

The hopes of defeating France militarily that had been so marked in 1742–3, especially after George II's victory over the main French army in Germany at Dettingen on 27 June 1743, were replaced by the realisation that it would be difficult to stop the French triumphing by land. Dettingen itself was politicised, with the failure to achieve the desired military consequences linked, in the public mind, to agitation over the favour George had shown his Hanoverian troops on the battlefield, a linkage that underrated the inherent difficulties amply seen during the War of the Spanish Succession of knocking France out of the war. This strategy as a whole was politicised with the argument that success could have been secured had the maritime war with Spain been pursued more vigorously. Before the 1744 campaigning started, *Old England*, an opposition London newspaper, in its issue of 10 March (os) declared:

> It is not much above a year since we were told by our politicians of the first rank that France was so exhausted and impoverished by her late exploits that we might not only safely undertake to draw her teeth and pare her nails, but with certainty of success in the operation. Upon this principle, which was urged with that dictatorial air which will not admit of disputation, which cannot bear contradiction, we neglected the *People's War*, which these very politicians, had once patronised with as much zeal, as if the very being of the nation depended on it, and madly embroiled ourselves in a land-war on the Continent.

The notion of a 'people's war' or a 'nation's war'[31] was a definite criticism of ministers, especially Carteret, supposedly serving the cause of Hanover by focusing on the war on the Continent, but the options apparently available to Britain greatly diminished when Louis XV declared war on Britain on 15 March 1744, and sought to invade both then and in the winter of 1745–6.[32] The 1744 invasion attempt was defeated by bad weather, but it was a valuable testimony to the extent to which neither the maritime strategy (a large navy), nor its Continental counterpart (a substantial army in the Low Countries), could deter the French from attempting an invasion of Britain, rather than one of Hanover.

The same was to be true of a Jacobite attempt, for in 1745, 'Bonnie Prince Charlie', Charles Edward Stuart, was transported with French help to the west coast of Scotland. The nature and severity of the resulting crisis provides a perspective on Britain's Continental commitment. The prospect of French military assistance was one of the major factors that led the Scots to follow Charles Edward south on his overland invasion of England, and indeed it was a prospect. Under the Treaty of Fontainebleau of 24 October 1745, Louis XV recognised James Edward Stuart as King of Scotland, and promised to send military assistance and to recognise him as King of England as soon as this could be shown to be the wish of the nation. An expeditionary force, under the Duke of Richelieu, was prepared at Dunkirk, but delays in its preparation, poor weather, British control of the Channel, and news of the Jacobite retreat from Derby on 6 December (os) led to its cancellation. The very threat of French intervention in what was a War of the British

Succession, however, arose directly from Britain's intervention against France in the War of the Austrian Succession. Far from addressing the problem of national security, interventionism had led to a dangerous commitment, because it was clear from French policy over the previous three decades, particularly after the Anglo-French alliance came to an end in 1731, that France would not support the Jacobites unless provoked.

This was not the sole challenge facing the Continental commitment. When, in August 1744, Frederick II attacked Austria, he prevented the Austrians from maintaining their military pressure on eastern France. George II and his Hanoverian ministers wanted Prussia defeated, and devoted much diplomatic effort to sustaining an alliance against Frederick, George maintaining a secret correspondence via Hanover with Hyndford, British envoy in St Petersburg from 1744 to 1749, unbeknownst to the British government.[33] This *secret du roi* sought to pitch Russia against Prussia. Frederick's success in forcing Austria and Saxony to terms in December 1745 (the Treaty of Dresden) was a considerable blow to George.

In 1745, the French also conquered much of the Austrian Netherlands (Belgium). As the British also captured the French base of Louisbourg on Cape Breton Island the same year, the proposition of an exchange as a key element in any peace emerged speedily, but this made it necessary for the British to defend their gain, which placed a strategic burden on the navy, while, at the same time, underlining the difficulties, and relative failure, of Britain's Continental commitment.

The distinction between policy, and how best to implement it, was one that could be elided in political discussion, with critics using failures in the latter to question the direction of policy; but there was also a difference. 'Blue Water' versus interventionism were, at once, differences of emphasis and contrasts of substance. As far as the first was concerned, commentators were aware that, when the enemy was France, it was necessary both to oppose her at sea and to challenge any attempt she might make to expand her power in the Low Countries. Any French advances there provided not only a means to endanger links between Britain and the Continent, including Hanover, but also naval bases from which the French could challenge Britain's naval dominance of the North Sea and, more particularly, increase the danger of an invasion attempt. Nicholas Rodger has cogently argued that 'The political nation at large may not have realised it, but a plain choice between military and naval strategy was never in fact available ... Real policy was based on a distribution of commitments afloat and ashore, aimed at preserving the balance of power in Europe and upsetting it overseas.'[34]

While correct, this conclusion also underrates the importance of the issues in debate. There were contrasts of substance over the distribution, and, more particularly, prioritisation, of commitments, and also over how best to fulfil them. Thus, neither diplomatic nor military tasks were clearcut. To provide another instance of this issue of the scale of contemporary prioritisation and the perspective of historical judgement, while it is true that there was rarely a choice between military and naval strategy (policy in the Baltic was resolutely navalist, as was intervention in support of Portugal in 1735), there was frequently a bitter conflict over priorities. This was not simply a matter of political point-scoring, for there was no obvious answer to questions about best practice in the shape of force structure and military planning. The same was true of diplomatic strategy, more particularly the degree of support owed to the interests of allies.

Emphasis on the political nature of the debate between American and Continental strategies serves, like that on the political character of the critique of Hanoverianism, both to make an accurate and pertinent point, and, less profitably, to divert attention from the extent to which, in both, there were real issues. This was not simply due to the political importance of the debate, but also because there were serious differences of emphasis in strategy.

The tension over goals made, and makes, discussion in terms simply of naval or military priorities less than helpful. This is readily apparent if the security implications posed by the Jacobite challenge and the possibility of French invasion are considered. When William Hay defended the army estimates in 1738, he told his fellow MPs: 'It may be thought, and I have often heard it said, that our fleet will protect us: but our fleet is not always sure of meeting an enemy; and if that expectation should fail what reserve have we then left but our land forces?'[35] In short, the army was not simply there to pursue the Continental schemes of monarch and ministers. The account of commitments focused on defence provided a narrative and an analysis of strategic goals and means that differed from those involving power projection. Again, this was not a matter of simple opposites – the Low Countries, or at least its coastal parts, particularly invasion ports such as Ostend, acting as a fulcrum of both defence and offence – but there were important differences in emphasis.

If by no means all differences in strategy focused on whether the stress should be on American or Continental goals, many did. Richard Harding uses an assessment of policy and strategy in 1739–42, specifically the enthusiasm felt by Carteret and the Pelhams for war in America in 1739 and war in Europe in 1742, to cast 'doubt upon the alleged division between Continental and American war strategies' and subsequently asserts, 'The American versus Continental war division was not of great significance in the 1740s in determining policy, and indeed it is doubtful if it ever was'. Instead, he argues that policy was influenced by many factors, public debate being only one of them.[36] Yet, the controversy over focusing military operations on Canada or Europe in the latter stages of the war, and that over the return of Cape Breton in the peace treaty, certainly saw a charged American versus Continental debate.[37] Even for the early 1740s, contemporaries could discern important differences, and this gave them political impact. If these differences could be stigmatised as opportunistic in Pitt's case – a charge that in fact fails to give sufficient weight to his distinction between help to

Hanover and a national commitment to the anti-French cause on the Continent – that charge can less fairly be applied to differences within the ministry. The issues at stake between Carteret and the Pelhams were not restricted to strategy, and it would be misleading to see them as supporting either Continental or American policies without qualification, but there were important differences that could be related to this continuum between Continental and maritime war. To that extent, the public debate captured a real rivalry in measures as well as men, and deepened its political resonance. The debates of 1742–4 had shown that a distinction between a Flanders (Low Countries) and a Hanover war had real political resonance, which had to be managed by the ministry in relation to the other realities of war in Europe and the colonies. Ministers had to take the broader matter of fighting the war into consideration and present it to the political nation at large in a way consistent with attitudes towards Hanover and the Low Countries. Policy thus responded to the practicalities of making war in a way and place to bring about the best results, as perceived by contemporaries.[38]

A further element of complexity can be added by noting that the American strategy was a later iteration of the 'Blue Water' emphasis and that, whereas the former was focused on France, the latter owed its historical resonance and political weight to confrontation and conflict with Spain. The Spanish strand in British foreign policy varied in intensity but was particularly important from the late 1710s until 1742, the year in which, as hopes of conquests around the Caribbean receded, confrontation with France moved up the political and military agenda. Many of the issues ventilated in discussion about policy toward Spain were to be translated to the French case, and it is important not to segregate them.

With Spain as with France, it was possible to emphasise either a 'Blue Water' strategy or an attempt to benefit from a Continental strategy, which in the case of Spain meant focusing on her opponents in Italy: Austria and Savoy-Piedmont (the Kingdom of Sardinia). The Italian possessions and pretensions of Philip V's sons acted as an even stronger distraction to Spanish policy than those of George II as Elector did to that of Britain. During the Anglo-French alliance, France indeed had been an important ally for Britain against Spain, militarily so in 1719–20. Seeking to secure the co-operation of France, played a major role in British relations with Spain from 1716 until 1729. When war broke out in 1739, however, the government responded to international and domestic circumstances, took a unilateral stance and pursued a 'Blue Water' policy towards Spain.

It is sometimes claimed that Britain only fought alone that century during the War of American Independence, and that failure then demonstrated the need for allies. In fact, Britain alone fought Spain from 1739 (though Spain, subsequently, chose to attack Habsburg interests in Italy in the War of the Austrian Succession), and, as with the War of American Independence, failure was due not to an inability to distract Bourbon resources by means of an alliance system but rather because of the inherent difficulty of the strategic task combined with military mismanagement. The leading government newspaper, the *Daily Gazetteer*, in its issue of 24 July (os) 1740, declared that it was best to fight Spain alone:

> This war, as it has been, and very likely will be carried on by sea, can never materially affect us; but should it become a complicated war, a war both by sea and land, as it unavoidably would if any power on the continent openly took our part, we should then be obliged to tread the same expensive circle as we did in the reigns of King William and Queen Anne. What foreign addition of strength do we want to humble Spain, and reduce her to equitable terms of peace?

If France helped Spain, according to the anonymous writer, then it would be necessary for Britain to seek the assistance of allies; but not otherwise. This argument clashed with that of opposition speakers, such as John, 2nd Duke of Argyle, in the House of Lords in April 1740,[39] and also with the *Craftsman* of 12 July (os) 1740, which claimed that, even if France backed Spain, there was 'no occasion for our making war on the Continent, unless France should attack the Dutch, or any other neighbouring powers; then we may be sure of their alliance'. Fleury, indeed, said that if France helped Spain, it would only be at sea; in short, that there would be no attack on Hanover. François de Bussy, French envoy in London, was convinced that, as long as the war was only by sea, and only with Spain, then it would always be popular.[40]

The debate over means had become more complex as the situation on the Continent moved toward war, because objectives became far more complex. In turn, the crisis of the Walpole ministry in 1741–2, and the subsequent reworking of British government and politics, led to a more frenetic and demanding attitude[41] towards options, especially on the part of opposition spokesmen keen to reject the Walpole years and eager to exploit what they saw as a new start. This desire extended to the far recesses of the country. On 20 August (os) 1742, the General Session of the Grand Jury of Montgomeryshire drew up an Address to their MP, Robert Williams, urging not only the repeal of the Septennial Act but also the pursuit of 'such measures, as in the end, may render this nation once more the terror of the Continent, masters of the ocean, and the real arbiters of Europe'. The press ensured that the news of such resolutions spread, and this helped maintain heady enthusiasm, but Williams, himself a member of the Jacobite Cycle of the White Rose, was happily freed by his opposition preferences from the need to think about how best to execute such nostrums: voting against the ministry in all recorded divisions, his most senior post was Recorder of Oswestry.

As, from 1743, the war with Spain was matched by conflict with France, the priorities of policy became a matter of complaint. The emphasis on conflict on the Continent led to charges that the war with Spain had been neglected,[42] and this became more serious because failure there accentuated the claim that the Continental commitment itself was foolish. In 1744, Edmund Waller, an opposition Whig MP, attacked 'the manifest neglect not to say worse of the navy the only proper defence of this country, whilst they were pursuing chimerical schemes of settling an impracticable balance of power on the Continent'.[43] This sense of a policy too far was not only expressed in Parliament. The *Daily Post* of 3 October (os) 1744 claimed: 'View the disputes on the Continent in what light you please, it will be found an undertaking past our skill and strength to compose them: consequently we have no business there, let who will be in the right or wrong.'

At the same time, it is necessary to note shifts in the debate. If Continental interventionism was unpopular, it was less so if, as it was to be in 1758, it could be dissociated from the charge of Hanoverianism, and, as in 1758, this required a domestic political solution that made the defeat of George II explicit. In 1758, this was to be Pitt's role as Secretary of State, while in 1745 the defeat of Carteret the previous year was a crucial factor. So also was the degree to which the Continental commitment could be located attractively. If in 1758 this was to mean in defence of Prussia's western approaches, from 1744 until 1748 it involved the defence of the Low Countries. On that basis, Pitt came, from 1744, to support the purpose of keeping British troops on the Continent. In January 1745, Pitt, distancing himself from the Tory position, spoke in the Commons in support of Pelham's proposal to increase the British force in the Austrian Netherlands, and Harrington drew attention to 'that important affair having passed with so great unanimity'.[44] The following month, Pitt supported the ministry in a debate over the proposal to increase Maria Theresa's subsidy, in order, as was generally understood, to enable her to take over the financing of the Hanoverians from the British Treasury. In 1746, support for the hiring of Hanoverians was made more explicit. On 11 April (os) the Commons agreed, by a majority of 255 to 122, to pay £300,000 towards the support of 18,000 Hanoverians who were to serve in the Austrian Netherlands.

In place of Carteret's desire to redraw boundaries, and George II's wish to act against Prussia, the ministry was now concentrating on a traditional geopolitical theme, firmly located within the parameters of widely accepted strategic culture. Subsidised foreign troops, such as the Hanoverians, whose extraordinary expenses for the 1746 campaign even Cumberland found questionable, were clearly designed to protect the Low Countries, and thereby British security. Trevor referred to the Austrian Netherlands and the United Provinces as 'outlying counties of England'.[45] If Britain abandoned her allies, the French might negotiate peace with them, make unacceptable gains, and help the Stuart cause. As a result both of this and of the defeat of Carteret's attempt, at George II's behest, to return to power and form a ministry in February 1746, the public debate over foreign and military policy became less charged, not least because George's attempt to create a defensive alliance against Prussia was kept from the public arena.

Prefiguring the shift that was to occur in the two following coalition wars against France, the non-interventionist agenda now seemed less appropriate. Concern over the Low Countries indeed took priority over governmental and public anxiety and anger about the effort made by Britain's allies,[46] although the latter issue helped ensure that the non-interventionist strand continued buoyant.[47] Furthermore, it became stronger in 1747 because the war went on going badly, even after William IV of Orange gained power in Holland and Zeeland that May, leading to a Dutch commitment that initially had seemed to offer a return to the days of the first Duke of Marlborough. The practicability of 'going on with a prospect of success'[48] became a key issue, one even doubted by key ministerial figures, especially after the major fortress of Bergen-op-Zoom fell to the French on 16 September 1747,[49] and foreign diplomats were in no doubt that support for peace was related to the progress of the war.[50] The subordination of foreign policy, and indeed military strategy, to the fate of military operations was both narrowing and depressing, although, fortunately for the British, the French were also under great strain.

The nature of this strain is a matter for scholarly debate, and was unclear to contemporaries. It was understandable that it was viewed in Britain in terms primarily of the British contribution to the war. As far as success was involved, this appeared to mean not the defensive gain of restricting the pace of French expansion in the Low Countries, an advantage compromised by defeat, but rather the value of naval victory, particularly the two battles off Cape Finisterre in 1747. Newcastle observed 'I believe we have done their trade and marine more hurt this war than in all the foregoing ones'.[51]

Indeed, these victories helped answer vociferous criticism of the Continental commitment, such as that published in a collected edition of pieces from the *Westminster Journal*, an opposition newspaper:

> Our interest, with respect to ourselves, and to the other nations of Europe, is so obvious, that what unbiased man can hide his astonishment and indignation when he sees it totally neglected? We have a prodigious fleet, and can we think matters are well conducted if it does us scarce any service in time of war? We are a mercantile nation, and have beyond all other powers the means of extending our commerce.[52]

Naval victories, however, did not fully cover the government politically, not only because of the issue of securing colonial gains, especially the much-desired retention of Cape Breton,[53] but also because success at sea encouraged an expectation of such gains.

Irrespective of this, it is unclear that the navy was the war-winner (as opposed to colony-gainer) envisaged by the British. French trade was indeed hit by the British navy,[54] but other factors contributed to serious economic and fiscal problems. French finances were hit by the cost of the war,[55] and most of this was in Europe, not at sea. Government expenditure had risen to 300 million livres in 1742 and 350 million in 1744, a sum that exceeded those of Austria and Britain combined. As was reported to the British government,[56] particular problems were caused by the poor state of the French harvest.

Whatever the fiscal position, the diplomatic situation was not propitious for France. All alliance systems appear weak from the inside, and those of Britain's Continental commitment were no exception. All systems, however, should be put in a comparative context. That of France was gravely weakened, because Spain, from July 1746 under its new ruler, Ferdinand VI, no longer supported French schemes, despite promises to the contrary. Indeed, Spain negotiated independently with Britain in 1747. France concluded an alliance with Sweden and Prussia that May, but this did not prevent Russia sending troops west and, in the aftermath of the Anglo-Russian subsidy treaty of 1747, the French were concerned at the prospect of British-subsidised Russian intervention on the Rhine.[57] In Hanoverian eyes, the purpose of this treaty was to deter Frederick II from aggressive steps, either directly against Hanover or those that would weaken the Electorate's relative position in the Empire, and represented a crucial British commitment to the Continent. The prospect of France accepting peace was also enhanced by her successes in the Low Countries, not only because conquests there provided valuable bargaining counters in negotiations, but also because the successes brought the prestige that made a compromise settlement at the end of a long conflict bearable.

The preliminaries of the Treaty of Aix-la-Chapelle were signed on 30 April and the definitive treaty on 18 October 1748. France made no territorial gains, recognised the Protestant Succession in Britain, expelled Bonnie Prince Charlie (Charles Edward Stuart), and regained Cape Breton, the British East India Company regained Madras, the disputed Canadian border was referred to commissioners, and there were relatively minor territorial changes in Italy. Both in Britain and in France, Aix-la-Chapelle was heavily criticised as an inglorious peace, and this was accentuated in 1750 when the Spanish claim to a right to search British merchantmen was not explicitly denied in the Anglo-Spanish commercial treaty. Exhaustion, however, made the absence of glory acceptable. The exuberant demands for action – against Spain in 1738–9 and, far less exuberant, in support of Austria against France in 1741–3 – were now replaced by a muted pleasure at the coming of peace. Pelham visited his constituency, Sussex, reporting, 'we had a full meeting of gentlemen, and almost all in good humour, our peace is popular with all parties'.[58]

7 Revived tensions, 1748–58

Under the direction of Providence, this nation has after a course of sixty years bad policy in the support of the popish house of Austria, been forcibly driven by her natural enemies to an alliance with the only power upon Earth that is capable of assisting us in the defence of the Protestant faith, and, by his military capacity, to reduce the common enemy . . . to an incapacity of disturbing the peace of his neighbours for the future. Such alliances are agreeable to the constitution and interest of these kingdoms. They are according to that model of sound politics, which were laid down by the ministers of our Elizabeth [I], who could never be persuaded to take any further share in the troubles on the continent, than was necessary to facilitate the schemes of their own government. But it is very wide of those continental measures, which of late years have loaded this nation with heavy debts for the support of armies in the time of peace, and for taking upon us the greatest burden in every quarrel raised by the house of Austria.

(*Monitor*, 22 April 1758)

Far from being fixed, the link between Hanover could have come to an end in 1760. In his will, George I had stipulated an eventual division of Britain and Hanover after the death of his then sole grandson, Frederick, later Prince of Wales, the Electorate going to Frederick's second son, if he had one, and, failing that, to the Brunswick-Wolfenbüttel branch of the house of Brunswick, but the will was suppressed by George II. Had the will stood when Frederick died in 1751, then William, Duke of Cumberland, would have become heir to Hanover on the death of George II, and this might have led him to marry and have an heir, which he did not do. Had he not married, Hanover could have become a secondgeniture, as the grand duchy of Tuscany became for the Habsburgs from 1765, so that, on Cumberland's death in 1765, it would have passed to Frederick's second son, Edward, Duke of York, and, on his death without heir in 1767, to George III's second son, Frederick, Duke of York.

Frederick, Prince of Wales, in turn, considered a division of the inheritance, with his second son, Edward, becoming Elector,[1] but neither he nor George II made any arrangements to that effect. George II took the idea seriously, as he feared the anti-Hanoverian attitudes of George III as Prince of Wales, but he tended to think Hanover's territorial integrity best served by the maintenance of the British connection, and in 1744 received this advice from the Hanoverian Privy Counsellors when he consulted them. In 1759, however, George was driven by anger at what he saw as the neglect of Hanover to advocate a division. The occasion was Newcastle's response to the King's question about the prospect of Hanover gaining territory as a result of the Seven Years' War. The Duke argued that there would be a return to the pre-war territorial status quo in Europe in the eventual peace, upon which George II let vent:

> after expressing great dissatisfaction with us, our ingratitude in doing nothing for him, who had suffered so much for this ungrateful country. To which I took the liberty to reply that this war had been most expensive to this nation; that it would increase our national debt 30 millions; that it would be impossible for us to retain all our conquests at a peace; and that whatever advantages the Electorate should gain, would be thought, by everybody, to be so far a diminution of what might have been retained for this country; and that *that* was the *point*; and the apprehension of all his servants. His Majesty then said, since you will do nothing for me, I hope you will agree to separate my Electorate from this country . . . pass a short Act of Parliament, that whoever possesses this Crown, shall not have the *Electorate* . . . *George* will be King; and his brother Elector.

Philip, Earl of Hardwicke, the former Lord Chancellor, replied:

> As to the question of *separation of the Electorate*, your Grace knows it has been seriously talked of before, but nobody could see their way through it either *here* or *in Germany*. There can be no other way, but passing an Act of Parliament laying disabilities upon that *branch*, which should be in possession of the Electorate, unless they should renounce and abdicate it; and there recurred the danger of creating *Pretenders* even in the family of Hanover itself. Consent of parties now in being would not help this in future. But I perfectly agree the thing is extremely to be wished.[2]

This was not taken further under George II, and George III did not pursue the idea of dividing the inheritance; instead, the will he drew up in 1765 stated that his eldest son would inherit both Crown and Electorate. The Hanoverian inheritance, which, in the case of the Electorate was itself the recent product of the fusion of the inheritances of several branches of the house of Brunswick, as a result of the maintenance of the primogeniture introduced by George I's father, Ernst August, did not divide until 1837.

Sensitivity in the mid-eighteenth century over the dynastic connection was fostered by the continued vulnerability of Hanover, which was demonstrated anew in 1753 and 1757. On the former occasion, there were fears of a Prussian invasion. In 1757, this was not an issue, as Prussia was an ally, although it was unable to provide the promised support,[3] but the ability of France to strike across the Rhine was evident when a French army defeated outnumbered Hanoverian and allied German forces under Cumberland at Hastenbeck on 26 July and overran the Electorate. This led to the signature on 8 September of another neutrality convention, that of Kloster Zeven.[4] Indeed, convinced that Hanover had become a target for France because of the latter's war with Britain, the Hanoverian Geheime Rat (ministerial council) in the autumn of 1757 debated its support for the maintenance of the personal union with Britain.[5] George, himself, had earlier expressed much anger about the lack of urgency in preparing for conflict shown by his Hanoverian ministers: 'I never saw His Majesty more concerned than at the accounts received of the dilatory proceedings at Hanover.'[6]

The two neutrality agreements, of 1741 and 1757, created considerable international difficulty and domestic embarrassment for British ministers, and these agreements showed that, irrespective of George II's ability as King to influence the direction of British diplomacy, the policies of the Electorate had immediate implications for this diplomacy. As a consequence, Newcastle, the minister most influential in British foreign policy from the fall of Carteret in 1744 to the establishment of the Pitt–Devonshire ministry in 1756, devoted considerable effort to the creation of an international system that would, among other goals, deter attacks on Hanover. Indeed, Horace Walpole complained in 1749 that Newcastle 'Hanoverizes more and more each day'.[7] Newcastle's concern indicated the shifting nature of the British response to Hanoverian issues.

This issue of how far Britain's identity and interests were bound up with the Continent was a major one in the mid-eighteenth-century debates over foreign policy, but it was also a theme that was played out in various contexts. On the one hand, the defence of interventionism was a support for the Hanoverian dynasty, and for the government's backing of this interest. There was also, however, the problem of how best to explain this support in terms of wider issues of British foreign policy. In 1753, Pitt, then Paymaster General, was keen to do so:

> If the Russian treaty is agreed upon; to treat it, as a defensive measure, for the preservation of the peace of Europe; and as a provisional force, in case a rupture with France, and a general war in consequence of it, should become necessary, on account of the affair of Dunkirk ... To adhere to our points with France, as to Dunkirk and the West Indies – in which case, the [Russian] army on the frontiers of Livonia, will have its weight.[8]

Newcastle was more realistic when he saw alliance with Russia as likely to restrain Prussia, rather than as influencing its ally, France:

> nothing would tend so much to keep His Prussian Majesty [Frederick II] quiet, or to discourage other powers from supporting him, as the seeing so considerable a strength, as a body of 70,000 Russian troops, on the frontiers, ready to act, in case the King of Prussia shall think proper to make any attempt upon His Majesty or any of his allies.[9]

On another level, the defence of interventionism was less specifically concerned with Hanover or the exigencies of British politics, and, instead, was a politicised response to the apparent dynamics of international relations, and, specifically, to the threat allegedly posed by France. Indeed in 1748, Sir Everard Fawkener, a former diplomat, threw light on the views of his influential patron, William, Duke of Cumberland:

> whatever the conditions of the peace may be, they will be rendered better or worse by the terms upon which the Allies may remain with regard to each other, and it is now more than ever necessary not only to maintain and cement the present alliance, but to receive into it all such powers as may take umbrage at the growing and dangerous power of France. This seems to His Royal Highness so essential a point that he thinks it is all we have to rescue Europe from that dependence on France, which so many and so long and bloody struggles have been made to prevent.[10]

Diplomacy was thus designed to keep the wartime alliance potent and pointed.

The domestic implications of policies were also an issue. In 1752, Newcastle wrote to Gerlach Adolf von Münchhausen, the leading Hanoverian minister, who had close relations with the Duke, that criticism in Britain of the anti-French and anti-Prussian direction of foreign policy had become stronger as a result of the need to pay peacetime subsidies in order to win foreign support for the policy.[11] Ministers involved in foreign policy were alive to the problems posed by such subsidies. Responding to Russian and Saxon expectations, Holdernesse complained in 1750, 'Sure they imagine guineas grow in our streets'.[12] Newcastle was irritated by pressure from Austria and the Dutch for Britain to pay subsidies to other powers.[13] The British ministry was not alone in facing such pressures. Responding to Saxon requests, Puysieulx, the French foreign minister, referred to the obdurancy of the Contrôleur Général and the state of French government finances.[14]

It is also necessary to consider the degree to which views and their expression were refocused due to the exigencies of wartime and to the character of wartime politics. Thus, in 1762, Newcastle mounted a defence of wartime intervention:

the recalling our troops from Germany, and abandoning the continent entirely would now render the House of Bourbon absolute master of all Europe, enable them to oblige every neutral power to submit . . . We should be reduced to that miserable condition of defending ourselves at home, with our wooden walls [the navy], our militia or perhaps our own troops, excluded from all commerce abroad, and all connection with the other powers of Europe.[15]

In peacetime, in contrast, the time-scale of policy options – specifically the likely timing of particular crises – was unclear. If, in the early 1750s, the crucial issue to Newcastle was the Imperial Election Plan – the wish to avoid fresh instability in the Holy Roman Empire by securing the election as King of the Romans (heir to the Holy Roman Emperor) of Archduke Joseph, the elder son of Emperor Francis I and Maria Theresa of Austria – the urgency of this was by no means clear to British and foreign contemporaries. Indeed, Francis was not to die until 1765, by which time Anglo-Austrian relations were cool. Although less prominent, the Polish Succession was also an issue, widely seen by British ministers as likely to lead to war,[16] but, in fact, Augustus III of Saxony-Poland was not to die until 1763, and, unlike with the death of his father and predecessor in 1733, this did not lead to a full-scale conflict.

These were instances of a more general unknowable which affected foreign policy. As the aspirations of foreign rulers, and their responses to developments, were unknown, so it was very difficult to assess likely changes. As Joseph II, Archduke Joseph, indeed, was to be no friend to Britain. The difficulty of assessing likely changes made it hard to discuss policy options other than in hypothetical terms, but that did not accord with the desire of ministers to appear to be in command of events. This desire was encouraged by strident criticism from politicians and polemicists, and thus by the need for ministers to respond to the public debate. Furthermore, the mental equipment of the period, more specifically the belief in mechanistic, rather than organic, theories of states and the state system, encouraged an approach to international relations that was instrumentalist: by means of adopting a specific policy, there would be assured outcomes (and therefore that the failure to adopt the policy would lead to certain failure). Thus, in 1754, Holdernesse wrote to Joseph Yorke that the possibility of Britain settling differences between Russia and the Ottoman (Turkish) empire

would naturally be productive of the happiest consequences, as His Majesty's influence at the Ottoman Porte will thereby be greatly increased, and the designs which the French may, at any time, have, to create disturbances, between the Grand Signior and either of the Empresses [Maria Theresa of Austria, and Elizabeth of Russia] will be rendered more difficult for the future.[17]

The confidence in this instrumentalist approach can be seen as a product of the Whig mind; the particular characteristics of this mind stemmed from a confidence, born of the mathematisation of experience in the 'new science', that rational calculation could be applied to understand and solve problems. This habit of thinking was not only associated with Whigs, but, nevertheless, there was a marked congruence that is worthy of comment.

Such an approach might be comforting for abstract speculation, but proved far less so for ministers and diplomats struggling with the unwillingness of foreign powers to conform to such calculation. Thus, throughout the early 1750s, what seemed to the British to be obdurate Austrian policies made it difficult to maintain enthusiasm for the 'Old' or 'Grand' alliance of Britain, the Dutch and Austria, which, to the British, represented both national interests and those of the international system. Joseph Yorke complained from The Hague in 1752, 'I see that the King of Prussia is upon the watch to pick us up, he is smoother than he has been a great while, and from no other motive, but because he is wise enough to see, that if the Imperial court drives us much farther, we must change our system whether we will or no'.

Yorke argued that, if her policy did not change, Austrian interests would be challenged – 'there will be no King of the Romans, nor no Barrier, the Austrians to save a penny will lose many a pound sterling, and the whole system of Europe will be overthrown'. Although he did not see it as likely, Yorke also suggested that Austria was not going to respond to Britain's agenda unless France drove the two together: 'In this situation of affairs, it is a fortunate circumstance that France wants peace, and will go some lengths to preserve it, and I don't know whether she won't get more ground by it, than by a rupture, which might unite us all.'[18]

The sense that powers had interests that should be combinable to produce a coherent and rational states system carried with it the consequence that if they did not act as anticipated, then this was a consequence of error – a foolish or wilful failure to understand interests. As a result, there was a frequent complaint about the views of individual members of foreign governments and, thus, an interest not so much in what would now be termed regime change, but rather in the removal of specific flawed ministers. This accorded with the use of the idea of evil ministers in British political imagery; although government apologists, of course, took an historical perspective to this issue in Britain. In 1756, Holdernesse wrote to Robert Keith, the British envoy in Vienna, of 'the necessity the King is under to use his utmost efforts to destroy Count Kaunitz's credit at the Court of Vienna'. Unlike Alberoni in 1720 and Chauvelin in 1737 (not that his fall was due to the British), Kaunitz's position, however, was far too strong for such efforts to succeed.

Reason in the form of intellectual speculation tended to suggest a benign order in which well-meaning states ought to co-operate; but this was not the best basis for the cut-and-thrust of self-interested diplomacy that appeared to prevail. The *Herald* warned on 22 December 1757 that the alliance with Frederick II could not be expected to bear too much weight:

> Thus does our security . . . depend at present on our keeping firm in our union with that heroic monarch. But we should remember that his objects are the security of the German constitution and his own dominions. As soon as his arms obtain him satisfaction in these points, the war in the Empire will cease of course,

and France would concentrate on Britain. The newspaper drew the crucial distinction between key and ancillary interests, although that distinction rested on assertion and was subject to political contention:

> German affairs are indeed become, from the circumstances of things, essentially collateral to our interests, but far from being direct and entire to them. The victories effectually to serve us must be achieved either in America or on the ocean. Prussia may be prosperous while Britain is undone . . . Vain and absurd would be our expectation that the King of Prussia, when he has accomplished his own deliverance should turn a Don Quixote and fight our battles in a war that he has nothing to do with.

At the same time, in accordance with the intellectual preference for mechanistic ideas, a policy of international co-operation was to be based on the political arithmetic of accurate information. Thus, seeking to persuade Maria Theresa's husband, the Emperor Francis I, of the virtues of co-operating to push through the Imperial Election Scheme, Hyndford told him that he should 'examine France, on the side of its interest', to ascertain whether it was prudent 'at present to begin a war when neither its trade, marine, nor finances, have recovered their strength, when Louis the fifteenth's expenses exceed by a third the expenses of Louis the fourteenth'.

This mathematical approach to policy-making, while suggested by the language of the balance of power, was not, however, one that commended itself to most rulers and ministers, as they tended to make an intuitive response to the situation, and then, in seeking allies, to push forward the reasons that seemed most persuasive; a situation very similar to that today. In dealing with states with a public politics, most prominently Britain, Sweden and the United Provinces, it was particularly important to think of arguments that would be likely to work best for such a politics, but that was a reason why ministers accustomed to such politics did not always offer ideas that worked well for states where authority, power, politics and debate were very much focused on the sovereign. This indeed was glanced at in Hyndford's report for, in discussing what he saw as the obstinate Austrian response to British plans, he added:

Mr. Keith and I have reason to believe that this Court is persuaded that His Majesty's Electoral [Hanoverian] Ministry are rather averse than otherways to the [Imperial] Election at this time, and in this belief Mr. Vorster is sent to Hanover, in hopes that the ministers of that court will join with him to influence the King not to bring on the Election at this time, but as I am absolutely certain of the contrary, being fully informed of the way of thinking of these worthy Gentlemen.[19]

As Elector, George II did not have to face the public politics or constitutional restraints he experienced as King, and British ministers and commentators had to attend not only to the dual responsibilities of their ruler as King and Elector, but also respond to the extent to which he had different powers and commitments in his particular responsibilities. The tensions stemming from this situation continued to play a major role in the debate over foreign policy.[20] British public opinion had not learned to make allowance for the commitments that the Crown had as a result of its Electoral status, nor for the problems that affected Hanover as a consequence of the royal link. George II complained:

we were angry because he was partial to his Electorate, though he desired nothing more to be done for Hanover, than what we were bound in honour and justice to do for any country whatsoever, when it was exposed to danger entirely on our own account. That we were indeed a very extraordinary people, continually talking of our constitution, our laws and own liberties,[21]

and obviously not of those of Hanover.

The prejudicial view of at least part of the public was not a luxury permitted the ministry. That indeed gave point to the public debate because, although the contours of that within the ministry were different to public discussion, there were real problems for ministers in deciding how best to respond to the interests of the King as Elector and the public debate was an important aspect of them.

Here again, theory had its limitations, although the theory in question was not the balance of power, but the more monarch-centred idea of a Protestant ruler, who, by his very Protestantism, would ensure national interests at home and abroad. This was the necessary dynastic myth to counter the Jacobite claim, but it left scant room for the embarrassments and compromises arising from the King's views as Elector, just as, earlier, it had had drawbacks in the face of William III's mode of personal government. At least in William's case, it had been easy to defend his foreign policy as anti-French and therefore necessary due to Louis XIV's support for the Jacobite claim, but, although George II was the monarch challenged by the '45, no such defence was possible in the case of George's Electoral interests.

George II, by the 1750s one of the most experienced politicians in Britain, was alive to the variations in interest between Britain and Hanover, and evidence for blunt exchanges with his British ministers survives in the Newcastle–Hardwicke correspondence. Additional valuable clues to his insights are offered by the reports from foreign diplomats who had audiences with him. In 1740, George made clear to Ossorio, the Sardinian envoy, that he was angry about Austrian policy. In 1755, as relations between Britain (not Hanover crucially) and France deteriorated over North America, François de Bussy reported from Hanover being told by George that he did not doubt Louis XV's good intentions, and that his were the same, 'mais que le differend actuel entre les deux couronnes étoit une affaire nationale, et que je savois quelle étoit la vivacité de la nation Britannique surtout ce qui attaquoit son commerce'.[22] Ironically, as agent 101, Bussy provided secret intelligence to the British from the 1730s, his identity disclosed in the Newcastle correspondence.

This is a valuable instance of the importance of the multiple approach to archival research, as reading the same story from different series can provide significant additional information. Most Secretaries of State had foreign (and British) diplomats to whom they were particularly prone to convey their views. Thus, Newcastle was close to successive Sardinian envoys – Ossorio, Perrone and Viry – and their well-preserved reports in the Archivio di Stato in Turin are useful not only for British policy toward the Italian principalities, but also more generally. In 1756, Newcastle told Viry that Britain could not accept peace with France unless it regained Minorca, which it had just lost, as the island was necessary both for trade and for links with Italian powers.[23] The Sardinian envoys benefited from good relations between the two states, but their personal skills, and the degree to which they took care not to associate with opposition politicians, were also important.

Several foreign archives, however (for example the Danske Rigsarkiv in Copenhagen and the Hauptstaatsarchiv in Dresden), have not yet been systematically probed for these topics. It is important to bear in mind that the value of foreign ministry archives is not restricted to the correspondence of diplomats. For example, the Mémoires et Documents series in the archives of the French Foreign Ministry contain much relevant material, including the interesting journal of the Count of Gisors, who visited London in 1754.[24] It is also pertinent to try to track down the papers of diplomats and ministers, which, in the case of French holdings for relations with Britain in this period, includes material in the K series in the Archives Nationales that throws light on the crisis that led to the Seven Years' War.

Research on foreign diplomatic holdings also offers the opportunity for a comparative assessment of British policy and, more specifically, of Britain-Hanover.[25] Hanover indeed was seen by some as an adjunct of, rather than an obstacle to, British policy. Referring to a scheme by the Saxon envoy, at a time when British policy faced grave difficulties, Newcastle wrote in 1755:

The system, as far as it can be called an active one, is, and must by necessity be suspended for the present. But my friend Flemming wants to introduce it another way; he sees England will not enter into subsidiary treaties, and therefore the same thing shall be done in another shape, vis by the *King as Elector*. Coloredo, Haslang, and in consequence, the courts of Vienna, and Munich, with Saxony are to be parties ... [would] bring on a general war, particularly with Prussia, by means of this Electoral convention, and that will be worse than even if it was done openly and confessedly by England.

The same letter revealed Newcastle's continued closeness to the Hanoverian ministry, an important aspect of the mid-century relationship between Britain and Hanover: 'President [Gerlach Adolf von] Münchhausen writes me word that in his opinion there can be no solid security for the King's German dominions, but by the methods proposed in my letter to him.'[26]

To understand the foreign policy of the period, it is necessary to return it to its political context and, therefore, to make an effort to analyse the contours and contents of the varied, and interrelated, debates over policy. This directs attention away from the instructions in the National Archives (formerly Public Record Office), which represent the end-result of these debates, and, instead, to a more disparate collection of sources. Far from these being solely those of the culture of print, for example newspapers such as the *London Evening Post* and the *Monitor*, it is necessary to appreciate that these 'public' facets of debate in part took on their meaning alongside, and, in many respects, in response to, private or semi-private facets within the political and governmental processes that can only be recovered by archival research.

These sources throw considerable light on the extent to which George II was still able to instruct British diplomats to further Electoral goals, a situation that helped, as much as clashes with Hanoverian diplomacy, to sustain criticism by British envoys, who found it time-consuming and irritating. In October 1747, Sir Charles Hanbury-Williams reported 'I have the Hanover affairs at this court [Dresden] put into my hands', adding, in November, that it had obliged him to postpone a journey to Vienna.[27] The same year, Sandwich successfully pressed the Dutch to hire a German regiment in accordance with George's wishes.[28] The attempt in 1747–8 to persuade Spain to pay money it owed to Hanover was more time-consuming, and led Horace Walpole to complain that the ministry was seeking repayment of this debt, rather than reparation for attacks on British trade.[29]

It would be mistaken to suggest that ministers necessarily yielded to Electoral demands. In 1748, Newcastle encouraged Sandwich to ignore orders about preventing Frederick II from obtaining any guarantee from the peace negotiations at Aix-la-Chapelle for his recent acquisition of East Friesland.[30] Yet, co-operation between British and Hanoverian ministers was the dominant theme in 1748, one to which George II greatly contributed.

This set the scene for close relations between Newcastle and Münchhausen. In July, George sent Bussche, his envoy in Vienna, to the congress at Aix-la-Chapelle. Newcastle was not shown his instructions, but was informed that they related to the Elector's interests in Osnabrück and East Friesland. George, however, clearly did not wish to complicate Sandwich's negotiations with the French Plenipotentiary, St Severin, Newcastle writing to the Earl:

> I am persuaded you will give Mor. Busch all the assistance you can in carrying it through. But as it is a very nice and delicate affair and ought to be conducted with great prudence and discretion; I have the satisfaction to assure you that Mor. Busch is directed to take no step, nor make any application to Mor. St. Severin, but in concert with you and by your advice. And therefore, at the same time, that I am very earnestly to recommend to you, to give Mor. Busch all the assistance in your power; I am persuaded, you will take great care not to give Mor. St. Severin any advantage over you, nor to put it into his power to make any ill use of the confidence reposed in him: for His Majesty has the immediate conclusion of the general pacification so much at heart; and is so desirous, that the negotiation should not be obstructed.

In 1748, ministers praised their Hanoverian counterparts. Aside from Newcastle's high opinion of Münchhausen, he also found 'Mr. Busch a very sensible and discreet man . . . with the rightest notions . . . for supporting the true system, that ought to be observed and followed by the Maritime Powers'. Pelham was 'sorry to lose' Steinberg when he resigned his London post, because 'he was a good natured innocent man'. *En route* to take up his embassy in Berlin, Henry Legge was given very useful information about the situation there by Münchhausen.[31]

The implicit bargain between King and British ministers that had helped to bring governmental stability in the latter stages of the War of the Austrian Succession was to be sustained in the post-war years: a degree of mutual understanding and co-operation to which Newcastle's marked willingness to play an active role as standard-bearer of Continental interventionism and opponent of Prussia was crucial. Once a German league was seen as important, and the Imperial Election Scheme centred on just such a league, Hanoverian advice and assistance was valuable, to an extent that had not been the case for the British ministry for many years.

As already argued, Newcastle's post-war attempt to arrange a strong collective security system designed to prevent war, however misguided in diplomatic terms, rested on the political insight that, in terms of relations with George II, it would not be easy for ministers to refuse Hanover support in a conflict, but that such support might cause serious political problems in Britain. In the event, even Pitt, a noted critic of Hanoverian measures, had to accept the dispatch of British troops and money to Germany in 1758, although he was able to present it both in terms of assistance to Prussia, a reasonable claim, at least in so far as keeping Frederick II in the war was concerned, and, more problematically, also, as a means to conquer Canada in Germany.

Like Newcastle's approach, this policy was riskier, because more exposed to the uncertainties of international developments, than that of Walpole; whose attitudes had, instead, been carried forward by his protégé Pelham. Newcastle and Pitt were very different in their political methods and resonance, but, in office, they shared a commitment to action, and, indeed, as a minor ministerial figure, Pitt had supported Newcastle in the late 1740s and early 1750s, defending the subsidy to Maximilian Joseph, Elector of Bavaria in the Commons debate on 22 February (os) 1751, although, the following year, he did not support the Saxon subsidy treaty.[32] The commitment to action carried with it serious risks: in both peace and war, Newcastle's diplomatic schemes fell foul of the difficulties posed by obdurate allies, and of the Duke's failure to appreciate the direction of international relations; while, in 1758, Pitt had to commit British resources to the weaker of the two alliance systems in Europe. The joy that greeted Frederick II's victories was, in part, relief that the consequences of this could be avoided.

Both Newcastle and Pitt felt constrained by George II and his Hanoverian concerns, and this affected policy. It led in particular to pressure for interventionism. The last stages of the War of the Austrian Succession had indicated the disadvantages of alliance politics and Continental military commitments. Aside from Anglo-Austrian tensions and a failure to derive the anticipated benefit from the seizure of power in the Netherlands by William IV of Orange in 1747, there had been a serious military collapse in the Low Countries, with the French capture of Bergen-op-Zoom in 1747 and Maastricht the following year. The collapse of the Dutch frontier fortifications was a demonstration of vulnerability akin to that of the French coercion of Hanover in 1741, but one that was far more disturbing as it clashed with the experience of a much more durable defence for the Low Countries in the Nine Years' War and the War of the Spanish Succession. As such, the French success prefigured the far more rapid victory of the French Revolutionary forces in the Low Countries in 1792–5, particularly their rapid success in the Austrian Netherlands in November 1792.

Despite these failures, and the striking contrast with British naval success in 1747, over the next few years British foreign policy was to be dominated by an interventionist diplomacy that placed little weight on naval power, and, instead, entailed a large-scale commitment to Continental power politics. The bulk of British diplomatic attention in 1749–53 was devoted to attempts to improve the 'Old Alliance', a classic instance of preparing to fight the last war. Because the Imperial Succession had helped undermine Austrian strength in the early 1740s, the issue was to be settled for the future. Because the defence of the Low Countries had been inhibited during the same conflict by Austrian and Dutch weaknesses and commitments (a view that forgot the consequences of the Jacobite rising in 1745), both powers were to be strengthened.

The value of this engagement strategy to Britain's overseas interests appeared demonstrated by the need to return Louisbourg and Cape Breton, as part of the peace treaty at the close of the War of the Austrian Succession. In practice, the relationship between Continental diplomatic strategy and oceanic power politics was more complex; and also not easy for contemporaries to disentangle. For example, the deterioration in Franco-Spanish relations that led to the Austro-Spanish Treaty of Aranjuez of 14 June 1752 was an important factor behind British naval success in the Seven Years' War (1756–63). Spain remained neutral until 1762, and thus the arithmetic of naval confrontation that had in the previous war limited British flexibility was transformed, a change that helps to explain Vergennes' subsequent determination to gain Spanish assistance in the War of American Independence. The British government sought to further both the settlement of the Italian question by Austria and Spain, and the rift between France and Spain. The government offered naval assistance to the new Austro-Spanish alignment, Holdernesse writing, 'The very notion of His Majesty's supporting this great alliance, with his maritime force, gives the greatest weight and sanction to it'.[33]

This, however, was wishful thinking. The new system owed little to Britain, and indeed, in one respect, helped weaken the diplomatic and strategic significance of British naval power. The challenge that Spain posed to Austrian defensive and offensive interests in Italy had given British naval power a major role in Anglo-Austrian relations in the 1700s, 1710s, early 1730s, and 1740s. That this was no longer the case was an important aspect of the degree to which the powers of Central and Eastern Europe were less impressed by, or interested in, British naval power than the British anticipated.

Naval power was seen as important in the Baltic, where there was a confrontation between Russia and Sweden in 1750, but the prospect of a war there diminished, and that year attention shifted to the Empire (Germany) where British naval power was of little value. Instead, the British relied on financial inducements and talk of shared interests, while militarily they referred to the support of Austria and Russia. Nevertheless, naval strength was still seen of value thanks to the interconnectedness of alliances. In 1753, Joseph Yorke was confident that Frederick II would not attack Hanover as he was sure that he would not act alone and that France would not 'enter into a war just now to please [Frederick] . . . Spain is not disposed to act with them, and they are too sensible of the weight of England by sea, to risk their marine before it is recovered'. Instead, Yorke thought that intimidation on the Continent was designed to offset British naval power:

> The preparations, rumours of encampments, magazines, augmentations, and many other such articles, I attribute to the persuasion they are in

at the Court of Versailles because we are attentive to our navy, that therefore we meditate some great design by sea, I have many proofs of their suspicion, and if that is so, does not good policy require that they should keep us in check by demonstrations towards the Empire, and Flanders, which last is our weak side and therefore the most likely to draw our attention, and prevent us from going to great lengths.[34]

As foreign envoys pointed out,[35] ministerial politics played a major role in policy choices. Newcastle was greatly influenced by his visit to Hanover in 1748, not least by meeting Münchhausen; and his ministerial allies in Britain drew attention to the Duke's new-found clarity. Newcastle's concern to rout his ministerial rival, Bedford, Secretary of State for the Southern Department, as indeed happened in 1751, was also important, as he needed royal support to this end. A sense of dependence, indeed anxiety about George's opinions, continued, thereafter, to characterise Newcastle's views. Thus, in 1755, he wrote to Holdernesse, the Secretary of State then with George in Hanover, 'I am sure you will take a lucky moment, when *we* are in good humour to lay the letters before the King . . . His Majesty must see the regard we have had to His German dominions'.[36] In his turn, Pitt was obliged to back help to Hanover if George II was to be persuaded to disavow the Hanoverian neutrality of 1757, which threatened the coherence of a foreign policy that then rested on alliance with Prussia alone.

Although this neutrality greatly alarmed British ministers, it alone was far from responsible for the difficulties facing British foreign policy in 1757; and, indeed, the vulnerability of the Electorate was not the sole problem stemming from the Hanoverian connection. Instead, there was a more general difficulty with the direction of post-1748 British policy, one that owed much to royal concerns, not least hostility to Prussia. George II had no hesitation in making these clear. In an instructive letter, that underlined the importance of clear royal support for policy, Newcastle had sought, in 1753, to reassure Britain's Dutch allies about George's commitment to getting Austria to meet Dutch goals:

> The King's view is to lay before the Court of Vienna the fatal consequences which must necessarily arise to them, and the whole alliance, if they do not determine to give satisfaction to the Maritime Powers [Britain and the Dutch], upon the two great articles of the Barrier and the commerce of the Low Countries; and His Majesty has chose to do this previously, and by himself, that the Imperial ministers may see that these are the King's own thoughts, and that His Majesty is determined to act pursuant to them.[37]

The 'Old System' – Britain's alliance with Austria and the Dutch, served royal and Hanoverian ends by essentially acting as a military deterrent to Prussia, while appearing also as an anti-French step, and thus matching the assumptions of British politicians. The clash between hostility to France and opposition to Prussia had led to significant political and diplomatic difficulties during the War of the Austrian Succession, but the coming of peace in 1748 permitted the shelving of the apparent differences between the two goals. However, securing the peace by restraining France and Prussia through a collective security system made Britain dependent on her partners, left it unclear whether France or Prussia were the major challenge and made it uncertain whether, in the event of war, intervention could surmount the problems of Hanoverian vulnerability and British political ambivalence toward the Electorate, and win success. As a consequence, British ministers, such as Holdernesse and Newcastle, were to be very free in their criticism of their Hanoverian counterparts in 1757.[38]

Anger with Hanover was in part a product of disappointed hopes. The response of the ministry to the worsening of relations with France over North America in 1754–5 was a determination to strengthen Britain's Continental alliances. Far from there being any notion that maritime strength could bring conquests that would compensate for Continental vulnerability, the ministry had based its diplomacy on the defence of Hanover, and this policy had failed. Seeking in the growing crisis in relations with France to protect Hanover from France's ally Prussia, and fearful of a French invasion of the Low Countries, the British turned to Austria and to Russia. The Austrians were unsympathetic, although, on 13 August 1755, the French envoy in Vienna reported that, if Hanover was attacked, Austria would act, adding that Maria Theresa would never abandon George II.[39]

Closer Anglo-Russian relations in late 1755 led Frederick II, unimpressed anyway by French policy, to accept British proposals to guarantee their respective possessions. The security of Hanover, however, became at this point a bitterly divisive point in Britain because the opposition chose on 10, 12 and 15 December 1755 to attack the subsidy treaties with Hesse-Cassel and Russia. This led to an inter-penetration of policy and politics both with relations within the Whig establishment and between the courts of George II and his grandson, the future George III, each of which were as vexed as the more conventional political battlelines.[40]

The Convention of Westminster of 16 January 1756 – between Prussia and Britain – was seen as constraining French strategic options by ending the threat to Hanover. Henry Fox, the Secretary of State for the Southern Department, testified to the sense of relief gained from pleasing George II, but also to a new feeling of strategic vulnerability:

> Our treaty with Prussia does us great honour and great service here, and will prevent an expensive war and more subsidy demands from Germany. But then, by doing this, it confines and almost obliges France to make some attempt on England or Ireland or both.[41]

The convention, however, also greatly angered Austria and Russia, and helped drive France towards Austria. On 1 May 1756, Austria and France signed a defensive alliance, known as the First Treaty of Versailles, which specifically excluded the Anglo-French conflict that had begun over North America, which had escalated on 18 April when French troops landed on British-held Minorca. Austria benefited most from the defensive agreement, because her position with regard to Prussia made her more vulnerable to attack than France, but France was freed for war with Britain, prefiguring the situation during the War of American Independence. Allied now to Austria, she did not have to worry about attack by her, or indeed by British forces operating from the Low Countries.[42]

Frederick II's unexpected invasion of Saxony on 28 August 1756 led to the Austro-French alliance being focused on war with Prussia, and thus diverted French attention from the struggle with Britain in a way that had not been anticipated when the Convention of Westminster was negotiated: that agreement was intended to secure Hanover. Frederick, however, had already warned Andrew Mitchell, the British envoy, in May 1756 that France might attack Hanover in 1757 'especially if the attempts she is now making in America and in Minorca should fail, or if their fleet should be beaten at sea, for it will then be the only card France has to play'.[43]

The outbreak of war in Germany further exposed Hanover, first because it lay athwart or close to routes along which the French could advance if they attacked Prussia. Prussia was also bound up with the defence of Hanover because of its territories in the Rhineland and also the possibility that it could send troops to the assistance of Hanover. An angry Frederick II, concerned about the prospect of no help from Britain, accordingly threatened at the start of 1757 to pull his troops out of Wesel, his main Rhenish base.[44] Concern about the possibility of Frederick making his peace with France helped encourage the British ministry to offer help to Prussia. Wesel itself fell to the French on 8 April. On 17 February 1757, the Commons agreed a request for £200,000 for an 'Army of Observation', composed mostly of Hanoverians and Hessians, to meet the French threat 'against His Majesty's Electoral dominions and those of his good ally the King of Prussia', an army that was presented as a means to enable George to fulfil his engagements to Frederick. In the event, this army was found wanting, in large part because it was outnumbered, although, as Puysieulx, the French foreign minister, had anticipated in 1750, the rapidly assembled nature of units of often indifferent troops was a problem with subsidy forces.[45]

Secondly, war in Germany exposed Hanover because it ended the possibility of neutralising the Empire, a goal George sought. Indeed, in January 1757, he proposed a league of Hanover, Bavaria and the Palatinate designed to try to end through their good offices the conflict in the Empire. In expressing opposition to Frederick's attack on Saxony, George made it clear that he thought Prussia was partly in the wrong.[46] In 1756, Austria opposed French plans to attack Hanover and, instead, wanted Hanover neutral.[47] The Austrian government was in touch with its Hanoverian counterpart, which, fearful of attack, was keen to satisfy demands for its neutrality. The British ministry, however, as it reassured Frederick, was unwilling to accept a Hanoverian neutrality. There was considerable British anger at the stance of their Hanoverian counterparts, and a view that Hanoverian security must rest on the Prussian alliance.[48] The negotiations for a Hanoverian neutrality harmed British relations not only with Frederick but also with other powers. This was true of Denmark, which played a role in the neutrality negotiations, and which Britain was trying to win over,[49] and of Hesse-Cassel, which was also being pressed to accept neutrality.[50] In 1757, in response to the formation of the Army of Observations, French forces overran the Electorate while acting as an auxiliary of the Empire against Frederick. Maria Theresa took the view that British willingness to pay subsidies to Prussia represented a breach of British treaty obligations to Austria, and left Austria free to back French schemes for the partition of Hanover.[51]

Holdernesse detected a political shift in Britain, writing of a parliamentary debate in the House of Lords:

> Many Lords of great weight openly expressed their opinion, that the utmost efforts should be made for the defence of His Majesty's Electoral dominions, attacked solely in consequence of measures taken for the defence of the rights and possessions of the Crown of Great Britain; for assisting the King of Prussia, and for supporting the Protestant cause in the Empire; and many other Lords, who had not an opportunity of speaking, expressed their approbation of the measure, and of the principles, upon which it was founded.[52]

In contrast, the vigour and coherence of the opposition stance can be detected in the *London Evening Post* of 23 April 1757:

> At present surely all parties have rid themselves of these Continent prejudices, and stand convinced that our only effectual barriers against France are a good navy and a national militia. With these, properly settled, we shall be always respected, our friendship courted by the powers on the Continent, and our resentment feared. We may then make what alliances are necessary for the sake of trade, without encumbering ourselves with foreign guaranties, or draining our almost exhausted treasure, in the payment of fruitless and foolish subsidies, paid to princes who will act with us, if it is their interest, without such subsidies.

The neutrality convention dissolved the Hanoverian army, left the Electorate occupied, and exposed Prussia's western frontier. Alongside the imperious manner in which French generals and diplomats proposed to employ their power in north-west Germany, the convention would not have been inappropriate a half-century later during the heyday of Napoleonic power.[53] Occupation of Hanover gave the French a powerful negotiating counter in any future peace settlement with George II, a repetition of the use of French conquests in Europe as a factor in the peace negotiations in 1748. Indeed the *London Chronicle* of 14 April 1757 had suggested that France would return Bremen and Verden to Sweden. Occupation of Hanover threatened to destroy the Anglo-Prussian alliance. There was a danger that Frederick, his western flank exposed, might accept peace terms and abandon Britain,[54] while, as Elector, George displayed an interest in negotiations with Austria for a neutrality for the Electorate, much to the concern of his British ministers.

Pitt refused to accept such a prospect, and, instead, pressed George hard for the rapid disavowal of the convention, refusing in October to pay the Hanoverian troops while they remained inactive. The Hanoverian government also angered Frederick II, who resisted pressure to attack Richelieu in Hanover, preferring to act against the Austrians.[55] In the winter of 1757–8, Pitt played the major role in securing a political settlement that tied the defence of the Electorate to British direction and identified it with the Prussian alliance. This was crucial to George's disavowal of the neutrality convention. At the Cabinet of 7 October 1757, Pitt's suggestion that Britain agree to pay the entire cost of the Army of Observation provided the convention was disavowed, was adopted. That winter, however, he refused to accept Prussian pressure for the dispatch of British troops to cover Frederick's western flank. This policy, agreed at the cabinet of 23 February 1758, was reversed under the pressure of apparent military necessity, and in the end, Pitt was willing to commit such troops to defend the Prussian North Sea port of Emden, presenting it as a step that did not divert manpower from North America. On 19 April 1758, the Commons voted a subsidy to Frederick and money to support 50,000 troops under Duke Ferdinand of Brunswick, Cumberland's successor, without a division. Frederick himself warned that if France triumphed in Germany it would then invade Britain.[56]

The alliance with Prussia served to legitimate interventionism for Pitt and many others: it diverted attention from the issue of Hanover and provided a plausible basis for policies that would have been condemned had they been linked only with the Electorate. The Prussian alliance provided the possibility for bridging the traditional antithesis of pro-Hanoverian, ministerial, Continental interventionism, and 'Patriot' isolationism, a bridging that Pitt represented and helped to popularise. Frederick II also had an aura of success to commend him; one that the Hanoverians did not gain with the British public. Fame was won by Ferdinand of Brunswick, but this did not reflect credit on the house of Hanover.

Pitt made a series of public defences of his policy, presenting Continental operations as a diversionary and defensive part of a strategic whole, rather than an unnecessary and separate conflict, and this theme was taken up by his supporters. The *Monitor* of 6 September claimed:

There is no doubt of the hazard which Britain runs by neglecting her naval power. To measure swords with France on the continent, while her marine and navigation are suffered to prosper, is ruinous: but this is not the case. Our navy triumphs over the Main, and the marine and navigation of France are totally ruined and cut off: now therefore is the time also to check the land force of our enemy, when he has lost the chief resource for carrying on those mighty armaments by which he has so often defied and baffled our forces on the Continent. Britain therefore, by her present conduct, has neither the same strength, nor the same hazards to encounter, as when France had nothing to fear from our naval power.

It is difficult to know how far this thesis related to the strategic (as opposed to political) practice of policy. Indeed, it is hard to establish the contours of this strategy except through drawing attention to what actually happened during the war. The ability to check the French in Germany certainly compromised France's acquisition of a major bargaining capture, greater than Minorca which they had seized in 1756,[57] to exchange for colonial losses in the eventual peace negotiations,[58] and at the start of 1760 Choiseul stated that France was no longer able to sustain war on both land and sea, although he also drew attention to the possibility of overrunning Hanover,[59] and thus improving France's negotiating position. Fortunately for the British government, the French were held in check. Victory at Minden on 1 August 1759 was particularly important, not least because it followed the dismal record of British forces on the Continent during the War of the Austrian Succession. Diplomatic strategy certainly did not focus on Hanoverian interests. Whereas Newcastle and Pitt could see that the security of the Electorate was important, neither was prepared to lend support to its aggrandisement. This was linked to a shift in the conceptualisation and use of British naval power, away from a Continental theme and towards a stronger emphasis on the struggle with France.

The absence of any commitment to allies in the Mediterranean or Baltic, despite strong Prussian pressure,[60] helped to release naval power to concentrate on the challenge from France. Frederick II would have preferred assistance against Russia in the Baltic, but he saw British naval action elsewhere as a help to Prussia. In July 1756, he told Mitchell that he wanted the British fleet 'to attack the French, this would give them occupation, and he mentioned St. Domingo or some other of their possessions in the West Indies'. Later in the year, concerned about the prospect of a French attack on Prussia, Frederick pressed the British to make threatening moves as if they planned to land at Ostend or on the coasts of Normandy or Brittany.[61] British ministers accordingly argued that attacks on the French coast were an important contribution to the war in Germany,[62] a clear example of the pursuit through military means of a political strategy. Focusing on the challenge from France helped to make naval operations less contentious, and therefore more popular. The assessment of national interests is always controversial, but once

Pitt had successfully explained the commitment to Germany it was easier to see the war, especially its naval dimensions, in terms of national interests. Maritime strategy was still contentious, not least the extent to which the British should focus on attacks on the French coast, and this was accentuated by the mixed success of this policy. Nevertheless, amphibious operations outside Europe had a good record. Furthermore, the absence in colonial operations of any need to consult the views of allies helped greatly to contribute to this popularity, as did the lack of any Hanoverian angle. This greatly affected the political context within which strategic choices were framed and discussed. Experience was transformed into expectations, encouraging a view of strategic options in which the navy was dissociated from Continental power politics. As Britain was now less relevant to the states of Central and Eastern Europe, this was a two-way process. It made Continental interventionism less viable politically and diplomatically, and this was to become abundantly clear in the 1760s.

8   Hanover to the background, 1759–71

> complained, but with great moderation of the little attention that England seemed to have to the affairs of the Continent, and this he candidly imputed to the great occupation that our internal divisions must necessarily give to His Majesty's ministers.
>
> (Andrew Mitchell reporting the comments of Frederick II[1])

Ironically, it was the future George III who most powerfully represented the ambivalence toward Hanover in the late 1750s. He took up the critical attitudes of Sir Robert Walpole toward an active foreign policy,[2] and, in doing so, linked royal authority to non-interventionism. As Prince of Wales, and influenced by the problems of the Seven Years' War, George criticised the partiality of his grandfather, George II, for Hanover, and, as King from 1760, he was determined to disengage from the 'German war', the German part of the Seven Years' War, and to avoid loading Britain with subsidies.

This aspect of George's policy risks being overshadowed by current interest in his subsequent support for Hanover. In practice, this support did not amount to what had been seen under his two predecessors, and George III had a clearer sense of Britain as a separate entity with its own political interests. George III sought to defend his rights, and his concern to defend his position as Elector, for example in response to the Emperor Joseph II's attempt to oversee the regency arrangements for Hanover when George became seriously ill in the winter of 1788–9,[3] matched his determination, as King, to protect his position in North America and over Catholic Emancipation. More significantly, he did not share his predecessors' zeal for the expansion of the Electorate.

Prior to his accession, there had been a conviction that the relationship with Hanover would alter under George. In 1751, the diplomat Sir Charles Hanbury-Williams had written:

> The grief at Hanover for the death of the late Prince of Wales [Frederick] is very great. They look upon themselves (and I hope with reason) as likely to become in reality a province subservient to the interests of

Great Britain, and it is high time they should be so for during my stay at Hanover last summer I saw so much of the insolence of those ministers that it made me sick. But now I think the scene must change for 'tis impossible that a Prince [George III] not born there can possibly like such a poor scrubby town and such barren and melancholic country.[4]

Indeed, as heir, the future George III wrote to his confidant, John, 3rd Earl of Bute, in August 1759, 'as to the affairs on the Weser they look worse and worse; I fear this is entirely owing to the partiality the King [George II] has for that horrid Electorate which has always lived upon the very vitals of this poor country; I should say more and perhaps with more anger did not my clock show it is time to dress for Court'. As King, George III showed his determination to end Britain's involvement in the German part of the Seven Years' War:

> though I have subjects who will suffer immensely whenever this kingdom withdraws its protection from thence, yet so superior is my love to this my native country over any private interest of my own that I cannot help wishing that an end was put to that enormous expence by ordering our troops home . . . I think if the Duke of Newcastle will not hear reason concerning the German war that it would be better to let him quit than to go on with that and to have myself and those who differ from him made unpopular.

Conscious of the importance of popularity, George informed Bute in 1762 that he would 'never wish to load this country with' subsidies.[5] In the 1760s, George was not conspicuous as an advocate of Hanoverian interests and of British commitments to aid the Electorate. As a consequence, the King's views on foreign policy were not as politically contentious as those of his grandfather and great-grandfather had been. This owed much also to the dominance of colonial, commercial and maritime issues in both foreign policy in the 1760s and in the political and public discussion of it. In addition, after 1763, foreign policy ceased to be such a consistently contentious sphere for, and source of, political debate. Domestic and American constitutional, fiscal and political issues helped to divert attention from foreign policy, with which it was difficult to link them. Those who challenged George III or his ministers did not need to refer to foreign policy. The collapse of Jacobitism and the political shifts of the 1750s helped further to create a new agenda in which Hanover and the royal role in foreign policy played little part. This argument must not be pushed too far – foreign policy was not forgotten and reference was made to George's views, but a substantial change followed his accession.

George's address to his first Privy Council reflected his determination to break with the past, while George made his views clear in his addition to the draft for his first speech from the throne:

Born and educated in this country I glory in the name of Britain; and the peculiar happiness of my life will ever consist in promoting the welfare of a people whose loyalty and warm affection to me I consider as the greatest and most permanent security of my throne.[6]

This attitude led to concern. One of Newcastle's supporters, Charles, 2nd Marquess of Rockingham, displayed concern over the terms of a likely address from Yorkshire:

I could wish that the words *Native Country* and *Truly English* were not echoed back from Yorkshire – as indeed it strikes me as carrying with it a signification that that was wanting in his late Majesty . . . Queen Anne on the death of King William in her declaration set forth that *Her Heart was entirely English* which gave great offence to the Whigs at that time.[7]

This break with his grandfather's ministers was intertwined with the break with the policies of the 1750s. It was not only that the alliance with Prussia was abandoned, but that the gap was not filled by an alliance with another major Continental power. The motive for such a course of action, royal anxiety about Hanover, ministerial concern about this anxiety, and the sense that defensive arrangements for Hanover could and should serve as the basis for a British alliance system, had been largely lost.

So also had the interventionist habit of mind and the concomitant diplomatic assumptions. Newcastle had written of the response of the elderly George II to a Prussian victory:

The King, who gives the tone to the nation, and is the foremost to extol and admire the great actions of this great prince, talks of this victory with the affection of a friend and near relation; the satisfaction of an ally, highly interested in the same cause; and with the praise, and admiration, of a general, who knows the real merit of it, and the extent of the genius which must, under God, have brought it about.[8]

The views of George III were very different. George might be very gracious to Carteret soon after his accession, but he had only limited interest in the views that that minister had once stood for. In March 1761, Baron Haslang, the Palatine envoy in London, pointed out that the prince-bishopric of Hildesheim, which George II had sought to acquire, was both vacant and actually occupied by George III's forces. George III, however, did not share his grandfather's views. Three weeks after reporting that Hildesheim was vacant, Haslang observed that the predilection for Hanover was no longer so strong, and also suggested that there would be no territorial cessions elsewhere in order to make gains for the Electorate.[9] This was at a time when the Electorate of Saxony was seeking territorial gains from the Archbishopric-Electorate of Mainz.

When, in June 1761, François de Bussy began peace negotiations with the British ministry, he was told by Carteret that the British had little interest in Hanoverian affairs. When Bussy told Pitt that France would expect compensation for her Hanoverian conquests, on the grounds that in order to pursue her operations on the Continent, France had diverted resources from the defence of her colonies, Pitt replied that the argument would have had a great effect during the reign of George II, but that the situation had changed. This was a position that Choiseul found it difficult to accept, though he had already commented in February 1760 that it would not matter to Pitt if France devastated Hanover.[10]

Bussy returned to the subject when he saw Pitt on 23 June 1761. He claimed that the Electorate should be regarded as a province of England, because George II, as King, had broken the 1757 Convention of Kloster Zeven for the disbandment of the Hanoverian Army of Occupation, and because the army commanded by Prince Ferdinand of Brunswick for the defence of Hanover acted in accordance with George's orders and for 'the cause of England'. Bussy reiterated the charge that French losses in the colonies were due partly to their operations on the Continent. Choiseul was determined to establish the principles of compensations and equivalence.[11] Pitt was willing to moderate his attitude and offer the return of Guadeloupe and Martinique as compensation for the French evacuation of her gains in Hanover and the territories of the latter's allies. He also insisted that France evacuate Prussia's Rhenish territories and Frankfurt.

In the end, however, the negotiations failed as a result of the Third Franco-Spanish Family Compact signed on 15 August, the deterioration of Anglo-Spanish relations, and the British delay in offering acceptable terms to France. Although Pitt had shifted his ground on Hanover, it was clear that George and his leading ministers were not willing to allow Hanoverian concerns to play a major role in the negotiations. Haslang had noted in July 1761 that whatever happened in the Empire would have little effect on British government policy, adding that it was no longer the time of George II. Three months later, Bute told Viry, the Sardinian envoy, that France would not gain better terms if she took Hanover. In November, Newcastle wrote to Rockingham, 'There are *many* who are for abandoning the German war, and giving up Hanover, and our allies. That is what I can never consent to, nor, I believe, any of our friends. I have talked very plainly to the King, and Mylord Bute upon it.'[12]

Two months later, as war with Spain led to new military commitments, Newcastle opposed Bute's wish to recall the troops from Germany 'with great force and warmth'.[13] Newcastle feared isolation:

abandoning the Continent entirely would now render the House of Bourbon absolute master of all Europe, and enable them to oblige every neutral power to submit to such conditions as they should think proper to impose upon them. The other maritime powers would be obliged to shut up all their ports against us.

He was concerned in particular that the Dutch would be coerced into joining the Bourbons. To Newcastle a 'Blue Water' policy would lead to exclusion from all connections with Europe.[14]

Indeed, worried about the state of Prussia, Newcastle, still keenly committed to a Continental policy, unsuccessfully sought in early 1762 to negotiate an alliance with Austria which could be used to settle Prusso-Austrian differences and thus present a better basis for Britain and Prussia to continue the war with their other enemies.[15]

Pitt's resignation, and the collapse, amidst serious recriminations, of the Anglo-Prussian alliance helped ensure that in 1761–2 commitment to the Continent was discussed in terms of shifting British political alignments. By 1762, the defence of the Prussian alliance was no longer easy. War-weariness and the greater popularity of 'Blue Water' policies sapped public support for the commitment to Prussia.[16] Pitt's intransigence, and the obvious preferences of George III and Bute, further reduced political support for the commitment, as did concern about Frederick's apparent willingness to support Peter III of Russia in his confrontation with Denmark.[17]

In so far as the cause of allies won favourable attention, it was that of Portugal, threatened by Spain, rather than Prussia. Joseph Yorke thought that the issue had not been anticipated 'by the red hot partisans of the Spanish war'.[18] Portugal was a crucial and apparently vulnerable trading partner of Britain, although even British help was not to stop 'the vexatious manner in which our trade to Lisbon is treated'.[19] The Bourbons sought either to force her to cut her links with Britain, or to make conquests that could be exchanged at the subsequent peace.[20] Interest in cutting Anglo-Portuguese trade links was an aspect of a strategy that prefigured Napoleon's more sustained and systematic attempt, with the Continental System, to blockade Britain. In 1761, the Spaniards also proposed Bourbon action to limit British trade with Livorno and Naples, while Choiseul suggested that an attack on Rio de Janeiro should accompany one on Portugal and also wanted the outbreak of war with Spain to hit British chances of raising the funds necessary to sustain the war.[21]

The war seemed a diplomatic coup for the Bourbons, a way to inflict military damage on Britain and to weaken her in peace negotiations. Indeed, in September 1761, Bute had told Newcastle that Britain could not wage a Spanish and a Continental war simultaneously.[22] Choiseul pointed out that, however many troops the British sent there, Spain would still enjoy a numerical superiority,[23] while Charles III of Spain argued that it would prove a costly diversion for the British, not least because it would help the French in Germany and prevent Britain from mounting major attacks in the New World.[24] Indeed, Choiseul feared that if freed from a Continental conflict,

Britain would be not only strong enough to prevent France from regaining her lost colonies, but would also be able to attack Spanish America.[25] Charles III was to be proved totally wrong, although it is unclear that this demonstrates the accuracy of Pitt's strategy in another context. In practice, the war (which still lacks a systematic study) was waged in Portugal, Cuba and the Philippines as a series of separate conflicts. In the event, the Spaniards proved far worse prepared than they had assured the French, and, instead, as Frederick II had anticipated, the British gained fresh opportunities for trans-oceanic triumphs.[26] In the face of British successes against Havana and Manila, and the failure of the Franco-Spanish invasion force to overcome Portugal, Choiseul came to appreciate that France had gained little from the alliance.

Yet, this failure led to an underrating of the vulnerability of Portugal and thus to the potential risk of that aspect of the Continental strategy. Critics of the British military presence in Germany had also been opposed to the dispatch of troops to Portugal,[27] while Newcastle had been concerned about the prospect of a land war in Portugal.[28] The Portuguese ministry itself argued that Britain ought to move troops there from Belle Île off the Breton coast which had been captured in 1761. As so often, an alliance meant clashing military priorities.[29] Coming, however, towards the end of the campaign, to the conclusion that even the fall of Lisbon would not stop Britain, Choiseul claimed that the British cared more about another colony in the New World than all the devastated provinces of Portugal.[30]

Having served to distract attention from Hanover and to limit antagonism towards Continental engagements, the disintegration of the Prussian alliance was linked to a revival of this antagonism. In contrast to earlier periods of marked hostility towards such engagements, however, in 1762 Hanover played only a minor role and the King was not criticised on its account. This was because the move to restrict commitments, and to limit policy to recognisably British goals, came from the monarch. The *Briton*, a weekly newspaper established by Bute, admitted in July 1762 that there was a danger of Hanover being invaded if Britain refused to assist Prussia, but added:

> it is the duty, the interest of the Germanic body to see justice done to any of its constituent members that shall be oppressed: but should they neglect their duty and interest on such an occasion, I hope the Elector of H—r will never again have influence enough with the K—g of G—t B—n, to engage him in a war for retrieving it, that shall cost his kingdom annually, for a series of years, more than double the value of the country in dispute.

The paper calculated the annual cost of the 'herculean task' of the defence of Hanover as £6 million.[31] The Continental commitment had also become far more unpopular. Israel Mauduit's pamphlet *Considerations on the Present German War* (1760), with its call for isolationism and the end of a military commitment to the Continent and, specifically, to Hanover, had caught a developing mood.[32] Writing in the *London Chronicle* of 26 January 1762, 'Nauphilus' attacked Pitt's arguments:

> America being conquered in Germany is a proposition so strangely absurd ... Germany has swallowed up not only more than all our Indian and American conquests, but more than all our former colonies, or all our trade in all parts of the world beside is able to supply. Almost all our Portuguese coin, the proof of our former wealth, is vanished.

In the *London Evening Post* of 30 November 1762, 'Cimon' criticised Pitt's strategy, not least by claiming that exhaustion stemming from the German war had led to the return to the Bourbons of some of Britain's wartime conquests:

> Was it worth launching out into such immense expenses of men and money in Germany, the more easily to make such conquests in America (as was unfairly given out, and as ridiculously and absurdly boasted of in a hyperbolical phrase of the great haranguer of the time) and to give up afterwards what had cost us so many millions, and so many thousand lives there to obtain, and in Germany also, so immensely much more, to facilitate such conquests, because the millions we had spent in Germany had put us out of a condition for keeping them, or from going on with the war, as is pretended.

The cost of 'the German war' was an issue that continued to echo for years, being the subject for example of an attack on Pitt in the *St. James's Chronicle* of 22 March 1766.

The Continental commitment was also linked to high taxes and high interest rates in Britain, and to Dutch commercial competition, while, more generally, as the *Briton* of 15 January 1763 noted, the army and navy had both been weakened by the continuation of the war, not least with a shortage of men. 'We are low indeed, but, thanks to Heaven, our German expences over,' exclaimed Bute in 1763.[33] The definitive treaty was signed in Paris on 10 February, to the delight of George III.[34]

At the same time as George and the British government he helped reconstitute disentangled themselves from the 'German war',[35] there was an instructive sign that George was not without concern for the position of the Electorate, albeit a concern in which territorial aggrandisement played a role. In September 1762, the Hanoverian minister, Baron Behr, suggested to Haslang that once a general peace had been made, a German league, of at least the leading Electors, should be formed so that the participants were not always at risk of being invaded on the slightest pretext. He added that George would seek agreement first with Maximilian III Joseph, Elector of Bavaria.[36]

The same month, Louis-Jules, Duke of Nivernais, the French envoy sent to London to negotiate peace in the autumn of 1762, was reporting that George and his British ministers wished to make the fewest links possible in the Empire and to spend no money there, and that peace was likely to be followed on the part of Britain by 'un sistème d'indifférence' towards the Empire.[37] There was no real contradiction between Behr's approach and Nivernais's report, given that George both seemed determined to retain the distinction between Britain and Hanover and revealed little interest in territorial acquisitions for the latter. Furthermore, Newcastle's charge that the British government was intent on 'abandoning the Continent'[38] was true only in so far as the war in the Empire was concerned. The personal, indeed emotional, attachments to Hanover of George II and to Continental interventionism of Newcastle, were not matched by their successors. Newcastle saw victory at Wilhelmstahl on 24 June 1762 as a vindication of his strategy,[39] but both were now largely irrelevant. Once freed of the incubus of the war, however, George III and his British ministers were willing, and, in some cases, eager, to revive the search for allies.

The attempt to revive negotiations with Austria and Russia was not matched by any comparable attempt to use British diplomatic assistance to support Hanoverian interests in north-western Germany. The death, on 7 February 1761, of the Wittelsbach episcopal pluralist Clemens-August, Archbishop-Elector of Cologne and Prince-Bishop of Hildesheim, Münster, Osnabrück and Paderborn, produced a tremendous opportunity not only for ecclesiastical place-seekers and advocates of secularisation, but also for those who wished to enhance their influence in this region. In 1753, a Dutch approach for British support in elections to vacant positions in the cathedral chapters (which chose the bishops) led Newcastle to reflect, 'it is certainly of consequence, to have a well-intentioned person choose Prevot of the Cathedral Chapter of Munster'.[40] George III, however, made little attempt to intervene in the elections in marked contrast to the position in the 1720s when they had last been conducted. His second son, Frederick, became Prince-Bishop of Osnabrück (shortly after his birth in 1763) under the system for the alternate filling of the see by a member of the house of Hanover, but, although in 1763 the Hanoverian attitude to the position in Osnabrück gave rise to some concern, secularisation was not pursued.[41] Indeed, the French government thought it possible to press George III and his British ministry for support for the episcopal claims of Clement of Saxony, the brother-in-law of the Dauphin, Louis.[42]

Haslang was told that George would go to Hanover in the summer of 1763, and he suggested that this would be not only a great consolation for his subjects but also an opportunity to arrange many things for the general good of the Empire.[43] George himself argued that an heir to the throne should visit 'the different parts of the dominions',[44] and, if he never travelled to Hanover, the same was also true of Scotland, Ireland, Wales and northern England.

In practice, George's failure to visit Hanover ensured that it was more difficult in the course of British foreign policy to further Electoral interests. Because George did not visit the Electorate, his British ministers did not go there, and thus Hanover ceased to be the episodic focus of British foreign policy. The possible importance of royal visits was indicated by the role of Frederick, Duke of York and Prince-Bishop of Osnabrück, who went to Hanover in 1781. From 1783, his presence and actions helped to improve relations between George and Frederick II. It is open to speculation whether a visit by George would have served for the negotiation of an improvement on earlier occasions. Imminent visits to Hanover by George were reported on a number of occasions, for example by *Owen's Weekly Chronicle* on 17 and 31 March 1764, but he never went. In a powerful commitment, however, George himself abandoned the idea of separating Hanover from Britain, for his Testament of 1765 established the succession of George, his firstborn, as heir to both.

Hanover did not play a major role in foreign policy in the 1760s, and, as Elector, George did not take the forceful part of his two predecessors, although he was interested in the Electorate and communicated regularly with his Hanoverian ministers, writing in German, at which he was adept.[45] Hanoverian issues and those relating to nearby territories continued to crop up in diplomatic correspondence, and British ministers were approached, sometimes unwillingly, by foreign envoys accordingly.[46] Hanover became a less contentious public issue,[47] and Newcastle worried about Bute, not the King's Hanoverian advisors. Haslang reported that the British ministers were not informed about German affairs.[48] In 1766, George, 3rd Earl of Albemarle, blamed the replacement of the Rockingham ministry by that of Pitt, now Earl, of Chatham, on George's concern for Hanover:

> You will stare and perhaps shake your head when I tell you it was by the advice of his German ministers. The King of Prussia, tired of soliciting England for the arrears due to him, informed the Hanoverian ministers that unless he was paid (or indemnified . . .), and immediately, that he would seize upon the Duchy of Lunenbourg and immediately. This so alarmed Munchhausen that he sent an express to the King with his alarms, and saying at the same time that no man could deal with the King of Prussia but Mr. Pitt . . . This determined the King so suddenly, and so unexpectedly to send for Mr. Pitt.

The more experienced Newcastle was more sceptical.[49] Similarly, the report in the *St. James's Chronicle* of 23 January 1766 that 'the treaty lately concluded with Russia, is said to be for the mutual defence of the German dominions of both powers' was wrong and although the issue of 29 April 1769 reported that 'considerable bets are laid near Coventry Street [in London], at a certain Military Coffee-House, that English troops will set their feet in Germany before the 1st of August next', none did so.

Angered by George's lack of interest in backing the Elector Palatine against the decision of the Imperial Aulic Council in the Elector's dispute with the city of Aachen, the Palatine foreign minister complained that George was overly pro-Austrian and insufficiently forceful.[50] The Hanoverian government was scarcely in a position to be the latter. Participation in the Seven Years' War led to an increase in the size of the army to 37,146 in 1763, but peace brought a reduction, as financial exigencies hit home, and the peacetime strength was only an average of 14,218 men. Just as for Prussia[51] and Saxony, the aftermath of the war saw reconstruction at home and caution abroad.

Hanover, moreover, was not near the centre of international contention as far as Britain was concerned. Indeed, in the decade after fighting in the Seven Years' War drew to a close, British foreign policy focused on opposition to the Bourbons and that centred on colonial and naval rivalry. Joseph Yorke, an experienced diplomat, observed in 1763: 'the interval between the treaties of peace, and the commencing new connections and negotiations is the golden age for the Secretaries offices in Europe, and I hope that age will last a good while longer.'[52] In practice, although there was considerable reluctance about interventionism,[53] there were to be a number of important initiatives as ministers sought to develop a Continental alliance system.[54] On occasion, this course was supported by commentators on explicitly strategic grounds. In 1763, James Porter, a retired diplomat, urged the need for co-operation with Austria, claiming that if France was sure of Austria it would be able to cut the army and in five years have a fleet of 100 ships of line, whereas 'if you are in friendship merely with that house, that of Bourbon will not be secure under such a reduction but be obliged to keep up their land army and they cannot supply for both'.[55] In reality, the capacity of the French naval system to support a large fleet for any length of time was limited.

The international situation, however, was particularly adverse to the British tendency, displayed by ministers, parliamentarians and commentators, to imagine that other states should, and therefore would, follow Britain's lead. Harnessing the resources and obtaining the backing of the Eastern European states had long been a major theme for their Western European counterparts, particularly after the new-found Russian dynamism of the 1690s. In 1756, France had won this struggle, displacing Britain from her Austrian alliance and, through that, acquiring links with Russia. Whereas France had been allied to the weaker alignment from 1742, from 1756 this was no longer the case. This provided the background to post-war diplomacy. After the collapse of the Anglo-Prussian alliance in 1762, it was France, alone, among the powers of Western Europe that had a strong ally further east.

The durability of the alliance between Austria and France proved a particular reproach to British assumptions. A pamphleteer of 1739 had explained of the Third Treaty of Vienna of the previous year:

there is very little foundation to be made upon treaties so extraordinary in their nature ... the different pretensions of the two Houses of Austria and France have always been thought, even by the most skilful and experienced ministers, of such kind, as never to be amicably accommodated.[56]

In practice, as so often, public statement was misleading. There had been ministerial anxiety about the prospect of such an alignment, especially in 1715 and 1728. Yet, at the same time, the assumption that it could not be amicable, and therefore strong, did affect ministerial assumptions.[57] British hopes, from 1756, expressed for example in the *London Chronicle* in early 1757, that the Austro-French alliance would disintegrate[58] proved misplaced, and, whatever the tensions between the two powers, Austria was unwilling to co-operate with Britain against France until the era of the French Revolution. The other pillar of the Old Alliance, the United Provinces, had also changed policy. Britain and the Dutch had been linked in wartime since 1689, but, in the Seven Years' War, the Dutch had been neutral and had complained bitterly about the British attempt to prevent their handling French trade. Relations did not improve subsequently.

Foreign states saw no need to alter alliances in order to accommodate British interests, while the specific demands of these potential allies proved unacceptable. British approaches to Austria, Prussia and Russia proved unavailing. For example, the Russian terms for an alliance were unanimously rejected by the ministry in September 1763.

This meant that Britain had no effective allies in the event of her disputes with the Bourbons leading to war. Apparently vindicating claims, for example in the Commons on 4 March 1763, that the peace would be no more than an armed truce, there were a number of disputes, notably over the French purchase of Corsica in 1768 and the Spanish seizure of a British settlement on the Falkland Isles in 1770, but they did not lead to conflict. In 1764–5, the British used intimidatory gunboat diplomacy to defend their position successfully in colonial disputes in West Africa and the West Indies,[59] but Choiseul's decisive actions over Corsica pre-empted effective opposition in a situation poorly handled by the British ministry.[60]

In 1770, Choiseul eventually supported Spain, but Louis XV's unwillingness to fight defused the crisis and Choiseul was dismissed. As a result of the absence of war, it is impossible to gauge the impact of British isolation in wartime circumstances until the very particular case of a revolution in some of Britain's American colonies broke out in 1775 and led to hostile French intervention. As far as peacetime confrontation is concerned, it is unclear that Britain would have been more successful in protesting about the fate of Corsica had she had allies, while over the Falklands she gained her ends without any allies.

The reshaping of interventionism under both Pitt and his successors had affected the parameters within which the policy had to be presented. The stress on the part of Pitt's defenders, such as the *Monitor*, was that Britain was linked to a major European state, and not to minor rulers that had to be bought, that this link served Britain's trans-oceanic goals, and that these were given priority in government policy.[61] Whether or not this was true of the Seven Years' War, it created post-war problems. Any major state was going to be better able to defend its own interpretation of its interests and to seek to drive the alliance that way. Secondly, not only were expectations of how any alliance should now appear to be directly helping British interests now greater, but these interests were also more closely focused on trans-oceanic goals than had been the case earlier in the century.

Furthermore, this pursuit increased Continental concern about British policy. Indeed, in 1761, Bedford had warned of the danger of exciting 'all the naval powers in Europe to enter into a confederacy against us, as adopting a system, viz. that of a monarchy of all naval power, which would be at least as dangerous to the liberties of Europe, as that of Louis the 14th was'.[62] This prescient warning, which echoed one made by Newcastle in 1740,[63] was not of interest to most of his compatriots. It was, however, a theme the French repeated, presenting their naval and commercial policy as determined by the necessity to put just limits on what Bernis saw in 1758 as the imperial power which Britain wished to exercise on all seas and over all trading powers, a theme repeated by Choiseul in 1761 and 1770. In 1755, Rouillé had argued that Britain sought to destroy the balance of power in the New World.[64]

The British ministry presented itself as pacific. Earl Harcourt, the envoy in Paris, told Choiseul in 1769 'that we did not desire to see any change or alteration in the political system of Europe; that England had no views of aggrandisement, and it was to be wished that other powers would show the same moderation'.[65] To critics, however, Britain's European policy, whether interventionist or isolationist, was a cover for a dangerous, indeed destructive, global strategy: and one that had worked. Opposition to this provided a rationale for maritime alliance against Britain. Cutting Britain down to size was seen as a prelude to France taking her rightful place in Europe: the British would be unable to support her opponents.

British diplomacy in response could be directed at the maritime powers – especially France, Spain and the Dutch – or at other states that could supposedly put pressure on them, but the latter proved ineffective during the War of American Independence and did not really work, apart from in the case of the Dutch crisis of 1787 (see p. 163). Instead, talks with the maritime powers were the best option, in order to help prevent them co-operating. Indeed, there was no such large-scale co-operation between 1762 and 1779, although this owed little to British diplomacy. Britain was to be alone against the maritime powers both in 1780–3 and in 1796–1802, but, although the first reflected diplomatic isolation, the second was a product of the failure of interventionism: Britain had allies but they were defeated and unable to influence the progress of the maritime conflict.

Shifts in the perception of British interests reflected the development of the public debate, and, as a result, European interventionism as both goal and strategy had become both marginal and more difficult. This can be readily seen in the case of naval power. In the 1720s, statesmen had discussed whether British naval power could affect actions by Austria and Russia that essentially owed nothing to maritime considerations and opposition spokesmen had bitterly condemned a misguided navalism, criticising fleets for achieving little,[66] which created pressure for success in later confrontations.[67] In contrast, during the Seven Years' War the central question was one of the direct impact of naval power. Instead of discussing whether bombardment of Naples or Riga might influence policy, it was possible to discuss the actual implications of seizing particular colonies.

An active post-war alliance system leading to Continental interventionism would have compromised this shift, which was as advantageous in politics as in strategy. As a result, the British government was fortunate in 1766 that fears of a projected Spanish attack on Portugal[68] proved groundless, as that would have compromised British policy and also left Britain alone against Spain and her backers, which were assumed to include France and Austria. This was a more serious prospect militarily than the one that was to face Britain in 1778–83, as Portugal could be invaded overland.

In a recent overview, François Crouzet has argued that as 'sea power could not conquer a continent ... most British governments were far-sighted in their policies of a Continental commitment'. He adds, 'On the other hand, it was a serious drawback for France to have to fight, except in the American War, on both sea and land',[69] which begs the question of whether the same was not true of the British. As far as the question of goals was concerned, the British did not want France to dominate Western Europe, let alone the entire Continent, but this was far less of a prospect in 1714–92 than consideration of the periods on either side might suggest. At the same time, Bute's hope for a true friendship and sincere liaison with France was misplaced.[70]

A more immediate potential threat posed by the French had been displayed by the French invasion plan of 1759, and was to be repeated twenty years later. It proved all too easy to minimise this threat, as part of a wider public perception of the Seven Years' War. Joseph Yorke saw 'the hand of God' in 'the wonderful distribution of earthly advantages by Providence, for it would be highly presumptuous in any man to say that he ever expected such an end when the war commenced'.[71] For most commentators, the glow of eventual success shadowed the problems and failures of the early stages of the conflict with France. This led to a post-war confidence, indeed complacency, as well as, in the eyes of critics, a willingness to focus on domestic divisions,[72] that were to have serious consequences.

9   Interventionism, George III and the Hanoverian connection, 1772–93

> By an intercepted letter from Count Kageneck [Austrian envoy] to Prince Kaunitz, I find the Count has had a conversation with Mr. [Charles James] Fox ... Mr. Vorontzov [Russian envoy] was of the party. The German League [Fürstenbund] as you may easily imagine made a material part of the conversation. Mr. Fox seems to have been infinitely more severe upon the King than upon the ministers in his remarks upon the subject, stating it as a measure which had been planned and completed without any communication whatever with Administration. That he [Foreign Secretary in 1782 and 1783] as well as his predecessors in office had frequently experienced the King's reserve respecting Hanover in measures and his fixed determination to pursue such plans as he thought proper in his Electoral capacity at the same time affecting to keep his English ministers totally ignorant of the nature and extent of them.
>
> (Marquis of Carmarthen, Foreign Secretary, 1785[1])

Hanover played a more prominent role in British foreign policy in the 1770s than the Electorate had done in the late 1760s, although it was still very much a secondary role. Hanover first featured in 1772, when the possibility that Britain would take a firm line in response to the seizure by Austria, Prussia and Russia of much of Poland in the First Partition of Poland was regarded as lessened by the threat of an attack on Hanover. A London report in the *Bristol Gazette and Public Advertiser* of 30 April noted:

> It is generally imagined by those who seem best acquainted with the secret springs of government, that the dread of a Prussian army in the Electorate of Hanover has altered the intentions of our court relative to the propriety of sending a squadron up the Baltic.

Nevertheless, there is little sign that this was a key element in policy. D'Aiguillon, the French foreign minister, had set out deliberately to make concessions in colonial disputes with Britain in order to improve relations, and in March 1772 he proposed concerted pressure on Austria and Russia in order to dissuade them from partitioning Poland. Interventionism was to be encouraged by making 'Blue Water' unnecessary. George III, however, responded coolly, and, when the French-backed Gustavus III staged a coup to strengthen monarchical authority in Sweden in August 1772, seizing power from a ministry inclined to Britain and Russia, suspicion of France increased in Britain.

The failure to establish satisfactory relations with France reflected and established the parameters for debate over policy in Britain. The mode and goals of any Continental commitment were at issue: it was easy for observers to suggest that Britain and France might be able to reach an understanding, but suspicion of France remained strong, and, although the British ministry was concerned about the policies of the partitioning powers, it had no wish to allow France to commit Britain to opposition to them. However poor British relations with the partitioning powers might be, it was more reasonable to hope that they could be improved than that a successful Anglo-French alliance could be created. These attitudes led the British to use threats in 1773 to dissuade the French from deploying their navy against Russia in the Baltic and Mediterranean.

Relations between Hanover and Austria deteriorated in the 1770s, as the Electoral government opposed what it saw as the Emperor Joseph II's dictatorial attitude in the Empire, while Joseph was angered by Hanoverian independence in the Imperial Diet. In 1774, the Austrian envoy in London threatened to suspend all relations with Hanover, while in Vienna they were regarded as broken. Repeating a theme from the 1720s, the Hanoverian minister attached to George in London from 1771 until 1795, Johann Friedrich Carl von Alvensleben, declared that Joseph was the chief, but not the master, of the Empire. Tension was reflected in the British press, with a report that the Austrian envoy had declared that: 'If the King of Great Britain avowed the language lately held by his Electoral minister, he must expect the Emperor to oppose him in every step he took in the Empire.'[2]

Fortunately for Hanover, the War of American Independence (1775–83) did not lead to any attack on the Electorate. France joined in on the American side in 1778, Spain in 1779, and the Dutch in 1780, and foreign intervention was to make the perhaps impossible task of conquering the Thirteen Colonies completely impractical. Until then, it had been feasible to imagine that British success might lead to a negotiated end to the war and thus obviate the need for total victory by Britain, but the French role helped make American independence a reasonable goal.

All struggles are of course unique, but the comparison often made with the Seven Years' War, with the resulting apparent conclusion that Britain's failure was due to a lack of allies, is invalid on both political and military grounds. In the War of American Independence, the British had been unable to win prior to French entry, and, in so far as British failure in the conflict was a matter of the inability to subjugate the Thirteen Colonies, then French entry was not the key element. Instead, the inherent problems of subduing the revolution were central. These were military as well as political. America, even during the Revolutionary War, was a Continental power and the same strategic lessons about the limits of naval capability applied to operations against America as they did to operations against France and Russia. A maritime power, such as Britain, could raid, blockade, send fleets and even occupy strategic points, such as New York and Charleston, but the issue could not be decided unless an army could be put ashore which could defeat the Americans. This is what was to happen to the Confederacy during the American Civil War and to Germany in 1944–5. Fleets with small armies could not achieve this. The problem was to get the Americans to consent to rule by London. Any policy or strategy which did not destroy George Washington's army and conquer the country, forcing consent on the Americans, would not have worked. In this analysis, fleets, raiding, blockades and the occupying of cities could not have achieved this end.[3]

As far as the wider war from 1778 was concerned, then Britain certainly did not do as well as in the Seven Years' War, but many factors played a role other than that of the absence of any diversion for Bourbon strength by a British alliance system on the Continent. First, the need for the British to commit much of their strength to garrison duties and counter-insurgency operations in the Thirteen Colonies was crucial, and, again, a distinctive feature of the conflict. There was no Bourbon equivalent, and this helped leave the initiative with France and Spain.

Secondly, the outbreak of the War of the Bavarian Succession between Austria and Prussia in 1778 indicated that any British alliance system would entail countervailing, and unpredictable, demands, and not simply those of the defence of Hanover. Thirdly, alongside the management of alliances, there was the issue of the management of the war. As Nicholas Rodger has cogently argued, the problems of British naval strategy in 1778–81 were in large part the consequences of mismanagements in naval preparation and in subsequent operations.[4] The difficulty of sustaining naval strength, not least as a consequence of the natural decay of what were the organic working parts of ships and also due to the strains on the naval dockyards, was also an issue.[5]

Fourthly, although French troops (and cannon) played an important role at the British defeat at Yorktown in 1781, the major French military effort overseas was naval. Indeed, at the Battle of the Chesapeake on 5 September 1781, the French fleet thwarted the British attempt to relieve the force blockaded at Yorktown. Both in India, with the Sultans of Mysore, and in North America, the French were able to rely essentially on local allies for the bulk of the land forces of the alliance in which they were involved.

France's prime commitment to the war was naval strength, but, as it is a counterfactual, it is unclear how far this effort would have been compromised by French involvement in Continental conflict, a claim made on several occasions during the century.[6] In 1755, Newcastle was not sure if it would be good for Britain if France fought only her.[7] French finances, liquidity and credit would all have been affected had garrison forces within France been marched into Germany; but, as Frederick II argued in 1755,[8] the conquest of Hanover would have left France with a powerful asset at the end of the campaign and one that could have been bargained in any subsequent peace treaty against British gains, risking a recurrence of the political difficulties in 1748 caused by the need to make such concessions.

Even more seriously, in the absence of gains during the War of American Independence, there would have been a need to consider handing over pre-war British territories in order to obtain the return of Hanover, and the legality of such a course was far from clear, while politically it would have been disastrous for the British ministry. In 1782, indeed, the possibility that the Cabinet would agree to the Spanish demand to cede Gibraltar led to criticism in Parliament that December, although, in fact, the Spanish demand was rejected. The loss of the Thirteen Colonies itself led to the raising of the question of whether the Crown had the right to part with territories without parliamentary authority. Thus, even had George III decided, as Elector, to bring Hanover into the war, such a decision risked serious political consequences in Britain. Furthermore, had Hanover remained neutral, then alliance with Prussia would still have left the Electorate vulnerable to attack and occupation by France as in 1757. British military strength was sufficiently stretched to make any return to the 1758 policy of sending troops to Germany highly unlikely and unwelcome. War on the Continent, indeed, would have necessitated the recall of Hessians and other German auxiliaries from North America, and of Hanoverians from Gibraltar, placing a still greater burden on the British military.

George III's concern for his Electorate makes such an instrumentalist account of strategy – risking Hanover for the sake of Britain – implausible, but, even ignoring that, the optimistic account of the interventionist option in 1778 is implausible as it underrates the risks of needing to support Hanover and of having to send troops to Germany. Indeed, twenty years earlier, Cardinal Bernis, the French foreign minister, had responded to the suggestion from the French envoy in Madrid that France make peace in Germany in order to gain against Britain the support of a Spain encouraged by the resulting French freedom to spend more on her navy. Bernis argued that, no longer obliged to help Hanover or Prussia, Britain herself would be able to spend more on her navy.[9]

Had France chosen in 1778 to support Austria in the War of the Bavarian Succession (and not used that as an opportunity to attack Hanover), then the situation would have been far more benign from the British perspective; but that was a possibility far removed from British interventionism, and one that the British were not in a position to secure. In the event, French caution and concern for the complexities of German politics discouraged intervention in the Empire.[10] British failure in the War of American Independence cannot therefore be readily used as a justification for an interventionist strategy during the century. Furthermore, to assume that it could be presupposes an ability to direct the responses of other European powers.

Hanover remained neutral, which was just as well as its vulnerability was acute, leading to an unsuccessful British approach to Russia in February 1778 and to interest in alliance with Prussia in early 1778. George III was very opposed to Austrian policy in the Empire and, combined with concern over the security of Hanover in the developing crisis with France, he, as King, offered Prussia an alliance and, in return for Prussian protection of Hanover, a subsidy. Reassured about Russian and French attitudes, Frederick II did not respond positively, while his expectation of Hanoverian support against Austria was unacceptable to George. Antagonism between Joseph II and George as Elector led the latter, however, towards Frederick, and it is not surprising that, during the War of the Bavarian Succession (1778–9), the Elector adopted a pro-Prussian position, to the anger of British diplomats such as Robert Murray Keith, envoy in Vienna, who feared that this policy was needlessly irritating to Joseph II.[11] This was at a time when France's refusal to support her ally was a serious blow to Austria, leading British diplomats to see an opening, unrealistically so.

The inclusion, for the first time since 1674, or, more problematically, 1688, of the United Provinces in the list of Britain's opponents underlined the difficulties of Hanover's position. Its army remained small, and did not increase in size to the extent seen in the War of the Austrian Succession and the Seven Years' War. Instead, it rose from 15,503 men in 1775 to 23,197 in 1783. The dispatch of Hanoverian troops to Gibraltar and to India, however, helped the cause of British imperial security. Including replacement recruits sent out, the two regiments that served the British East India Company from 1781 to 1792 totalled 170 officers and 2,800 men. Due largely to disease, 69 of the officers failed to return, only four of whom were killed in action, while only about half the men returned fit for further service.

George's growing interest in German politics reflected, to a considerable extent, his opposition to change in the Empire, a sentiment that most German rulers shared. This helped to perpetuate the decentralised Imperial political system at a time when, in most of Europe, attempts were being made to strengthen central government. Just as George I had opposed the efforts of the Emperor Charles VI to stress the authority of Imperial courts over disputes between German rulers, and George II had sought to stop Frederick II's invasion of Silesia and the development of two-power Austro-Prussian preponderance in the Empire, so George III was concerned about Joseph II's attempt to increase Austrian power within the Empire. Generally happy to see Austria strong in Italy and Eastern Europe, the Electors of Hanover were deeply concerned about Austrian power and the use of Imperial authority inside the Empire. There was a genuine problem in combining Hanoverian policy and, in particular, the need to respond to specific issues and initiatives by other German states, with the British aspiration for better relations with Austria. It was too easy to British diplomats and ministers who sought the latter, and who believed that it was in Austria's interests to blame their failure on Hanover, underestimating the impact of other factors that lessened the chance of better relations.

In the aftermath of the War of American Independence, there was an opportunity for the ministry of William Pitt the Younger, which came to power in December 1783, to make a new start in foreign policy. Alliance with Austria and her ally Russia was one of the major options, but this was complicated by the policy of George III as Elector. Although suspicious about Prussian intentions, George and his Hanoverian ministers moved closer to Prussia in 1784,[12] and news of the Austrian plan to exchange the Austrian Netherlands for Bavaria, a measure seen as likely to increase greatly Austrian power within the Empire, lent urgency to this attempted alignment. Frederick, Duke of York, George's favourite son, who was resident as Prince Bishop of Osnabrück, was tangible proof of George's growing personal commitment to Hanover, and played a major role in the negotiations. He also warned George that Joseph II's brother, Max Franz, who in 1784 became Archbishop-Elector of Cologne and Prince-Bishop of Münster on Hanover's borders, was also seeking the coadjutorship (succession) of the prince-bishoprics of Paderborn and Hildesheim.[13] The latter extended to within a few miles of the city of Hanover and helped separate it from the southern portion of the Electorate. Habsburg power so close was very unwelcome.

George responded rapidly to Prussian approaches in early 1785,[14] more so than his Hanoverian ministers, who had to be pushed on by George and York, a contrast that was hardly new; indeed, the tendency in British public debate to treat Hanover as a unit motivated by clear Hanoverian concerns was generally inaccurate. At Berlin, on 23 July 1785, representatives of Prussia, Hanover and Saxony signed a treaty agreeing to the preservation of the Imperial system as currently constituted, to co-operation at the Imperial Diet, and to opposition to the Bavarian exchange and any similar further projects.[15] The resulting Fürstenbund, or League of Princes, which grew rapidly in the following months as other German princes acceded, met with serious Austrian and Russian complaints which were held to harm British diplomatic interests, particularly the hope of improved relations with the two powers. It also led to parliamentary attacks. Charles James Fox, the opposition leader in the House of Commons, declared there:

> As it was obvious that the Regency of Hanover ought neither to form laws nor enter into any treaties which might prove injurious to Great Britain, consequently it behoved the ministers of this country to have prevented their entering into any alliances which might involve serious consequences to the interests of England.[16]

Hanoverian participation in the Fürstenbund led to an upsurge of criticism in the British press of specific aspects of the Hanoverian connection, such as the patronage of German plays, music and army officers by the royal family, and the 'Germanic' habit of excluding the public from royal gardens. This was extended to the education of royal princes at Göttingen: in 1786, Princes Ernest, Augustus and Adolphus were sent there to university. George, however, never went to the Electorate and the impact of this was commented on by British travellers. In his *A Tour from London to Petersburg* (1780), John Richard noted:

> The absence of the Elector renders the court of Hanover exceeding gloomy . . . Party matters formerly carried some Englishmen so far as to treat Hanover with the greatest contempt, and the Hanoverians do not mention England with any marks of cordial friendship. They seem to consider the absence of their Elector as a disadvantage to them, and this is probably true.[17]

The Fürstenbund also led to a widely held view that George was controlling British policy for the benefit of Hanover and Prussia, while moves against British trade in both Austria and Russia were blamed on the Fürstenbund.[18] George indeed took an active role in seeking the support of German princes for the league. Fox and Viscount Stormont, both leading opposition politicians, told the Austrian envoy that George was not only very attached to Hanover but also kept his British ministers in the dark about German affairs. The leading Austrian minister, Prince Kaunitz, also asked how the British ministry could believe an Austrian alliance possible, given George's views.[19] More than the Fürstenbund, however, lay between Britain and an anti-French alliance system. Joseph II and his ally Catherine II were unimpressed by George III, while, conscious of Anglo-French antipathy, Joseph and Kaunitz regarded the prospect of a British alliance with disfavour. Although the French alliance was devoid of much positive content, the Austrian government saw no reason to replace it with a British one. Friedrich, Count Kageneck had reported in February 1785 that domestic problems would prevent Britain from taking an active part in a Continental war.[20]

The Russian envoy in London, Count Vorontsov, reported George as greatly influenced by Alvensleben and York, both of whom had Prussian links, and as overriding Pitt. In practice, this *secret du roi* was largely restricted to German politics, rather than dominating the whole of foreign policy. Thus, at a crucial moment in the Dutch crisis in 1787, York saw Frederick II's nephew and successor, Frederick William II, on behalf of George, but it was to discuss the coadjutorship of Mainz, on which Hanover and Prussia were co-operating, not Dutch affairs.[21] In 1791, Frederick, Duke of York married Frederica, Princess Royal of Prussia, although they swiftly separated.

This marriage, which involved trying issues of etiquette as well as practicalities, such as Frederick's concern that Frederica's trousseau should not incur import duties,[22] is a reminder, like the dispatch of the princes to

Göttingen, that the links between the royal family and Germany were many and varied. As Elector, George III encouraged the development of Hanover, particularly its economy and its educational facilities, although this was largely a matter of responding to initiatives by the ministerial council in Hanover. George's personal commitment emerges more clearly in cultural matters, as he wished to ensure a princely effect in his Hanover palaces. Aside from having the palace of Herrenhausen restored, and having two carriages made in London and sent over to Hanover in 1781, George played an active role in creating the largest and best-documented silver service of any made for a German court in the eighteenth century: he was determined on a new service in Hanover, and one in the new Neoclassical style, rather than a Rococo one. Most of the inherited silver service, a Rococo design, was melted down to pay for the new service. Sample designs for a new service were commissioned from the French goldsmith Robert-Joseph Auguste in 1772, and the first pieces were sent to London for George to approve them. The last delivery was made in 1786, by when a service for seventy-two people was available. All was prepared for George's long-promised visit. More mundanely, George had turnips and ham imported from Hanover for the royal table in England.[23]

An episode of Continental interventionism which did assist the British in maritime terms was provided by the Dutch crisis of 1787. The Peace of Versailles of 1783 did not end Anglo-Bourbon tension. Instead, the vigour of French activity in Indian waters at the end of the war under the dynamic command of Suffren helped to exacerbate British concern that France would soon seek to deprive Britain of India as she had of America. The argument of John Trevor, envoy in Turin, in 1786 that 'we cannot keep too strict an eye upon every motion of the French in the East Indies' was commonplace. This concern explained British anxiety about closer Franco-Dutch relations, as, in Cape Town and Sri Lanka, the Dutch had crucial bases on the route to India which complemented those of France in Mauritius and Réunion, and the Dutch were also an important naval power. George Rose, an MP who was Joint-Secretary to the Treasury and a confidant of Pitt, wrote to William Wilberforce, a fellow-member of Pitt's circle: 'The struggle is whether this country or France shall have the assistance of Holland in future contests; I do not scruple to say that almost our existence both at home and in the East Indies depends upon that.'[24]

Press comment suggested a clear linkage between France's Continental position and the naval threat she posed. The *Daily Universal Register* of 25 August 1786 noted:

> situated as France is at present with all the powers around her in the strictest alliance with or dependence upon her, except Britain, she has nothing to dread from a continental war; and if she can acquire a decided superiority of naval strength, which, considering her revenue, is far from impossible; especially if she considerably diminishes her force

by land, she may with care deprive us of our distant possessions one
after another . . . No expense therefore ought to be thought too great for
our Navy, on which, as we stand alone in Europe, our very existence as
a nation must depend.

The ousting of the pro-French 'Patriot' government in the Dutch crisis of
1787 helped to alter the naval balance considerably in Britain's favour. This
was achieved by a Prussian invasion supported by British naval preparations
and by the encouragement and funding of anti-Patriot groups. In some
respects, this was the most decisive instance of successful British interventionism during the entire century, but it would be mistaken to make a
general case from this instance. Far from being a unique instance of the
willingness of the Central European monarchies to act in Western Europe,
the Austrians or Prussians were to do so on several occasions in 1787–92
(the Austrians in the Austrian Netherlands and France, the Prussians in
Liège and France), but they did so in accordance with their own interests,
and not at the behest of Britain. Indeed, although Britain encouraged the
Prussian intervention in the United Provinces in 1787, Frederick William II
was not actually allied to Britain at that juncture. The Prussian army played
the key role; Britain's contribution was less important.

There was an understandable degree of hesitation on George's part over
using Hanoverian forces in the crisis. In 1787, as conflict with France over
the future of the United Provinces seemed imminent, Charles, 3rd Duke of
Richmond, the Master-General of the Ordnance, suggested to William Pitt
the Younger that it would be 'wise to take this opportunity of immediately
entering into a treaty with the King as Elector of Hanover and with the
Landgrave of Hesse and such other German princes as can be got, for a
supply of an army of at least 50,000 men to be ready to march at a day's
notice'.[25] An agreement with the Landgrave of Hesse-Cassel was indeed
signed, but George, although pressed by Pitt to prepare a Hanoverian force,
was less than helpful. He sought information about how far Britain would
pay and stated that he could not leave Hanover undefended.[26] This remark
indicated George's hesitation, as Prussia was a supporter of the assault
on the French-backed Dutch Patriots, and indeed there was no need for
Hanover to act, as Prussian intervention, when it came on 13 September,
was speedily successful.

In the aftermath of the Dutch crisis, reports were spread of an army of
50,000 Hanoverians, Hessians and Brunswickers (Brunswick-Wolfenbüttel
was now generally known as Brunswick) designed to support Prussia and
paid for by a Prussophile George as Elector of Hanover.[27] These reports
were inaccurate, for, although George sought an alignment of Britain, the
United Provinces and Prussia,[28] which was indeed negotiated in 1788,[29] he
did not see Hanover as playing an active role. Nevertheless, the linkage
with Prussia was strengthened as a result of George's anger with the unsuccessful attempt by Joseph II to take the Regency of Hanover into his own

hands in response to George's breakdown in mental health in the winter of 1788–9.

Caution, however, was one of George III's watchwords. Although in 1788 there had been suggestions that George as Elector took an aggressive stance in the Baltic crisis,[30] in which Christian VII of Denmark was threatened with attack by Britain and Prussia in order to force it to peace with Sweden (then at war with Russia), in fact George was opposed to war breaking out. Rather, however, than this being a case of King versus British ministers, the latter were divided on the wisdom of a policy that might lead to war.[31] The prospect of a Baltic war was not seen as an opportunity for Electoral gains, a major contrast to the situation under George I.

Thus, interventionism had been separated from Hanoverianism. This was a process facilitated by the lesser emotional commitment of George III to the Electorate compared to that of his two predecessors, although this was not the sole political factor at play. The greater unity of the ministry, which stemmed from the increased practice of Cabinet government and from the continuity of the Pitt the Younger ministry, was also significant, making it less likely that George could have prevailed, had he wanted to stress Hanoverian interests. Tension over foreign policy also declined because of the lesser experience of the Continent on the part of British ministers. Recently, there has been a welcome rediscovery of Britain's eighteenth-century links.[32] At the same time, it is necessary to note variations in the relationship. Whereas most of the leading ministers directly involved in foreign policy under George I and George II, with the conspicuous exception of Walpole, and of Newcastle prior to 1748, had played a prominent personal role in Continental power politics, this was less the case under George III. Furthermore, the political and governmental influence of Secretaries of State was greater under the first two Georges than under George III. The net effect was that the discussion over interventionism was less intense than that under the first two Georges, as was seen with reference to the Triple Alliance negotiated with Prussia and the United Provinces in 1788.

The value of the recently acquired Dutch support was shown in 1790 when Britain came close to clashing with Spain, and her ally France, in the Nootka Sound crisis. This had been touched off by the seizure by Spanish warships of fur-trading British vessels on Vancouver Island, part of the extensive American territories Spain claimed, and the subsequent crisis indicated the possibilities of Britain's alliance system. The Dutch sent a squadron to join the British warships assembling at Spithead. Their role has been treated as largely inconsequential, but this is the perspective of hindsight. Had the French fulfilled their promise to come to Spain's assistance in 1790, or had the confrontation reached the stage of conflict, then Dutch assistance might well have been valuable, and it would anyway have been a factor in the arithmetic of relative naval strength that played such an important part in naval and political attitudes towards commitments, deployments and operations.

Other allies, in contrast, were less forthcoming. Although the British envoy was instructed to ascertain if the Portuguese government would let British warships into Lisbon, Portugal was exposed to Spanish pressure. Even had it been willing, Prussia was in no position to help against France, to anticipate as it were the invasion of 1792, because two years earlier, Frederick William II was close to war with Austria. As a consequence, had war broken out, there would have been no landward diversion of French (or Spanish) strength. That, however, was not the issue, as the crisis resolved into the question of whether the French would be able to fulfil their promise to help Spain. The Spanish sense that they could not do so played a major role in their decision to settle with Britain, while the fact that the British had the same view encouraged them to persevere. Furthermore, unlike in the War of American Independence, the colonial dimension of the crisis could be limited, not least as the British decided not to embark on a war of conquest.

Their failure to do so suggests that it is important to consider the restraints that affected policy, and not helpful to consider international relations simply as if, due to inherent competition, states strove to maximise their territorial gains. Instead, as in 1770 over the Falklands, British policy was reactive. In 1790, the opportunity for deploying Britain's potential as a maritime power had possibly never been greater, and was certainly far greater than in 1739–41 or 1770. The Spanish empire was seen as weak and unstable, France, its government and military capability affected by rising domestic disorder, was unable to come to her assistance, and the British navy was at a high standard of preparedness. Yet, not only was there no war, but the settlement was not a complete abdication of the Spanish position. This was due not only to the essentially pacific intentions of the British government, which were particularly well developed in the ministry of the Younger Pitt, with his strong sense of economy, but also to Britain's diplomatic position. Britain was involved in complex negotiations designed to end, on the basis of the status quo before the conflict, the war in the Balkans that had begun in 1787. Weakened by internal discontent, especially in Belgium and Hungary, Austria had been persuaded to accept these terms, but Russia under Catherine the Great was determined to preserve some Balkan conquests. Frederick William II of Prussia was ready to use the threat of force to stop Russia making gains. This was the international background against which Britain decided not to strike at Spain, despite the possibility of gains in Latin America. The idea of conquering 'America' while France and 'Germany' were taken care of, not by diversionary British and British-subsidised troops but by internal and other rivalries, did not convince the ministry. Instead, in the second half of 1790, the idea developed of using the naval power that had been mobilised against Spain in order to give force to the intimidation of Russia.

The subsequent Ochakov crisis, however, demonstrated some of the political and military fallacies of interventionism. The potential alliance against Russia was weak: Prussian policy was quixotically unstable, there was justified uncertainty over Austria's position, and Gustavus III of Sweden ended his war with Russia in 1790. In contrast, during the Crimean War of 1854–6, France was to be a firm ally, while Russian strength then was also absorbed in fighting the Turks in the Caucasus. Furthermore, in 1791 as in 1854–6, as a Continental power without a trans-oceanic colonial empire, other than in Alaska, Russia was not particularly vulnerable to attack by a naval power, and there were no really plausible targets for an amphibious attack that could alter her policy.

The role of naval power had been central in all British confrontations with other European powers since 1763, although, earlier, the successful outcome of the Seven Years' War had suggested that deficiencies as a land power could not be compensated for by maritime success: instead, it had been necessary to fight France successfully in both Germany and Portugal. British policy-makers were not old enough to remember a different strategic world. George III had been born in 1738, his Foreign Secretary, Francis, 5th Duke of Leeds, in 1751, and William Pitt the Younger in 1759. They had to relearn the two crucial strategic lessons of the first half of the century, both of which focused on the limitations of what naval power could bring to an interventionist strategy. The first was that naval power was of limited value against a Continental power. This had been learned in the Great Northern War, and was demonstrated anew in the Ochakov crisis. It was not so much a question of the deficiencies of the navy in any war against such a power, because war was only the last option. Naval power, indeed, was most effective in international relations when it was used to intimidate and threaten, not to fight, but it was difficult to treat Continental powers successfully in this fashion.

The second lesson was that of 1745–8, that maritime success had to be assessed against failure on the European mainland. In the French Revolutionary and Napoleonic Wars, Britain was to learn that maritime and oceanic gains could not prevent the French from dominating Western Europe with all the strategic and economic dangers that that posed. George III responded to Nelson's victory at the Battle of the Nile in 1798 by suggesting that because of the international situation it was more valuable than a victory over the Brest fleet, which threatened Britain and, more particularly, Ireland: 'the beating and destroying the Brest fleet would be highly glorious and advantageous to this kingdom, but the success of this brave admiral is of more utility to the cause we are engaged in. If it electrifies Austria and Naples, it may save Italy.'[33] The failure on the Continent of the Second Coalition (against France), however, rendered such hopes fruitless, and, by the Treaty of Amiens of 1802, a by then isolated Britain returned her colonial conquests to France in order to secure peace.

Furthermore, Hanover continued vulnerable. The Hanoverian army numbered only 17,836 in 1789, but in the initial stages of the French Revolutionary Wars, which broke out in 1792 and which Britain took part in from 1793, conflict was restricted to France's borders, and France had no allies elsewhere. As a result, it was possible to deploy Hanoverian and allied-German forces in the Low Countries without apparent risk to the Electorate. The situation changed, however, when the French overran first the Austrian Netherlands (Belgium) and then the United Provinces, exposing Hanover to attack. This led George to press for British support for Hanover, but the situation was transformed in April 1795 when Prussia negotiated the Peace of Basle with France. Aside from French occupation of the left bank of the Rhine, this included the creation of a Prussian-controlled north German neutrality zone.

The creation of the neutrality zone ended the immediate threat of French attack but was to prove a stage to the conquest and absorption of Hanover into the French system. As Elector, George adhered to the neutrality, but the Electorate was still menaced.[34] In 1801, Prussia, which had long wished to seize Hanover, did so with the encouragement of Paul I of Russia and Napoleon, using the excuse of British actions against the Armed Neutrality of Baltic powers. Prussia restored control that October when Alexander I of Russia reversed his assassinated father's policies, encouraged by the entry of a British fleet into the Baltic. George himself was keen that any secularisation of ecclesiastical principalities should lead to the acquisition of Münster and Osnabrück, although the British government offered only limited support in negotiations.[35] Indeed, the negotiations in Germany in 1802–3 over territorial changes, which led to the Rezess of Regensburg of 25 February 1803, saw Hanover fulfil its long-held goal of acquiring Osnabrück, although Prussia and Bavaria gained more, the former acquiring much of the bishopric of Münster.

In 1803, however, when war resumed between Britain and France, the French rapidly occupied the entire Electorate, although it was supposedly neutral. It fell in June after scant resistance, although George III refused to ratify the Convention of Suhlingen by which the civilian government capitulated on 3 June. As a result, the French pressed the Hanoverian commander, Johann Ludwig von Wallmoden to capitulate, and he did so by the Convention of the Elbe, the second of George II's sons to do so, as the 77-year-old Wallmoden was the illegitimate half-brother of William, Duke of Cumberland who had accepted the 1757 neutrality convention.[36]

The vulnerability of Hanover was fully displayed in 1803, but this was the product of an international system different to that which had prevailed in Europe, not least the Empire, prior to the Revolution. The new system also accentuated differences between British and Hanoverian policy, Grenville, the Foreign Secretary writing in 1798 that George III was 'well aware that the instructions sent from the Hanoverian Chancery do not always exactly correspond with the sentiments or interests of the English government'.[37] 1795–1802 was the longest period in which Hanover was neutral while Britain fought France. Unlike in 1757–8, there was no rapid reversal of policy.

The last two decades prior to the outbreak of the French Revolutionary

Wars had highlighted some of the problems of British diplomatic and military strategy, but the absence then of war in Western Europe ensured that the full extent of the strategic dilemma that would face Britain in a major conflict was not grasped. Without a successful navy, the armies of the French Revolution in 1795–6 and again in 1801 could still destroy Britain's alliance system. The Franco-Austrian alliance of 1756, by keeping Western Europe peaceful, had insulated Britain from the dilemma of seeking to reconcile interests in Continental Europe with its navalist military capability. Although the alliance of 1756 might seem largely empty of meaning after 1763, in particular with French opposition to the Austrian acquisition of Bavaria and to the opening of the Scheldt for navigation in 1784, it kept the peace in the Low Countries and the Rhineland, and thus solved in an unexpected fashion the Western Question, which had been a central problem for British foreign policy since 1677: how best to respond to French expansionism on the Continent. This problem, and Britain's strategic dilemma, were posed from 1792 in an increasingly acute form, forcing new choices in foreign, strategic and military policy as Britain faced a crisis that was unprecedented in the experience of its governors.

10 Conclusions

Whoever reflects on the present alliances, projects, and conduct of the European princes will be forced to acknowledge the justness of the following remark made by that judicious statesman Sir William Temple . . . 'I have long observed from all I have seen or heard, or read in history, that nothing is so fallacious as to reason upon the counsels or conduct of princes or states, from what one conceives to be the true interest of their countries.'

(*London Chronicle*, 6 January 1757)

There were two major chronologies at stake in Anglo-Hanoverian relations, one focused on Hanoverian security and the other on Hanoverian expansionism. Although interrelated, they were also different, and this had important implications for British foreign policy, as well as for the debate within Britain about the impact of the Hanoverian connection. Furthermore, the distinction between policies to further Hanoverian security and those to aid its expansion opens a way for the disaggregation or dissection of Hanover as influence and concern for Britain.

To take the example of a key episode that can be analysed in very different ways, the British government responded to the crisis created by the diplomatic confrontation between the Alliances of Hanover and Vienna from 1725, negotiating a subsidy treaty with Hesse-Cassel in early 1726, but, although contentious, the goal of this treaty was defensive, not focused on Hanoverian expansion. Furthermore, the attempt to win the support of Hesse-Cassel was also linked to the successful British effort to gain the alliance of Sweden whose king, Frederick I, was the eldest son of Landgrave Karl of Hesse-Cassel, and this alliance could be presented in 'British' terms as designed to preserve the balance of power, as well as Baltic trade routes. The role of Hanoverian issues in the crisis awaits detailed study. At present, although the continued role of the investitures of Bremen and Verden and the Mecklenburg issue appear important in sustaining poor relations between George I and both Austria and Russia, the usual emphasis would be on more general diplomatic concerns arising from the Austro-Spanish Alliance of Vienna. Nevertheless, there is an interesting, if allusive, hint that it was believed inappropriate to differentiate 'British' from 'Hanoverian' issues too readily in relations with Austria, in that Hanoverian concerns were seen as playing a malign role in preventing the settlement of the former. With reference to concern about the Austrian establishment of the Ostend Company to trade to the Indian Ocean, a measure seen as hostile to British and Dutch commercial interests, it was suggested that this 'might have been soon stifled, had not the Germans [Hanoverian ministers] kept it on foot as a pretence to engage Great Britain to assist Hanover in the Bremen quarrel'.[1]

The sort of difficulties posed by Hanover were indicated, however, by planning for how best to protect the Electorate in the event of a full-scale war breaking out between the Alliances of Hanover and Vienna. This is not a topic that has been thoroughly studied (and indeed there is room for a systematic examination of British war-planning in the eighteenth century), but it is important as war plans indicate the problems, nature and views of alliances under strain. Hanover was greatly exposed by Prussia's switch from the Hanover to the Vienna Alliance in 1726, while the latter also won the support of Russia and of neighbouring Brunswick-Wolfenbüttel. The protection of Hanover thus required a pro-active British approach to Continental politics, rather than a non-interventionism possibly combined with a 'Blue Water' policy elsewhere.

The extent to which, in the absence also of intervention on behalf of Hanover, a 'Blue Water' policy was possible was controversial, and this controversy had direct relevance to the issue of the damaging (if any) consequences of the Hanoverian connection. Townshend indeed had already sought, in 1725, to justify a reluctance to rely solely on a 'Blue Water' policy against Spain when he presented an account of Spanish policy as motivated by the Queen's quest for Italian territories for Don Carlos, her eldest son by Philip V of Spain (Elizabeth Farnese was his second wife). Townshend very much offered a 'secret cabinets' view when he argued that the Queen had forgotten

> her husband's interest, Spain and the Spaniards; we may with great probability conclude that all our force used against Spain only and its dominions, even though it should go to the depriving them of their possessions in the East and West Indies, would not bring this mad woman to reason. The only way therefore to prevent the confusion into which we are like to be plunged, is, by well concerted alliances so to terrify the Emperor as that he may think it for his own interest to abandon the ambitious projects he is now forming, and consequently make it his business to appease and pacify this wild Queen.[2]

This was the view in 1725 from Hanover, to which Townshend accompanied George, but, alongside pressure on France to be able to assist Hanover,[3] the British government, the following year, in fact dispatched three large fleets, one to encourage Sweden and Denmark to accede to the Hanover Alliance, a goal in line with Townshend's emphasis on the need to consider Continental developments, but the other two against Spain: one to the West Indies to blockade the Spanish treasure fleet, and one to Spanish waters, not least to support Gibraltar in the event of attack. In short, in this crisis, naval strategy scarcely suggested the dominance of Hanoverian concerns, but nor either a focus on trans-oceanic goals and means at the expense of European counterparts.

This strategy, indeed, was in keeping with the possibilities of naval power, and with the political context within which British ministries operated. It would be incorrect to argue that more could not have been done to offer Hanover direct assistance. A large fleet in the Baltic, as was to be requested by Frederick II during the Seven Years' War, if it could have been kept supplied, might have influenced Russian and Prussian policy towards Hanover, although it could not have prevented overland attack on the Electorate.

Nevertheless, the prime Hanoverian commitment for British naval power was the protection of Hanoverian rule in Britain. This anti-invasion duty was not a new role for the navy, but a traditional one, although its importance was greatly accentuated as a consequence of the 'Glorious Revolution', both because this led to a Jacobite interest and also because it led to a more interventionist foreign policy on the part of Britain. In 1725–7, indeed, the availability of ports in the Austrian Netherlands led to Jacobite pressure for Austrian assistance in mounting an invasion.

As conflict apparently neared in the international crisis in 1726 – the first shots were not in fact fired until the Spaniards besieged Gibraltar in February 1727 – the tension over Hanoverian vulnerability increased, being exacerbated by reports of the build-up of Austrian forces in Silesia.[4] The British initially pressed for a camp near Nijmegen and for joint operations with French and Dutch forces, but concern about Hanover led to reiterated requests that the main French army cross the Rhine at once,[5] so as to be in a position to assist Hanover. Townshend pressed for greater vigour in the Empire than originally intended and, in particular, for the need to lay bridges over the Rhine towards Strasbourg and near Rheinfels, adding 'the French need not be scrupulous about passing the Rhine'.[6] Postal interception enabled the French indeed to know that their readiness to send an army to protect Hanover had been appreciated by the Prussians.[7]

As in other crises, the question of the most appropriate political and military strategy in 1725–7 rests in part on the quicksands of counterfactuals, but it is difficult to see the British government pressing for such a vigorous stance from its main ally, France, had Hanover not had to be defended, and it is unclear that this defence accorded with any particular national interests, other than concern for the ruling dynasty and its Continental possessions. But for this connection, it is difficult to see how a Whig ministry would have pressed for French forces to cross the Rhine. Indeed, British ministers had last been allied to a French government that had done so in 1672 when Louis XIV had attacked the Dutch in co-operation with Charles II. This alliance stemmed from the secret Treaty of Dover of 1670 which included a Catholic and autocratic prospectus for Britain,[8] not one welcome to the Whigs of 1725–7, nor indeed to George I.

Even if Townshend's argument in 1725 quoted above is not rejected as special pleading, it is clear that the particular direction given to interventionism by concerns about Hanover created grave problems. These concerns were accentuated by the possibility that Jacobite encouragement would lead to Austrian action against the Electorate.[9] While this was a clear sign of 'British' factors exacerbating Hanover's vulnerability, these factors were not the root cause of the latter.

It is also important in a crisis such as that of 1725–7, when George I was challenged by more than one power, to appreciate that the degree to which animosity might be regarded as 'British' or 'Hanoverian' in cause varied by potential opponent, in this case Austria, Spain, Prussia, Russia and Brunswick-Wolfenbüttel. In addition, 'British' and 'Hanoverian' can each be dissected in order to indicate variations between individual ministers. Thus, the argument that Hanover was under threat in 1725–7 because of British interests, whether British opposition to Charles VI's trans-oceanic commercial aspirations for the Ostend Company, or the threat to European security and the balance of power posed by the Austro-Spanish alliance, or the extent to which the latter might entail support for a Jacobite *revanche*, has to be considered not only in light of disputes between Electorate and Emperor, but also with reference to other powers, especially Catherine I of Russia, the widow and successor of Peter the Great (r. 1725–7).

Catherine's concern was primarily set by Baltic goals, and the point at issue with George I rose not from a supposed threat to the balance of power, although that was mentioned in the British press, but rather from the territorial interests of the Electorate, especially with reference to Bremen and Verden. Catherine continued Peter's support for Charles Frederick, Duke of Holstein-Gottorp and his claims to Sleswig, which threatened to undo the settlement under which George controlled Bremen and Verden, as Britain and France had guaranteed Danish rule of Sleswig. In June 1725, Charles Frederick, who had taken refuge in Russia, married Peter's daughter Anna, which further increased the possibilities of Russian intervention. Catherine I, indeed, proposed that Charles Frederick should be compensated with Bremen and Verden.

The extent to which concern over the latter (as well as over Mecklenbug) helped determine George's views toward Russia, and thus British policy, in these years tends to be neglected, due to the stress on relations with Charles VI (which were also the focus of the parliamentary debate), but it is difficult to see how policy toward Russia could be presented accurately as a concern set by 'British' goals. The expulsion of George from Bremen and Verden was viewed by opponents as necessary for the settlement of international disputes,[10] and was also seen as reflecting Russian animosity toward George as Elector, and not against Britain.[11] The British government certainly had to consider the possibility of a Russian advance on Sleswig and Hanover via

Poland and Prussia, as well as an Austrian advance on Hanover via Saxony.[12] This continued a theme of earlier concern about Russian views, one that focused attention on Bremen and Verden.[13]

Here, and more generally, however, concern over Hanoverian interests has to be scrutinised very carefully in terms of its importance relative to other concerns and interests. There is no clear way to rank significance, for evidence of policy prioritisation is limited to occasional memoranda by those very few ministers who liked to put pen to paper, while the actual process by which decisions were taken rests in the obscurities of unminuted meetings. As a consequence, it is helpful for scholars to be tentative in their judgements in this context. It is particularly necessary to be wary about applying remarks, whether supportive or critical, about the importance of Hanoverian interests, made at particular moments, as if they explained prioritisation more generally. This, indeed, is a major problem with the use of texts discussed in Chapter 1, and can lead to the situation in which foreign policy in a given period, such as the 1750s, is held to be motivated by such different priorities as Hanoverian security, trans-oceanic expansion, or both, equally, or unequally.

The same point relates to foreign comments about the impact of Hanover on British policy. These were frequent, as diplomats often sought the key to this policy in royal concern for Hanover (an analysis of which the British government was aware through postal interceptions and deciphering), and indeed could be encouraged in this direction by British ministers and politicians. It is necessary to treat each claim on its merits within a specific conjuncture; for example, on occasion, attempts were being made to ensure a more pliant foreign response to the pursuit of particular interests. Nevertheless, the belief that Hanover did have this effect on British policy encouraged its use as an issue by foreign powers, and thus offered an alternative to the exploitation of the Jacobite threat in order to lessen British resolve. This was particularly valuable for Prussia and Russia, neither of which posed an invasion threat to Britain itself.

Judgements of the relationship between Hanoverian interests and British foreign policy will continue to vary, but they need to rest on an awareness both of shifts in the relationship and of lacunae and nuances in the surviving evidence. Particular caution is required when reading from polemic and the particular to the general, for example in using passages in Pitt's speeches as an objective description of affairs.

The same is true for similar issues in other personal unions, such as those of Saxony with Poland, and of Hesse-Cassel with Sweden, each of which posed comparable issues for the conduct of foreign policy, for example the non-communication to the Swedish Senate of agreements entered into by Frederick I, King of Sweden, as Landgrave of Hesse-Cassel.[14] These comparisons were occasionally made by contemporaries, as in 1723 when the French foreign minister told the Hesse-Cassel envoy that Swedish suspicion of Hesse-Cassel was similar to British suspicion of Hanover, but that the latter was less intense as there was less Hanoverian meddling in British politics.[15] As yet, there is no systematic study that would permit the evaluation of such remarks.

The contentious character of interests and objectives has emerged repeatedly in this study. Just as Hanoverian ministers were divided, so their British counterparts split over the degree to which Britain should try to mould European affairs, and about how to respond if other powers did not match up to British expectations. The inclinations, as well as the views, of Stanhope, Townshend, Carteret and Newcastle were very different to those of Robert Walpole and Henry Pelham, and these inclinations were more important in framing policies and the response to crises than is generally appreciated. An experienced observer of his subject, Pelham, complained about his brother, Newcastle, in 1748:

> all this proceeds only from this active spirit, he wants to be doing, and the many interested parties he has been lately with, have found out that, and of consequence flatter him into their own measures. He always had a partiality and regard for the late Lord Stanhope [James, Earl Stanhope]. I know he thinks no minister has made a greater figure but him in the two reigns: he will therefore imitate him as far as he can, and I doubt, if he is not checked by somebody, will bring himself if not his country into the same distress that fertile but well intentioned Lord did before him.[16]

Pelham's tracing of pedigree was particularly appropriate. It was doubly noteworthy as Pelham looked back to Walpole, who had consciously and explicitly rejected Stanhope's policies and legacy. Whereas Walpole had benefited from the death of Stanhope in 1721, and had played a major role in the fall of Townshend in 1730, Pelham did not come out from under Newcastle's shadow as far as foreign policy was concerned. Had Pelham been as influential as Walpole had been in the 1730s, then it is likely that there would have been far less interventionism from 1748: Pelham was opposed to the costs involved in the Imperial Election Scheme. This might well have ensured that the crisis with France over North America that developed from 1754 followed the lines of that with Spain in 1739, with trans-oceanic conflict not being matched by warfare in Europe involving Britain for several years, if indeed at all.

It is also necessary to be aware that a subjective response toward the character of policy plays a part in judgement. As interventionism, not least in the case of Newcastle's policies, was linked to Hanover, with Hanoverian concerns and ministers both playing a role, and George I and George II sponsoring the nexus, it is scarcely surprising that modern judgements of the Hanoverian link in part stem from views on the value of British interventionism. This is only a problem if, as too frequently, the element of preference on the part of the scholar is ignored, and the identity of national interests in the period under study simply asserted. To do so is mistaken, and neglects the widespread evidence of well-informed clashes over interests and policy. The differences of contemporaries should not be overlooked, or minimised, by reference to factious opposition. Indeed, these differences still resonate today, and play a role in contrasts between the views of scholars.

Judgements were also affected by institutional preferences: Horatio Walpole drew attention to a frequent difference when he remarked of one diplomat urging policies that were not politically feasible, François, Seigneur de St Saphorin, envoy in Vienna from 1718 to 1727: 'St. Saphorin is a good judge of the Court of Vienna, but not of the House of Commons.'[17] Like George I's Hanoverian advisers, St Saphorin was not British and could never be an MP. Horatio Walpole, in contrast, was both MP and diplomat. Again, there is a difference between scholars who applaud fertility of diplomatic imagination and deplore the constraining role of Parliament, and others who see the parliamentary role as more positive, not least in helping cause the shaping of more acceptable policies. To address such issues openly, rather than placing them in a historiographical side-chamber, is uncommon in scholarship on eighteenth-century international relations, but existing conventions are misleading, and, as this book indicates, the situation benefits from re-examination.

The wider question posed at the outset of the book of the relationship between the Continental commitment and Britain's rise in this period to become the leading European power on the world scale repays consideration for the century as a whole. As already indicated, a close causal relationship was asserted at the time for political reasons, most obviously eventually by, and on behalf of, William Pitt the Elder. In many respects, this was the equivalent of the 'Whig myth' of constitutional and domestic change, in short of the assertion that the 'Glorious Revolution', and related subsequent events and institutions, had benign consequences. From the outset, because of the identification of both with William III, the defence of interventionism had a clear equivalence with that of the 'Glorious Revolution'. There was a political relationship that encouraged a political defence, but it is less clear that this should serve today as a means and conclusion of analysis.

The same is true of what might be termed the second stage of 1688, namely, in the domestic context, of the Hanoverian Succession and its consequences, and, externally, the international results of the Hanoverian link. It would be simple to refer to the latter in terms of the aggrandisement and defence of the Electorate of Hanover, but, as indicated in this study, the situation was more complex. For each of the Kings, the Electorate was not only a dynastic goal but also an aspect of Continental policies that were of wider import. These were separate to (though could also overlap with) what may be seen as British-based rationales for interventionism, although the latter should not be narrowly defined.

Furthermore, it is necessary to note the extent to which the British assessment of interventionism and its value was far from constant. An important aspect of this was provided by the rise of Russian power and assertiveness in the 1710s which posed new demands, not least making it clear that the British habit of viewing European relations in terms of hostility to Catholicism and/or Western European powers was inadequate. Secondly, there was the issue that apparently related more centrally to the debate about the merits of Continental interventionism, namely the consequences for Britain's interests and military needs of the growing commitment to trans-oceanic opportunities.[18] Newcastle's justification of the subsidy treaties with Russia and Hesse-Cassel that followed the breakdown of relations with France in 1754 drew attention to exigencies:

> Things were in such a situation, that when I could not do what I wished (owing to the faults of others and not my own) I was forced to do what I could ... With regard to public measures, I mean those of peace, and war; and the manner and means of obtaining the one, or carrying on the other, when I cannot do what I would I must do what I can. The notion of obliging France to confine war to the sea, and to America, I always thought difficult, if not impracticable; and might, as it certainly will, prove dangerous to this country at last; by forcing them in a manner to give their whole attention to their marine; which they now certainly do, and are, or I am afraid will very soon be, superior to us at sea. In what condition will this nation be then?[19]

Empire, in short, was a dynamic issue in the debate over foreign policy, but one for which the consequences in terms of clear-cut policy prescriptions in particular conjunctures were unclear. So, more seriously, was the relationship between empire and what is today called strategic culture, the set of assumptions that guided policy choice. This vocabulary is very much a modern one,[20] and the use of the concept may appear anachronistic, although it has been applied with considerable benefit.[21] The extent to which a strategic culture can be defined is limited by the nature of policy-discussion and formulation. The small scale of the governmental bureaucracy did not automatically preclude the institutionalisation of coherent analysis as an aspect of informed diplomatic and military decision-making, but that was not the route generally followed in Britain. Ministers and officials could offer some analysis, and some, such as St Saphorin under George I, and Horatio Walpole in the 1730s, did so with alacrity, but they were regarded as curiosities, even nuisances, and not as valued advisors taking part in a regular process.

It is possible, nevertheless, through an analysis of the surviving sources, especially correspondence between ministers, to recover aspects of the discussion of strategic culture. When diplomatic instructions offered, as some did, rationales of government policy, it might appear even more practicable to do the same, but some of these, instead, can be seen as aspects of the persuasive aspect of government: the instructions were designed to be communicated to the governments to which the diplomats were accredited, and should not therefore be used as a revealing account of the intentions of policy. In so far as strategic culture can be discussed, it is clear that, as in other contexts, this term is best employed not to suggest a clear-cut body of ideas and policies, but, instead, the parameters within which policy was contested.

Alongside this approach to the recovery of strategic culture, it is valid to engage with the configuration of the contemporary public debate, not least because of the close relationship between this debate and discussion in governmental circles. The politicisation of strategic culture in large part stemmed from the attempt to deny that interventionism and Hanoverianism were acceptable costs of the domestic situation stemming from 1688 and 1714, in other words the protection cost stemming from the Protestant Succession. This argument in fact was, and is, a plausible one, but it represented a contractual approach to the monarchy that was generally unacceptable. Indeed, the stress on royal *gloire* seen in some of the scholarship[22] and, more generally, on the positive aspects of dynasticism, was scarcely compatible with such a defence of foreign and strategic policy. Nor was such a defensive schema acceptable when contrasted with the arguments of Jacobite legitimism, not least because interventionism and Hanoverianism were deliberately focused on by Jacobite propagandists. As a result, it was necessary to defend both, and this need provided a political dimension that should not readily be abstracted from modern discussion.

In turn, the character of modern discussion has to be faced, not least the extent to which subsequent discussion of interventionism has affected the consideration of the eighteenth-century situation. This discussion was seen most obviously with the debates over both the appeasement of the dictators in the 1930s and British membership in the European Union. Within the eighteenth century itself, subsequent events indeed greatly affected debate. This was particularly the case because of the emphasis on consistency, although it was also necessary to defend the consequences, intended or otherwise, of policy choices. A good instance is provided by the extent to which the political exigencies of the Seven Years' War influenced discussion, both then and subsequently, of the earlier situation, but this process was even more marked earlier in the century, due in large part to the contentious nature of the Peace of Utrecht.

In 1741, for example, it was suggested that the anonymous pamphlet *The Groans of Germany*, one of the most interesting and well-informed opposition discussions of British foreign policy in the last years of the Walpole ministry, was written by Bolingbroke. Anton von Zöhrern, an Austrian diplomat in London, reported 'A pamphlet came to my hands yesterday, entitled *The Groans of Germany*. It meets with great ingress here and is ascribed to the famous Bullingbroke. I am now translating it from English into French.'[23] There was a determined effort in the pamphlet to trace faults in policy, not least in order to question competence. This also involved defending a particular interpretation. Thus, the author defended the Peace of Utrecht of 1713, which Bolingbroke had played a major role in negotiating:

> Her [Britain's] whole business was to have maintained things as they were settled by the Treaty of Utrecht, without the least variation. To this end the spirit of the Grand Alliance should have been kept up, and the strictest harmony preserved with the Emperor, Savoy, the States-General, Prussia, and all the ancient confederates. Upon the least motion of the House of Bourbon to enlarge itself either on this, or the other side of the Alps, or to disturb the public tranquility, the confederacy should be resumed and satisfaction demanded immediately and exacted.[24]

The pamphlet is instructive for the light it throws on other aspects of the public debate, not least its relationship with other sources. *The Groans of Germany* repeated themes advanced in the *Craftsman*, arguing that policy in the late 1720s had been overly pro-French, criticising the Treaties of Hanover (1725) and Seville (1729), anti-Austrian alliances entered into in concert with France, and condemning the provisions of the latter treaty by which Britain aided the introduction of Spanish garrisons into the duchies of Parma and Tuscany. This move, it was argued, had had serious consequences for the Austrian position in Italy when conflict began in the peninsula in 1733 and 1741,[25] and was attacked by opposition speakers in Parliament in the 1730s, particularly Tories such as Lord Bathurst and Bolingbroke's close ally, Sir William Wyndham, the Tory leader in the House of Commons.

A significant accusation in the pamphlet that reflected the author's interest in foreign policy was that Britain had made secret promises to France concerning the Polish succession:

> it has been rumoured at all the courts of the North, that to bring France into good humour, after the Second Treaty of Vienna, the court of London promised her interest and assistance to restore King Stanislaus [father-in-law to Louis XV of France] to the throne of Poland whenever King Augustus [II] should die; and that in consequence of this promise, the British Minister in Poland was ordered, and did actually co-operate with the French Minister after the death of the Prince [in 1733].[26]

The charge was false, although during the period of the Anglo-French alliance (1716–31), the British ministry had promised to assist Stanislaus. Suspicion of this suggests a high level of awareness of foreign policy issues in the author of the pamphlet, and an expectation that readers would be both interested and able to follow the argument. By 1741, discussion of foreign policy in pamphlets rested on a basis of an extensive coverage of the subject in newspapers. The principal reason for the extensive coverage of foreign

affairs was widespread national interest in European matters. The public
had been educated in the importance of foreign policy by the experience of
conflict in which Britain had been closely involved.

The Groans of Germany also indicates the problem of using texts.
Although others besides Zöhrern suggested that it was written by Bolingbroke,[27] there is no evidence to indicate that it definitely was: the ideas
advanced were the same as those offered by him elsewhere, but, equally,
they were the same as those advanced by the opposition Whigs. In late
1741, however, Bolingbroke showed interest in the idea that the disparate
elements in the opposition could combine in an attack on ministerial foreign
policy.[28] If *The Groans of Germany* was his contribution to the attack, it
showed that he had lost none of his ability to write well and persuasively on
the subject.

More generally, the role of the past in affecting both ministerial discussion
and public debate makes it dangerous to abstract short periods of time for
consideration. In one respect, this is necessary in order to recover the specificities of particular conjunctures, and the way they anchored, inspired and
coloured more general arguments. The latter, however, also resonated in
part thanks to their accumulated weight and resonance in debate, and their
location in pre-existing political contention. These provide the most appropriate context in which to consider the linked issues of interventionism and
the Hanoverian connection. Debates over policy were related to the development of public culture and politics. The need to define and discuss interests and policy in semi-public and public contexts raised a number of issues.
These included the questions of how best to discern national interests,
indeed of the validity and shaping of the concept, and then of the extent
to which it was proper and prudential, to explain, debate and invite discussion of them. This involved the dichotomy of prerogative and public, and
the need to consider strategies to link the two. Alongside this, there is the
significant issue of the way in which ideas and information, especially
international developments, were incorporated into the debate.

This public debate cannot be abstracted from the wider currents of politics.
As Nicholas Rodger cogently pointed out, 'what purported to be a strategic
debate was in many cases a disguised form of ideological contest, where
foreign policy acted as the surrogate of domestic politics'.[29] Indeed, ministers and diplomats were only too happy to emphasise the role of domestic
pressures when arguing their case with foreign representatives. This was
seen in 1726 when Palm reported a clash with Townshend who

> broke out with his usual warmth against the Ostend Trade . . . said that
> he saw no way to quiet and to pacify the nation . . . so long as the trade
> of Ostend remained as a stumbling block, and if the King and his minis-
> ters should try to come to an accommodation with your Imperial Majesty
> upon this subject, it was the furthest way to expose them to the hatred of
> the nation, and to bring on their own ruin.

Townshend added an instructive historical dimension. He told Palm what he had told Starhemberg, that the latter should reflect on the War of the Spanish Succession 'and enquire what was the true cause of that violent hatred between the English and the French nation, and then we should palpably find, that it had originally its beginning from the time when France set about doing all the prejudice they could to the trade of England'. Townshend also said that 'no good was to be expected, so long as this thorn was not taken out of the side of the English nation',[30] but that assertion is not evidence that should be abstracted from its context as an aspect of contention at a particular moment. The assessment of policy choices should not be treated as if diplomacy was separate from this. It is not appropriate to argue that national interests were as readily apparent as ministers and other politicians suggested or to ignore the extent of contemporary debate.

Eighteenth-century interventionism rested on a sense of optimism about the goals and means of foreign policy, and, as such, prefigured contemporary issues. Tony Blair falls squarely into the Whiggish tradition of interventionism and the creation of systems to solve problems and prevent their recurrence, and is apt to underrate the pragmatic and prudential approach to foreign commitments. Current engagement with the issue of 'Europe', for example, rests on excessive optimism about the possibility of moulding change. A government that came to power in 1997 on the basis of welcoming change and rejecting the past is necessarily one that is optimistic about the prospect for improvement and a better future. This has a partisan aspect, with the specific denial of attitudes and policies associated with either the Conservatives or 'Old Labour'. Indeed, Blair's presentation of himself as 'New Labour' encourages the rejection of established assumptions of national interests and policy. Europe as a governmental unit indeed bears little relationship to long-established British national interests. Instead, these are being reconfigured (or Europeanised) in a policy that testifies to the governmental view that Europe is the crucial international unit for Britain, and also the optimistic hope that it can be made to work as such.

Europeanisation reflects an old-fashioned emphasis on propinquity (nearness) that dates from mid-twentieth-century assessments of security and economic relations. In practice, this propinquity seems to have little to do with the global economics and geopolitics of the present day. Furthermore, the emphasis on Europe underrates the multiple links of Britain, which for centuries has been closer to Boston, Kingston or New York, than to Bari, Cracow or Zagreb.

A sense of optimism, however, can be reconceptualised in terms of a need to respond to problems and a determination to make the best solution work; and this presentation can be offered in defence of both eighteenth-century and contemporary interventionism. In both cases, there are military/security aspects as well as their diplomatic/geopolitical counterparts, although, to a considerable extent, this is a matter of distinctions along a continuum rather than sharp divisions.

The security dimension was the most urgent at both the outset and the close of the period of this study. If in 1714 it was the new dynasty that was most obviously at stake, its fate involved that of the Protestant Succession, the Revolution Settlement, and the position of much of the British social order. In 1792, the trial of Louis XVI again put the focus on monarchs, but the threat to, and in, Britain again encompassed the structure, character and ethos of the political and social order. In each case, security was seen to require more than a powerful navy. This prefigured British concerns about 'near-Europe' in the twentieth century. Security can be seen as the justification of the Continental commitment, both in the eighteenth and in the twentieth century, but, in the former, the goals, practice and politics of this commitment were at the least complicated, if not seriously compromised, by the Hanoverian connection. It is also important and instructive to probe the political context of contemporary rationales for intervention.

Notes

Preface

1 George Clarke to Edward Nicholas, 26 Mar. (os) 1726, BL. Eg. 2540 fol. 610.
2 Michell, Prussian envoy in London, to Frederick II, King of Prussia, 29 Ap. 1757, *Polit. Corr.* vol. 15, p. 36.
3 J.S. Brewer, *The Sinews of Power. War, Money and the English State, 1688–1783* (London, 1989).
4 D. Armitage, *The Ideological Origins of the British Empire* (Cambridge, 2000).

1 Britain and the rise to world empire

1 F. Braudel, *Écrits sur l'histoire* (Paris, 1969), pp. 41–83, and *La Méditerranée et le monde Méditerranéen à l'époque de Philippe II* (2nd edn, 2 vols, Paris, 1966).
2 H. Kleinschmidt, *The Nemesis of Power* (London, 2000), pp. 114–70, and 'Systeme und Ordnungen in der Geschichte der internationalen Beziehungen', *Archiv für Kulturgeschichte*, 82 (2000), pp. 433–54.
3 Haslang, Bavarian envoy in London, to Emperor Charles VII, 5 Mar. 1743, Munich, Bayr. Ges. London 208.
4 Also titled *Rape Upon Rape*. J.M. Black, 'Political Allusions in Fielding's "Coffee-House Politicians" ', *Theoria*, 62 (1984), pp. 45–56.
5 BL. Add. 10348 fol. 144.
6 Robert, 4th Earl of Holdernesse, Secretary of State for the Northern Department, to Thomas, Duke of Newcastle, 1st Lord of the Treasury, 6 Aug. 1755, BL. Add. 32858 fol. 14.
7 Charles DuBourgay, envoy in Berlin, to Charles, 2nd Viscount Townshend, Secretary of State for the Northern Department, 28 June 1727, NA. SP. 90/22; William, 1st Lord Harrington to Benjamin Keene, 30 Jan. (os) 1730, envoy in Spain, BL. Add. 32765 fols 232–3.
8 George Whitworth, envoy in Berlin, to Luke Schaub, 25 Oct. 1719, New York, Public Library, Hardwicke papers vol. 46.
9 Edward Sedgwick, former Under Secretary, to Edward Weston, his former colleague, 26 Nov. 1765, BL. Add. 57928 fol. 170.
10 Henry Fox to William, 2nd Earl of Shelburne, 4 Oct. 1762, London, BL, Bowood, papers of the 1st Marquess of Lansdowne, vol. 15 fol. 107.
11 K.W. Schweizer, 'Foreign Policy and the Eighteenth-Century English Press: the case of Israel Mauduit's *Considerations on the Present German War*', *Publishing History*, 39 (1996), pp. 46, 51.
12 Northampton, Northamptonshire CRO. L(C) 1734.
13 Bristol, Record Office, Mss. 40469/7.
14 Gregory to Addington, 22 Oct. 1807, Exeter, Devon CRO., Addington (Sidmouth) papers, 152 M/C 1807/OF 13.

15 P.J. Marshall (ed.), *The Oxford History of the British Empire, II. The Eighteenth Century* (Oxford, 1998).
16 Tyrawly to Sir Charles Wager, First Lord of the Admiralty, 10 May 1738, Washington, Library of Congress, Wager papers.
17 Lee to Addington, 16 Sept. 1807, Exeter, Devon CRO, Addington (Sidmouth) papers, 152 M/C 1807/OI 6.
18 For example, J. Brewer, *The Sinews of Power. War, Money and the English State, 1688–1783* (London, 1989).
19 E.g. re shortage of magazines and powder in Minorca, the major British base in the Mediterranean, Colonel Montagu, Commander at Mahon, to Newcastle, then Secretary of State for the Southern Department, 27 June 1729, NA. SP. 43/78.
20 J.M. Black, *Britain as a Military Power 1688–1815* (London, 1999).
21 Delafaye to James, Earl Stanhope, Secretary of State for the Northern Department, 29 Sept. 1719, NA. SP. 43/63.
22 F. Anderson, *A People's Army. Massachusetts Soldiers and Society in the Seven Years' War* (Chapel Hill, 1984).
23 *Wye's Letter*, 28 July (os) 1737.
24 M.S. Anderson, 'Eighteenth-Century Theories of the Balance of Power', in R. Hatton and M.S. Anderson (eds), *Studies in Diplomatic History* (London, 1970), pp. 183–98; Black, 'The Theory of the Balance of Power in the First Half of the Eighteenth Century: A Note on Sources', *Review of International Studies*, 9 (1983), pp. 855–61.
25 P. Schroeder, *The Transformation of European Politics 1763–1848* (Oxford, 1994), p. 393.
26 N.A.M. Rodger, 'The Continental Commitment in the Eighteenth Century', in L. Freedman, P. Hayes and R. O'Neill (eds), *War, Strategy and International Politics: Essays in Honour of Sir Michael Howard* (Oxford, 1992), pp. 39–55.
27 M. Roberts, *Splendid Isolation 1763–1780* (Reading, 1970); H.M. Scott, *British Foreign Policy in the Age of the American Revolution* (Oxford, 1990).
28 On which see recently, J.D. Grainger, *The Amiens Truce. Britain and Bonaparte, 1801–1803* (Woodbridge, 2004).
29 Stair to Robert Trevor, envoy at The Hague, 13 Jan. 1743, Aylesbury, Trevor, vol. 33.
30 Schweizer, 'The Non-Renewal of the Anglo-Prussian Subsidy Treaty, 1761–1762: A Historical Revision', *Canadian Journal of History*, 13 (1978), pp. 383–96.
31 J.M. Black, *British Foreign Policy in an Age of Revolution, 1783–1793* (Cambridge, 1994), pp. 382–403.
32 H.M. Scott, 'Great Britain, Poland and the Russian Alliance, 1763–1767', *Historical Journal*, 19 (1976), pp. 53–74; J.M. Black, *Parliament and Foreign Policy in the Eighteenth Century* (Cambridge, 2004), pp. 191–2.
33 S. Das, *Myths and Realities of French Imperialism in India, 1763–1783* (New York, 1992).
34 Tyrawly to Wager, 10 May 1738, Washington, Library of Congress, Wager papers.
35 *Weekly Packet*, 26 Sept. (os) 1719.
36 A. Cunningham, 'The Oczakov debate', *Middle Eastern Studies* (1964–5).
37 A. Burns and J. Innes (eds), *Rethinking the Age of Reform. Britain 1780–1850* (Cambridge, 2003), in particular Innes, ' "Reform" in English Public Life: The Fortunes of a Word', pp. 71–97.
38 M. Poovey, *A History of the Modern Fact. Problems of Knowledge in the Sciences of Wealth and Society* (Chicago, 1998); D.R. Headrick, *When Information Came of Age. Technologies of Knowledge in the Age of Reason and Revolution, 1700–1850* (Oxford, 2000), pp. 59–64, 68, 70, 77–8, 84. See, more generally, E. Higgs, *The Information State in England* (Basingstoke, 2004).
39 Newcastle to Philip, 1st Earl of Hardwicke, 26 July 1757, BL. Add. 35417 fol. 5.

40 R. Whitworth, *Field Marshal Lord Ligonier* (Oxford, 1958), p. 201.
41 Grenville to Lord Mornington, 5 Oct. 1798, BL. Add. 70927 fols 24–5.
42 Mirepoix, French envoy in London, to Rouillé, French foreign minister, 16 Jan., 8 Mar., Bonnac, French envoy in The Hague, to Rouillé, 21 Feb., Bussy, French envoy in Hanover, to Rouillé, 29 July 1755, AE. CP. Ang. 438 fols 18, 261, Hollande 488 fols 106–7, Br. 52 fol. 22; A. Reese, *Europäische Hegemonie und France d'outre-mer. Koloniale Fragen in der französischen Aussenpolitik 1700–1763* (Stuttgart, 1988), pp. 274–310.
43 William, Lord Auckland, envoy in The Hague, to Grenville, 29 Jan. 1791, BL. Add. 58919 fol. 33; Auckland to James Bland Burges, Under Secretary in the Foreign Office, 1, 9 Mar. 1791, Bod. Bland Burges papers, vol. 30 fols 129, 133.
44 Cobbett, vol. 29, cols. 204–14.
45 John, 4th Duke of Bedford, Secretary of State for the Southern Department, the Secretary of State with authority in colonial matters.
46 Knowles to Trelawny, 27 Nov. 1750, Washington, Library of Congress, Trelawny papers.
47 P. Gauci, *The Politics of Trade: The Overseas Merchant in State and Society, 1660–1720* (Oxford, 2001).
48 P.G.M. Dickson, *The Financial Revolution in England: A Study in the Development of Public Credit 1688–1756* (Oxford, 1967); D. Baugh, *Naval Administration, 1715–1750* (London, 1977); Brewer, *The Sinews of Power: War, Money and the English State, 1688–1783* (London, 1989); N.A.M. Rodger, *The Command of the Ocean: A Naval History of Britain, 1649–1815* (London, 2004).
49 For an early attempt, J.M. Black, *Kings, Nobles, and Commoners: States and Societies in Early Modern Europe, a Revisionist History* (London, 2004).
50 R. Bonney, 'Towards the Comparative Fiscal History of Britain and France during the "Long" Eighteenth Century', in L. Prados de la Escosura (ed.), *Exceptionalism and Industrialisation. Britain and Its European Rivals, 1688–1815* (Cambridge, 2004), pp. 201–3.
51 P. Taylor, *Indentured to Liberty: Peasant Life and the Hessian Military States, 1688–1815* (Ithaca, New York, 1994). An earlier version of part of this chapter appeared in the *British Journal for Eighteenth-Century Studies* 27 (2004), pp. 157–71.

2 Hanover and the debate over policy

1 W.C. Costin and J.S. Watson, *The Law and Working of the Constitution. Documents 1660–1914* (2 vols, London, 1961) I, 95.
2 J.J. Murray, *George I, the Baltic and the Whig Split of 1717* (London, 1969); J.M. Black, 'Hanover and British Foreign Policy, 1714–60', *English Historical Review*, 120 (2005).
3 H.M. Scott, *The Emergence of the Eastern Powers, 1756–1775* (Cambridge, 2001).
4 G. Meinhardt, *Die Universität Göttingen: Ihre Entwicklung und Geschichte von 1734–1974* (Frankfurt, 1977).
5 C. Borgmann, *Der Deutsche Religionsstreit der Jahre 1719–20* (Berlin, 1937); H. Naumann, *Österreich, England und das Reich*, pp. 43–58; H. Schmidt, *Kurfürst Karl Philipp von der Pfalz als Reichsfürst* (Mannheim, 1963), pp. 114–49.
6 Robethon to Stair, 16 Ap. 1716, NAS. GD. 135/141/7.
7 Count Albert, Bavarian and Palatine envoy in Paris, to Baron Malknecht, Bavarian foreign minister, 29 Jan. 1721, Munich, KS. 17076.
8 St Saphorin, envoy in Vienna, to Charles, Viscount Townshend, Secretary of State for the Northern Department, 26 Aug. 1722, NA. SP. 80/47.
9 Charles Whitworth, envoy at the Imperial Diet (1715) and in Berlin (1721), to

Townshend, 9 Dec. 1715, 18 Mar. 1721, BL. Add. 37362 fol. 193, NA. SP. 90/13; Albert to Malknecht, 3 Feb., 9 Ap. 1719, 16 Jan. 1724, KS 17072, 17083; Gansinot, Wittelsbach envoy at The Hague, to Count Ferdinand Plettenberg, leading minister of Clemens August, 13 Jan., 20 March 1722, 8 Jan. 1726, Münster, NB 259 I fols 39–40, 91, 147; Gansinot to Count Törring, Bavarian foreign minister, 5 Oct. 1728, Munich, KS 17306.

10 St Saphorin to George I, 7 Oct. 1719, Hanover, Cal. 24 Nr. 4913 fols 3–5.

11 Albert to Malknecht, 20, 28 Jan. 1726, KS 17087; Townshend to Plettenberg, 28 Jan. (os) 1726, NA. SP. 81/179.

12 Townshend to Plettenberg, 28 Jan. (os) 1726, Münster, 5474 fol. 4.

13 A. Rosenlehner, *Kurfürst Karl Philipp von der Pfalz und die Jülichsche Frage, 1725–1729* (Munich, 1906); Townshend to Count of Lippe, intermediary with Karl Philipp, 28 Jan. (os) 1726, NA. SP. 81/179; Albert to Max Emanuel, Elector of Bavaria, 12 Jan. 1726, Munich, KS 17087; Karl Philipp to Schmidmann, Palatine envoy at The Hague, 27 Mar. 1726, Munich, Kasten Blau 67/9.

14 Townshend to St Saphorin, 14 Jan. (os) 1726, NA. SP. 80/57.

15 Albert to Max Emanuel, 3, 12 Jan., 9 Feb. 1726, Albert to Törring, 24, 29 May 1726, Munich, KS 17087, 17091.

16 Charles Albert to Albert, 19 Nov. 1726, Munich, KS 17090; Gansinot to Plettenberg, 10 May 1726, Münster, NB 259 I fols 269–70.

17 Townshend to Horatio Walpole, 15 Sept. (os), 11 Oct. (os), Newcastle to Horatio Walpole and William Stanhope, 30 Sept. (os), 6 Nov. (os), Townshend to Philip, 4th Earl of Chesterfield, envoy at The Hague, 29 Nov. (os) 1728, BL. Add. 32758 fols 195–7, 333–3, 32759 fol. 116, 9138 fol. 11; Newcastle to Horatio Walpole, 11 Oct. (os) 1728, NA. SP. 78/189 fol. 428.

18 Törring to Plettenberg, 24 Dec., Chavigny, French envoy to the Imperial Diet, to Plettenberg, 26 Dec. 1729, Townshend to Plettenberg, 6 Mar., Albert to Plettenberg, 31 May, 3 July 1730, Münster, NA. 148 fol. 225, NB. 286 fol. 62, 5474 fol. 40, NB. 33 I fols 11, 22; Plettenberg to Törring, 18 Dec. 1729, 12 Feb. 1730, Albert to Törring, 20 Jan., 10 Feb., 15 Mar., 17 Ap., 31 May 1730, Munich, KS 17222; memorandum, Munich, Bayr. Ges. Paris 84.

19 Newcastle to Stephen Poyntz, envoy in Paris, 12 Feb. (os) 1730, BL. Add. 32765 fol. 322; Albert to Törring, 3, 10, 15 Mar. 1730, Munich, KS 17111.

20 Poyntz to Newcastle, 11 Jan. 1730, BL. Add. 32765 fol. 8.

21 Townshend to Horatio Walpole and Poyntz, 11 Dec. (os) 1729, BL. Add. 48982 fol. 205.

22 Whitworth to Stanhope, 26 Sept. 1719, New York, Public Library, Hardwicke papers vol. 46. Heinrich Rüdiger von Ilgen was the Prussian minister for foreign affairs.

23 Historical Manuscripts Commission, *Manuscripts of the Earl of Egmont, Diary of Viscount Perceval* (3 vols, London, 1920–3) I, 25–6.

24 Holdernesse to Andrew Mitchell, envoy in Berlin, 29 Ap. 1757, NA. SP. 90/68.

25 *Champion*, 27 Oct. (os) 1741; Anon., *Reflections upon the Present State of Affairs* (London, 1755), p. 19.

26 U. Dann, *Hannover und England 1740–1760* (Hildesheim, 1986), translated and slightly revised as *Hanover and Great Britain, 1740–1760* (Leicester, 1991).

27 J.M. Black, *The Hanoverians* (London, 2004), pp. 28–30.

28 Palm to Charles VI, 15 Feb., Riva to the Austrian diplomat Count Starhemberg, 5 Mar. 1726, NLA, Mss. 1458/9/8/1, 1458/9/4/12.

29 Schleinitz to Cardinal Fleury, 8, 12 July 1729, AE. CP. Br. 47; Charles VI to Fonseca and Stephen Kinsky, 31 Aug., 10 Sept. 1729, C. Höfler, *Der Congress von Soissons* (2 vols, Vienna, 1871–6) I, 144–6, 211.

30 Le Coq, Saxon envoy in London, to Augustus II of Saxony-Poland, 12 Feb. 1726, NLA. Mss. 1458/9/8/2.

31 J.M. Black, 'British Neutrality in the War of the Polish Succession, 1733–1735', *International History Review*, 8 (1986), pp. 345–66.
32 For the legal situation, I.B. Campbell, 'The International Legal Relations between Great Britain and Hanover, 1714–1837', (Cambridge University PhD., 1966).
33 J.M. Black, 'An "Ignoramus" in European Affairs?', *British Journal for Eighteenth-Century Studies*, 6 (1983), pp. 55–65.
34 J.M. Black, 'The Tory View of Eighteenth-Century British Foreign Policy', *Historical Journal*, 31 (1988), pp. 409–27.
35 The seriousness of which emerges from E. Cruickshanks and H. Erskine-Hill, *The Atterbury Plot* (Basingstoke, 2004).
36 J.M. Black, 'The Anglo-French Alliance 1716–31: A Study in Eighteenth-Century International Relations', *Francia*, 13 (1986).
37 J.M. Black, 'The Theory of the Balance of Power in the First Half of the Eighteenth Century: A Note on Sources', *Review of International Studies*, 9 (1983), pp. 855–61.
38 R. Rolt, *Memoirs of the Life of the Right Honorable John Lindesay, Earl of Crawfurd* (London, 1753), p. 359.
39 J. Shebbeare, *A Sixth Letter* (London, 1757), p. 17.
40 J.M. Black, 'The British Attempt to Preserve the Peace in Europe 1748–1755', in H. Duchhardt (ed.), *Zwischenstaatliche Friedenswahrung in Mittelalter und Früher Neuzeit* (Cologne, 1991), pp. 227–43.
41 George II to Frederick II, 7 Jan. 1757, *Polit. Corr.* 14 (1886), p. 251. On the Hanoverian Chancery in London, R. Grieser, 'Die Deutsche Kanzlei in London, ihre Entstehung und Anfänge', *Blätter für deutsche Landesgeschichte*, 89 (1952), pp. 156–68.
42 National Registry of Archives report 22339; K.W. Schweizer, 'A Handlist to the Additional Weston Papers', *Bulletin of the Institute of Historical Research*, 51 (1978), pp. 99–102.
43 For an introduction, L. Scott, 'Under Secretaries of State, 1755–1775' (MA. Manchester, 1950).
44 M.J. Cardwell, *Arts and Arms. Literature, Politics and Patriotism During The Seven Years War* (Manchester, 2004), p. 282. See also M. Peters, *Pitt and Popularity: The Patriot Minister and London Opinion during the Seven Years' War* (Oxford, 1980).
45 E.g. Newcastle to Pelham, 26 Sept. 1750, BL. Add. 35411 fol. 138.
46 E.g. Perron, Sardinian envoy, to Charles Emmanuel III, 12 Mar., 11 May 1750, AST. LM. Ing. 56; Alt, Hesse-Cassel envoy, to Landgrave of Hesse-Cassel, 16 July 1751, Marburg, England 248.
47 Holdernesse to Yorke, 30 July 1755, BL. Eg. 3446 fol. 182. For the papers of diplomats, Black, 'Non-Walpolean Manuscripts in the Lewis Walpole Library', *Yale University Library Gazette*, 67 (1992), pp. 58–67 and *British Diplomats and Diplomacy 1688–1800* (Exeter, 2001), pp. 177–98.
48 Holdernesse to Yorke, 23 Dec. 1755, BL. Eg. 3446 fol. 301.
49 J.M. Black, 'Pitt the Elder and the Foundation of an Imperial Foreign Policy', in T.G. Otte (ed.), *The Makers of British Foreign Policy. From Pitt to Thatcher* (Basingstoke, 2002), pp. 35–51.

3 Securing the new dynasty, 1714–21

1 Newcastle to Stanhope, 14 Oct. (os) 1719, BL. Add. 32686 fol. 152.
2 Memoranda on state of Hanoverian army joined to letters from Poussin, French envoy, 7 Jan., and from Rottembourg, 23 Mar. 1715, AE. CP. Br. 45 fols 4–5. I have also benefited from the advice of Peter Wilson.
3 P. Wilson, *German Armies. War and German Politics, 1648–1806* (London, 1998), p. 218.

4 Paul Methuen, acting Secretary of State for the Southern Department, to John, 2nd Earl of Stair, envoy in Paris, 2 Oct. (os) 1716, NAS. GD. 135/141/5; James Stanhope, Secretary of State for the Southern Department, to Methuen, 16 Oct. 1716, NA. SP. 43/1 fol. 101.

5 Temple Stanyan, Under Secretary in the Southern Department, to Stair, 24 Ap. (os) 1718, NAS. GD. 135/141/13B.

6 George I to Orléans, 22 Dec. 1719, New York, Public Library, Hardwicke papers vol. 54.

7 Anon. [possibly Bolingbroke], *The Groans of Germany* (London, 1741), p. 20.

8 St Saphorin, George I's representative in Vienna, to George I, 6 July, St Saphorin to Robethon, 9 July 1718, Hanover Cal. 24, Nr. 1619 fols 12–17, 18; J.F. Chance, *George I and the Northern War* (London, 1909).

9 Tilson to Whitworth, 16 Feb. (os) 1722, BL. Add. 37388 fol. 71.

10 Verses in papers of Lady Sarah Cowper, Hertford, Hertfordshire CRO. Panshanger Mss. D/EP F240, verse 10.

11 Stanhope to Stair, 31 May (os) 1718, NAS. GD. 135/141/13A.

12 Abraham Stanyan, envoy in Vienna, to Sunderland, 5 Jan. 1718, NA. SP. 80/35 fol. 225.

13 I would like to thank David Aldridge for letting me read his unpublished papers 'Czar Peter I and Admiral Sir John Norris 1715–1717' and 'George I's British Ministerial Crisis of 1716–17 Revisited'.

14 D. McKay, 'The Struggle for Control of George I's Northern Policy 1718–19', *Journal of Modern History* (1973).

15 Bolingbroke to Francis Atterbury, Bishop of Rochester, no date, BL. Stowe Mss. 242 fol. 212.

16 W. Coxe, *Memoirs of Sir Robert Walpole* (3 vols, London, 1798), II, 128.

17 Johann, Freiherr von Pentenriedter to Marquis Rialp, Secretary of Charles VI's Council of Spain, 26 Dec. 1717, HHStA. EK. 53.

18 Hugo Paterson to John, 11th Earl of Mar, 18 Nov. 1717, BL. Stowe Mss. 232 fol. 46.

19 George I to Daniel Erasmi von Huldeberg, Hanoverian envoy in Vienna, 12 June 1719, AE. CP. Br. 45 fol. 88.

20 Hanover, Cal. 24, Nr. 1987 fol. 62.

21 Stanhope to Pentenridter, 19 Aug. 1719, NA. SP. 43/2.

22 Whitworth to Tilson, 20 Jan. 1720, see also 24 Aug. 1721, NA. SP. 90/11, 15.

23 NA. SP. 90/11–12; Darmstadt F23 A 159/9. See also Whitworth to Bernstorff, 30 Sept., 10 Oct. 1719, New York, Public Library, Hardwicke papers vol. 46. J.M. Hartley, *Charles Whitworth. Diplomat in the Age of Peter the Great* (Aldershot, 2002), pp. 152–68.

24 K. Borgmann, *Die deutsche Religionsstreit der Jahre 1719–1720* (Berlin, 1937).

25 Whitworth to Tilson, 9, 13 Jan. 1720, 11 Nov., 27 Dec. 1721, Whitworth to Townshend, 18 Mar., 2, 11 Nov. 1721, NA. SP. 90/12–15.

26 St Saphorin to Schaub, 20 Nov. 1717, New York, Public Library, Hardwicke papers vol. 38.

27 Destouches to Dubois, 31 Jan., 9 Mar., Dubois to Destouches, 5 May, Dubois to Stanhope, 5 May 1719, AE. CP. Ang. 322 fols 154–60, 323 fols 35, 269, 276–7.

28 Destouches to Dubois, 9, 16 Mar., 23 Ap. 1719, AE. CP. Ang. 323 fols 36, 64, 257; Craggs to Dubois, 20 Jan. 1719, NA. SP. 300/3.

29 Hanover, Cal. 24 Nr. 1988 fols 7–8, 15.

30 Bonet to Frederick William I, 5, 23 May 1719, Berlin, Geheime Staatsarchiv, Preussische Kulturbesitz, Rep. XI vol. 41.

31 R. Hatton, *George I* (London, 1978), p. 243; Sunderland to Newcastle, 22 Oct. 1719, BL. Add. 32686 fol. 149.

32 For example, Mme de Schulenburg to Lord Chancellor Cowper, 25 Oct. 1717,

Hertford, Hertfordshire CRO, Panshanger Mss. D/EP F56 fol. 64; Chammorel to Dubois, 9 Mar. 1719, AE. CP. Ang. 323 fol. 30; Craggs to Schaub, 30 June 1719, Lord Mahon, *History of England from the Peace of Utrecht 1713–83* (3rd edn, London, 1853), II, lxxix–lxxx.

33 *A True Translation of Baron Bothmar's Letter to Monsieur Schutz* (London, 1717).

34 Craggs to Stanhope, 7 Aug. (os) 1719, NA. SP. 44/269A.

35 Le Coq, Saxon envoy, to Augustus II of Saxony-Poland, – May 1726, NLA. Mss. 1458/9/64.

36 von Schele to Görtz, 19 July, Görtz to Sunderland, asking for shares, 20 Aug. 1720, Darmstadt F23 151/30, 156/28; Couraud to Delafaye, 8 Oct. 1720, NA. SP. 43/3.

37 Couraud to Delafaye, 26 Aug. (os) 1720, NA. SP. 43/4.

38 R.R. Sedgwick (ed.), *The History of Parliament. The House of Commons 1715–1754* (2 vols, London, 1920), I, 438.

39 Mathy, French Consul in Gdansk, to Council of the Marine, 30 Dec. 1716, Duke of Huxelles to Council of the Marine, 2 Nov. 1717, Paris, Archives Nationales, Archives de la Marine, B^{1}17 fol. 51, B^{1}18 fol. 196; Court Karl Gyllenborg, Swedish envoy in London, to Georg von Görtz, Swedish minister, 29 Oct. 1716, NA. SP. 107/115 fol. 228; *Thursday's Journal*, 3 Sept. (os) 1719.

40 Frederick William I to Chambrier, 15 May 1723, AE. CP. Prusse 73 fol. 51.

41 Stair to Stanhope, 5 Feb. 1715, NAS. GD. 135/137 no. 41.

42 Anon. memo., no date but 1725–7, NLA. Mss. 1458/10/7/2.

4 Cold wars on the Continent, 1721–31

1 C.W. Ingrao, 'The Balance of Power: From Paradigm to Practice', in P. Krüger and P.W. Schroeder (eds), *'The Transformation of European Politics, 1763–1848': Episode or Model in Modern History?* (Münster, 2002), p. 81, quoting G. Mecenseffy, *Karl VI's spanische Bundnispolitik 1725–1729* (Innsbruck, 1934), p. 11.

2 Whitworth to George Tilson, Under Secretary in the Northern Department, 13 May 1721, NA. SP. 90/14.

3 The most important works, both brief in their coverage of the 1720s, are G.H. Jones, *Great Britain and the Tuscan Succession Question, 1710–1737* (New York, 1998) and J.M. Hartley, *Charles Whitworth. Diplomat in the Age of Peter the Great* (Aldershot, 2002).

4 K. Wilson, *The Sense of the People. Politics, Culture and Imperialism in England, 1715–1785* (Cambridge, 1995).

5 J.M. Black, *Kings, Nobles and Commoners. States and Societies in Early Modern Europe. A Revisionist History* (London, 2004), pp. 133–4.

6 For a defence of interventionism, R.M. Hatton, *War and Peace 1680–1720* (London, 1969), especially pp. 22, 26.

7 For earlier work, see G.C. Gibbs, 'Parliament and Foreign Policy in the Age of Stanhope and Walpole', *English Historical Review*, 77 (1962), pp. 18–37, and 'Newspapers, Parliament and Foreign Policy in the Age of Stanhope and Walpole', in *Mélanges offerts à G. Jacquemyns* (Brussels, 1968), pp. 293–315.

8 G. Syveton, *Une Cour et un Aventurier au XVIII siècle: le Baron de Ripperda* (Paris, 1896).

9 M.S. Anderson, 'Eighteenth-Century Theories of the Balance of Power', in Hatton and Anderson (eds), *Studies in Diplomatic History* (London, 1970), pp. 183–98.

10 James, Earl Stanhope, Secretary of State for the Southern Department 1714–16 and for the Northern Department 1716–17 and 1718–21.

11 5 February (os) 1721.
12 Townshend to Horatio Walpole, 27 Aug. 1725, BL. Add. 48981 fols 107–10; R. Geikie and I. Montgomery, *The Dutch Barrier 1705–1719* (Cambridge, 1930).
13 On the dispersal, A.H. Smith, G.M. Baker and R.W. Kenny, *The Papers of Nathaniel Bacon of Stiffky*, I (1979), xx–xxxvii. The records still in Raynham have been listed by the Norfolk CRO, Historical Manuscript Commission reference 86/14.
14 Walpole to 3rd Viscount Townshend, 14 Oct. 1754, reply 19 Oct. 1754, Bloomington, Indiana, Lilly Library, Department of Manuscripts, Walpole papers. All other Townshend references are to the 2nd Viscount.
15 Hatton, *George I* (2nd edn, London, 2001), pp. 216–42; R. Browning, 'The Duke of Newcastle and the Imperial Election Plan, 1749–1754', *Journal of British Studies*, 7 (1967), pp. 28–47; H.M. Scott, ' "The True Principles of the Revolution": The Duke of Newcastle and the Idea of the Old System', in Black (ed.), *Knights Errant and True Englishmen: British Foreign Policy, 1660–1800* (Edinburgh, 1989), pp. 55–91.
16 B. Williams, *Carteret and Newcastle* (Cambridge, 1943).
17 P.J. Kulisheck, 'The "Lost" Pelham Papers', *Archives*, 24 (1999), pp. 37–43.
18 Lord Tyrawly, envoy in Lisbon, to Admiral Sir Charles Wager, 10 May 1738, Washington, Library of Congress, Manuscript Division, Wager papers, reel 91.
19 Newcastle to William, Duke of Cumberland, 18 Mar. (os), John, 4th Earl of Sandwich to Cumberland, 7, 9, 17 Ap. 1748, RA. Cumberland Papers, 32/337, 33/272, 114, 112, 134, 295.
20 Memorandum of 17 May 1726 presented to Prince Eugene by 'Sir' John Graeme, Jacobite envoy in Vienna, HHStA. Staatskanzlei, England, Noten 2.
21 Hatton, *War and Peace 1680–1720* (London, 1969), esp. pp. 22, 26.
22 P.W. Schroeder, *The Transformation of European Politics 1763–1848* (Oxford, 1994), pp. 5–19.
23 Walpole to Townshend, 10 Sept. (os) 1725, BL. Add. 48981 fols 115–24.
24 Whitworth to Townshend, 6 May 1721, NA. SP. 90/14.
25 Walpole to Newcastle, 25 July (os) 1723, BL. Add. 32686 fol. 285; Walpole to Townshend, 23 July (os) 1723, NA. SP. 43/4 fols 116–17, 43/66.
26 Townshend to St Saphorin, 14 Jan. (os) 1726, NA. SP. 80/57.
27 Townshend to St Saphorin, 14 Dec. (os) 1722, NA. SP. 80/48.
28 On Austrian policy, H. Naumann, *Österreich, England und das Reich 1719–32* (Berlin, 1936); M. Braubach, *Prinz Eugen von Savoyen* (Vienna, 1963–65); A. Drodtloff, *Johann Christoph Pentenriedter* (PhD., Vienna, 1964). On Italy, G. Quazza, *Il Problema Italiano e l'Equilibrio Europeo 1720–1738* (Turin, 1965).
29 Sparre to Frederick I of Sweden, 16 Mar. 1720, Marburg, England 184.
30 Robethon to Dubois, 20 June 1721, AE. CP. Ang. 339 fol. 107.
31 Kent to Stanhope, 18 Aug. (os) 1719, NA. SP. 43/62; Craggs to Newcastle, 10 Aug. (os) 1719, BL. Add. 32686 fol. 137.
32 Stanhope to Dubois, 22 Aug. 1719, New York, Public Library, Hardwicke papers, vol. 54.
33 Newcastle to Abraham Stanyan, envoy in Constantinople, 24 Mar. (os) 1726, NA. SP. 97/25 fol. 258.
34 Marquis di Cortanza, Sardinian envoy in London, to Victor Amadeus II, 1 June 1722, AST. LM. Ing. 31. On relations later in the decade, R.A. Marini, *La Politica Sabauda alla Corte Inglese dopo il trattato d'Hannover 1725–1730 nella Relazione dell' ambasciatore piemontese a Londra* (Chambéry, 1918).
35 G. Symcox, 'Britain and Victor Amadeus II: Or, the Use and Abuse of Allies', in S.B. Baxter (ed.), *England's Rise to Greatness 1660–1763* (Berkeley, 1983).
36 Perceval to –, 14 Ap. (os) 1720, BL. Add. 47029 fol. 30.

37 For example, re Spain, John, 2nd Earl of Stair to Sir Luke Schaub, 19 May 1720, New York, Public Library, Hardwicke papers, vol. 54.

38 For discussion of the appropriateness of the term strategy in this period, J.B. Hattendorf, *England in the War of the Spanish Succession: A Study of the English View and Conduct of Grand Strategy* (New York, 1987).

39 Townshend to Newcastle, 24 Aug. 1725, NA. SP. 43/6 fol. 361.

40 Chauvelin, French foreign minister, to Chammorel, chargé d'affaires in London, 26 June, 7, 21 July 1729, AE. CP. Ang. supplement 8; Instructions to Chavigny, envoy to Hanover, 26 June, Chauvelin to Chavigny, 3, 24 July, 21 Aug. 1729, AE. CP. Br. 47.

41 St Saphorin to Townshend, 21 Feb. 1722, NA. SP. 80/46.

42 St Saphorin to Townshend, 25 Ap. 1722, NA. SP. 80/46; W. Mediger, *Moskaus Weg nach Europa* (Brunswick, 1952), and *Mecklenburg, Russland und England-Hannover 1706–21* (2 vols, Hildesheim, 1967).

43 William Stanhope, envoy in Spain, to Carteret, 3 May 1722, NA. SP. 94/91.

44 Dubois, French foreign minister, to Destouches, envoy in London, 21 Ap. 1722, AE. CP. Ang. supplement 7 fols 30, 32.

45 A. Baudrillart, *Philippe V et la cour de France* (5 vols, Paris, 1890–1901).

46 Dubois to Destouches, 30 July 1721, AE. CP. Ang. 339 fol. 162.

47 Duke of Bourbon to Dubois, 25 May, 1 June, 5 July 1722, AE. CP. Ang. 339 fols 289, 291, 308; L. Vignols, 'L'asiento française, 1701–1713, et anglais, 1713–1750, et le commerce franco-espagnol vers 1700 à 1730', *Revue d'histoire économique et sociale*, 17 (1929), pp. 403–26; G. Rambert, 'La France et la politique commerciale de l'Espagne au XVIIIe siècle', *Revue d'histoire moderne et contemporaine* (1959), pp. 269–83.

48 Destouches to Dubois, 20 Jan. 1721, AE. CP. Ang. 339, fol. 23; S. Conn, *Gibraltar in British Eighteenth Century Diplomacy* (New Haven, 1942).

49 M. Braubach, *Versailles und Wien von Ludwig XIV bis Kaunitz* (Bonn, 1952).

50 Horatio Walpole to St Saphorin, 27 May 1726, Hanover, Hannover 91, St Saphorin Nr. 3 fol. 7.

51 Carteret to Robert Walpole, 18 Oct. 1723, NA. SP. 43/5 fol. 152; J.F. Chance, *George I and the Great Northern War* (London, 1909).

52 Whitworth to Townshend, 12 Ap. 1721, NA. SP. 90/14.

53 Cortanza to Victor Amadeus II, 1 June 1722, AST. LM. Ing. 31.

54 Whitworth to Tilson, 7, 24 June, 1 July 1721, Whitworth to Townshend, 3, 27 May, 24 June, 2 Sept., 6 Dec. 1721, NA. SP. 90/14–15; Whitworth to Tilson, 1, 19 Sept. 1722, BL. Add. 37389 fols 153, 177.

55 Whitworth to Bothmer, 24 Feb. 1722, BL. Add. 37328 fol. 58; St Saphorin to Townshend, 11 Mar. 1722, NA. SP. 80/46.

56 Whitworth to Scott, 17 Mar. 1722, BL. Add. 37388 fol. 134.

57 Dubois to Destouches, 16 July 1721, AE. CP. Ang. 339 fols 121–2.

58 Tilson to Whitworth, 17 Sept. 1723, BL. Add. 32792 fol. 91.

59 Townshend to William Finch, envoy in The Hague, 7 June (os) 1726, NA. SP. 84/290 fol. 183; A.M. Wilson, *French Foreign Policy during the Administration of Cardinal Fleury, 1726–1743* (Cambridge, MA, 1936).

60 Horatio Walpole to Townshend, 14 Aug. 1725, BL. Add. 46856 fols 67, 70; Seysel d'Aix, Sardinian envoy in London, to Victor Amadeus II, 1, 5 May 1727, AST. LM. Ing. 35.

61 Horatio Walpole to Newcastle, 12 Nov., Newcastle to Horatio Walpole, 6 Nov. (os), Newcastle to Townshend, 8 Nov. (os) 1723, BL. Add. 32686 fols 381–2, 404, 406.

62 See e.g. Anon [Robert Walpole], *The Thoughts of a Member of the Lower House, in relation to a Project for Restraining and Limiting the Power of the Crown in the future Creation of Peers* (2nd edn, London, 1719), pp. 6–7.

63 Horatio Walpole to Newcastle, 20 Nov. 1723, BL. Add. 32686 fol. 417.
64 Horatio Walpole to Robert Walpole, 29 Jan. 1724, BL. Add. 63749.
65 Stanyan to Schaub, 3 May (os) 1721, New York, Public Library, Hardwicke papers, vol. 67; E. Cruickshanks, 'Charles Spencer, Third Earl of Sunderland, and Jacobitism', *English Historical Review*, 113 (1998), pp. 65–76.
66 Newcastle to Robert Walpole, 2 Nov. (os) 1723, BL. Add. 32686 fol. 387.
67 Sunderland to Dubois, 11 Feb. (os) 1721, AE. CP. Ang. 339 fol. 31.
68 Dubois to Chammorel, 7 Mar. 1721, AE. CP. Ang. 339 fol. 45.
69 Carteret to Schaub, 4 May (os) 1722, New York, Public Library, Hardwicke papers, vol. 67.
70 Schaub to Carteret, – June 1722, New York, Public Library, Hardwicke papers, vol. 67.
71 Newcastle to Robert Walpole, 2 Nov. (os) 1723, BL. Add. 32686.
72 J. Dureng, *Le Duc de Bourbon et l'Angleterre 1723–1726* (Paris, 1911).
73 E.g. George Woodward to Townshend, 16 Ap. 1727, NA. SP. 80/61; Horatio Walpole to Townshend, 17 June, Newcastle to Horatio Walpole, 30 Nov. (os) 1727, BL. Add. 48982 fol. 17, 32753 fol. 178; Waldegrave journal 8 Nov. 1727, Waldegrave to Townshend, 24 July 1728, Chewton.
74 Carteret to Newcastle, 28 Sept. (os) 1721, BL. Add. 32686 fols 206–7. For the Court context of policy-making, J. Duindam, *Vienna and Versailles. The Courts of Europe's Dynastic Rivals, 1550–1780* (Cambridge, 2003).
75 James 'III and VIII' to Charles Caesar MP, 21 Ap. 1721, RA. Stuart Papers 53/46.
76 Tilson to Delafaye, 20 Aug. 1723, NA. SP. 43/4 fol. 252.
77 Dubois to Destouches, 27 Jan. 1721, AE. CP. Ang. supplement 7 fol. 8.
78 Cruickshanks, 'Lord North, Christopher Layer and the Atterbury Plot: 1720–23', in Cruickshanks and Black (eds), *The Jacobite Challenge* (Edinburgh, 1988), p. 99.
79 Dureng, *Bourbon et l'Angleterre*, p. 33.
80 St Saphorin to Townshend, 3, 30 Jan. 1723, NA. SP. 80/49.
81 Whitworth to Tilson, 1 Sept. 1722, BL. Add. 37389 fol. 153.
82 Destouches to Dubois, 6 Ap. 1722, AE. CP. Ang. 341 fols 14–15.
83 Chavigny, envoy with George I in Hanover and then London, to Morville, French foreign minister, 15, 21 Oct., 17 Nov. 1723, 21 Feb. 1724, AE. CP. Ang. 346 fols 152–53, 170, 183, 266, 347 fol. 82.
84 Stanhope to the Austrian diplomat, Johann Christoph, Freiherr von Pentenriedter, 19 Aug. 1719, NA. SP. 43/2.
85 Horatio Walpole to Townshend, 18 May 1722, NA. SP. 84/278 fol. 122.
86 Horatio Walpole to Schaub, 3, 15 June 1722, New York, Public Library, Hardwicke Collection, vol. 67.
87 M. Hughes, *Law and Politics in Eighteenth-Century Germany: the Imperial Aulic Council in the Reign of Charles VI* (Woodbridge, 1988).
88 Tilson to Charles Delafaye, Under Secretary in the Southern Department, 9 Oct. 1723, NA. SP. 43/5 fol. 126.
89 Townshend to Robert Walpole, 18 Oct. 1723, NA. SP. 43/5 fol. 135.
90 St Saphorin to Townshend, 21 Feb., 6 Nov., 9 Dec. 1722, NA. SP. 80/47.
91 Bourbon to Dubois, 17 May 1722, AE. CP. Ang. 339 fol. 281.
92 Townshend to William Finch, 18 Mar. (os) 1726, NA. SP. 84/289 fol. 194.
93 Contrast Townshend to Robert Walpole of 18 Oct. 1723, NA. SP. 43/5 fol. 135, with Horatio Walpole to Newcastle, 20 Nov. 1723, BL. Add. 32686 fols 418–19.
94 Craggs to Newcastle, 10 Aug. (os) 1719, BL. Add. 32686 fol. 138.
95 Newcastle to William Stanhope, 17 Mar. (os) 1726, NA. SP. 94/97 fols 46–47.
96 Carteret to Schaub, 4, 12 May (os), 4 June (os) 1722, New York, Public Library, Hardwicke papers, vol. 67. On the burning of letters, see also Destouches to Dubois, 1 June 1722, AE. CP. Ang. 341 fol. 108.

97 Friedrich Thöm, Wolfenbüttel diplomat, report 7 May 1726, Wolfenbüttel, Staatsarchiv, 1 Alt 6 Nr. 86 fol. 143; R. Grieser (ed.), *Die Memoiren des Kammerherrn Friedrich Ernst von Fabrice* (Hildesheim, 1956); W. Coxe (ed.), *Memoirs of the Life and Administration of Sir Robert Walpole* (3 vols, London, 1798) II, 500–1; Chance, *The Alliance of Hanover* (1923), p. 412; Brigadier Charles Du Bourgay, envoy in Berlin, to Tilson, 6 Dec., Du Bourgay to Townshend, 25 Dec. 1725, NA. SP. 90/19; Baron Johann Christoph von Schleinitz, Wolfenbüttel minister, to Morville, 12 Nov. 1726, AE. CP. Br. 45 fols 210–12; Karl Joseph von Palm, Austrian envoy in London, to Charles VI, 23 Ap. 1726, W. Coxe, *Memoirs of the Life and Administration of Sir Robert Walpole, Earl of Orford* (3 vols, 1798) II, 498; Palm to Charles VI, 17 Dec., Giuseppe Riva, Modenese envoy in London, to Duke of Modena, 27 Dec. 1726, CUL, C(H) corresp., 1382, 1389. For tensions between British and Hanoverian diplomacy, Horatio Walpole to Tilson, 28 May 1727, BL. Add. 49891 fol. 234, Black, *British Diplomats and Diplomacy 1688–1800* (Exeter, 2001), pp. 26–8; for concern about the Hanoverian agent in Paris, Townshend to Robert Walpole, 24 Sept. 1723, BL. Add. 48981 fol. 13, and for better relations with another, Jean Louis Saladin, Hanoverian agent in Paris, to Johann Philipp von Hattorf, Hanoverian minister in London, 13 July 1733, Hanover, Cal. 24 Nr. 2002 fol. 11.
98 See, for example, Baron Dehn, Wolfenbüttel envoy in Vienna, to Count Konrad Dehn, Wolfenbüttel envoy to London, 20 Aug. 1727, PRO. SP. 84/294; Count Dehn to Ferdinand Albrecht, 2 Sept. 1727, Wolfenbüttel, Staatsarchiv 1 Alt 22, Nr. 534; Magnan, French envoy in Russia, to Chauvelin, 15 Nov. 1727, *Sbornik Imperatorskago Russkago Istoricheskago Obsshchestva* (148 vols, St Petersburg, 1867–1916), LXXV, 126.
99 E.g. Schleinitz to Morville, 17 Jan., 11, 18 Feb., 18 Mar., 18 Ap., Morville to Schleinitz, 6 Feb., 20 Mar. 1727, Schleinitz to Chauvelin, 6 Aug. 1728, AE. CP. Br. 46 fol. 8–12, 15, 42, 60–1, 80–1, 93, 21, 55–6, Br. supplement 2 fol. 525.
100 Schleinitz to Morville, 18 Ap. 1727, AE. CP. Br. 46 fol. 93.
101 Schleinitz to Morville, 11 Feb., 1 Ap. 1727, AE. CP. Br. 46 fols 26–7, 81.
102 Schleinitz to Morville, 10, 20 Dec. 1726, Schleinitz to Chauvelin, 17 June 1730, AE. CP. Br. 45 fols 231, 234, 48 fol. 61.
103 Schleinitz to Morville, 18 Ap., 30 May, 10 June, 11 July 1727, AE. CP. Br. 46 fols 93–4, 123–5, 136–7, 165.
104 J.M. Black, 'Fresh Light on the Fall of Townshend', *Historical Journal*, 29 (1986), pp. 56–7, and 'Additional Light on the Fall of Townshend', *Yale University Library Gazette*, 63 (1988–9), pp. 132–3.
105 Thöm report, 22 Jan. 1726, Wolfenbüttel, Staatsarchiv, 1 Alt 6 Nr. 86 fol. 46.
106 Du Bourgay to Townshend, 24 May 1725, NA. SP. 90/19.
107 Tilson to Delafaye, 1 Oct. 1723, NA. SP. 43/5 fol. 94. cf. Cyril Wich, envoy in Hamburg, to Tilson, 4 Feb. 1724, NA. SP. 82/41 fol. 15.
108 James Johnston to Friedrich Wilhelm von Görtz, 2 Feb. (os) 1724, Darmstadt F140/9; St John Brodrick MP to his father Alan, Viscount Midleton, Lord Chancellor of Ireland, 2 Mar. (os) 1724, Guildford, Surrey CRO., Brodrick papers 1248/5 fol. 381; Chavigny to Morville, 23 Mar. 1724, AE. CP. Ang. 347 fol. 133.
109 A.M. Starkey, 'La Diplomatie britannique au Congrès de Cambrai, 1722–1725', *Revue d'histoire diplomatique*, 2 (1971), pp. 98–115; Hartley, *Whitworth*, pp. 180–97.
110 G.H. Jones, *Britain and the Tuscan Succession Question*, p. 39.
111 C. Höfler, *Der Congress von Soissons* (2 vols, Vienna, 1871–6); Black, *The Collapse of the Anglo-French Alliance 1727–1731* (Gloucester, 1987).

112 E.g. John, Viscount Molesworth, envoy in Turin, to James Craggs, Secretary of State for the Southern Department, 25 Jan. 1721, Molesworth to Carteret, 28 Mar., 13 June 1722, NA. SP. 92/30–31.

113 Destouches to Dubois, 14 May 1722, 4 Jan. 1723, AE. CP. Ang. 341 fols 74–75, 344 fol. 12.

114 Chammorel, French chargé d'affaires, to Chauvelin, 9 Mar. 1730, AE. CP. Ang. 369 fol. 297.

115 For an acute discussion of the situation in the 1740s, B. Harris, *A Patriot Press: National Politics and the London Press in the 1740s* (Oxford, 1993).

116 E.g. D. Coombs, *The Conduct of the Dutch. British Opinion and the Dutch Alliance during the War of the Spanish Succession* (The Hague, 1958).

117 D. Armitage, *The Ideological Origins of the British Empire* (Cambridge, 2000), p. 182; B. Harris, *Politics and the Nation. Britain in the Mid-Eighteenth Century* (Oxford, 2002).

118 Benjamin Keene, envoy in Spain, to Newcastle, 19 Ap. 1728, BL. Add. 32755.

119 Craggs to Stanhope, 14 Aug. (os), 23 Oct. (os) 1719, NA. SP. 43/58, 44/269A; Craggs to Stair, 22 Oct. (os) 1719, NAS. GD. 135/141/19A; Destouches to Dubois, 23 Feb. 1722, AE. CP. Ang. 340 fols 960–1; A. Bakshian, ' "A Hangdog Whom I dearly Love": The Third Duke of Peterborough', *History Today*, 31 (1981), pp. 14–19.

120 Hoadly, *Enquiry*, p. 1.

121 Hoadly, *Enquiry*, p. 5–6.

122 Hoadly, *A Defence of the Enquiry into the Reasons of Great Britain* (London, 1729), p. 10.

123 Anon., *The Treaty of Seville, and the Measures that have been taken for the Four Last Years, Impartially Considered* (London, 1730), pp. 6–7.

124 John, Viscount Perceval to Philip Perceval, 19 Jan. (os) 1727, BL. Add. 47032 fol. 1.

125 Cowper, notes for parliamentary debate, 11 Jan. (os) 1722, Hertfordshire, Panshanger papers D/EP F182 fols 96–104.

126 Black, 'An "ignoramus" in European Affairs?', *British Journal for 18th-Century Studies*, 6 (1983), pp. 55–65.

127 The Infanta, who had been intended as a bride for Louis XV.

128 A reference to Elizabeth Farnese, Queen of Spain.

129 Duke of Bourbon.

130 Fleury, Bishop of Fréjus.

131 Perceval to Edward Southwell, 12 Jan. 1726, BL. Add. 47031 fols 73–4.

132 William Stanhope to Schaub, 16 Mar., Horatio Walpole to Townshend, 5 June 1722, NA. SP. 94/91, 84/278 fol. 44.

133 E.g. re the likelihood of war, Brinsley Skinner, Consul in Leghorn (Livorno) to Newcastle, 2 Mar. 1726, BL. Add. 41504 fol. 26, and re French factional moves, David, 6th Viscount Stormont, envoy in Paris, to William, 4th Earl of Rochford, Secretary of State for Southern Department, 16 Feb. 1774, NA. SP. 78/291 fol. 93.

134 Henry Davenant, envoy in Genoa, to Townshend, 25 Mar. 1721, NA. SP. 79/14; Destouches to Dubois, 4 Jan. 1723, AE. CP. Ang. 344 fol. 11.

135 Tilson to Whitworth, 27 Mar. (os), 13 Ap. (os) 1722, BL. Add. 37388 fols 216, 300.

136 Cortanza to Victor Amadeus II, 20 Ap. 1722, AST. LM. Ing. 31.

137 Paris, Bibliothèque Victor Cousin, Fonds de Richelieu 30 fol. 224.

138 Palm to Count Königsegg, Austrian envoy in Spain, 7 Mar. 1726, CUL., C(H) corresp., no. 1514.

139 Instructions for Broglie, 9 Mar. 1726, AE. CP. Ang. 354 fol. 170.

140 Chavigny to Lafitau, 2 Jan. 1720, J.G. Gossel (ed.), 'Correspondance de

Lafitau, évêque de Sisteron, et du Chavigny, ambassadeur à Gênes 1719–20', *Documents d'Histoire*, 1 (1910), p. 354.
141 Re Austria, St Saphorin to Townshend, 25 Ap. 1722, NA. SP. 80/46.
142 Philip Perceval to John, Viscount Perceval, 21 Feb. (os) 1727, BL. Add. 47032 fol. 7.
143 *A Letter from a Gentleman at Edinburgh* (London, 1719), p. 7.
144 The Tory ministry that negotiated the Peace of Utrecht.

5 Opposition to interventionism, 1731–40

1 J.M. Black, 'British Neutrality in the War of the Polish Succession, 1733–1735', *International History Review*, 8 (1986), pp. 345–66.
2 P. Woodfine, *Britannia's Glories. The Walpole Ministry and the 1739 War with Spain* (Woodbridge, 1998).
3 Though see D. Reading, *The Anglo-Russian Commercial Treaty of 1734* (New Haven, CT, 1938).
4 P. Vaucher, *Robert Walpole et la politique de Fleury* (Paris, 1924).
5 G. Quazza, 'I negoziati austro-anglo-sardi del 1732–33', *Bolletino Storico Bibliografico Subalpino*, 46 (1948), pp. 73–92, 47 (1949), pp. 45–74.
6 Pelham to Waldegrave, 23 Mar. (os) 1731, Chewton; Charles VI to Stephen Kinsky Fonseca and Königsegg, 27 Aug. 1730, C. Höfler, *Der Congress von Soissons* (2 vols, Vienna, 1871–6), II, 261; Black, *The Collapse of the Anglo-French Alliance 1727–1731* (Gloucester, 1987), pp. 194–6.
7 Robinson to Newcastle, 30 Sept., Newcastle to Robinson, 19 Ap. (os) 1732, BL. Add. 32778, 32776 fols 442–3.
8 Harrington to Robinson, 20 Nov. (os) 1733, NA. SP. 80/101.
9 Horatio to Robert Walpole, 10 July 1734, CUL. C(H) corresp. 2259.
10 Wych to Tilson, 20 Aug. 1735, NA. SP. 82/56.
11 Horatio Walpole journal, 20, 22 Ap. 1734, BL. Add. 9140 fols 127, 138.
12 Wilson, *German Armies*, p. 229.
13 General Ernst Diemar, Hesse-Cassel envoy in London, to the Austrian minister, Prince Eugene, 20 Ap. 1734, HHStA. GK. 85a; Diemar to Frederick I of Sweden, 23 Ap. 1734, Marburg, England 203; Edward Weston, Under Secretary, to Robinson, 16 Ap. 1734, BL. Add. 23790 fol. 401; De Löss, Saxon envoy in London, to Augustus III of Saxony-Poland, 21 May 1734, Dresden, 638 IIa fol. 458.
14 R.R. Sedgwick (ed.), *Some Materials towards Memoirs of the Reign of King George II* (3 vols, London, 1931).
15 Degenfeld, Prussian envoy in London, to Grumbkow, 13 Jan. 1733, NA. SP. 107/8.
16 Degenfeld to Grumbkow, 3 Mar., Frederick William I to Degenfeld, 3 Mar., Hendrik Hop, Dutch envoy in London, to Fagel, Dutch minister, 3 Mar. 1733, NA. SP. 107/10.
17 H. Gerig, *Die Memoiren des Lord Hervey als historische Quelle* (Freiburg, 1936); Diemar to Frederick I of Sweden, 27 Nov. 1733, 23 Ap. 1734, Marburg, England 203; De Löss to Augustus III, 30 Oct., 17 Nov. 1733, Dresden, 638, I; Diemar to Eugene, 20 Ap. 1734, HHStA. GK. 85(a); Count Ulfeld, Austrian envoy at The Hague, to Count Philip Kinsky, envoy at London, 30 Ap. 1734, Vienna, Palais Kinsky, papers of Count Philip Kinsky, Kart. 2d.
18 Eugene to Philip Kinsky, 29 June 1734, CUL. C(H) corresp. 2228.
19 Re George's declaration at Imperial Diet, Diemar to Frederick I of Sweden, 15 Jan. 1734, Marburg, 4f England 203.
20 Robinson to Harrington, 28 Oct. 1733, NA. SP. 80/100.
21 Diemar to Frederick I of Sweden, 23 Ap., 9 July, Frederick to Diemar, 22 June

1734, Marburg, 4f England 203. See also 4f Kurbraunschweig 96; Chavigny to Chauvelin, 7 May 1734, AE. CP. Ang. 384 fol. 19.

22 Horatio Walpole to Benjamin Keene, envoy in Spain, 29 Aug. 1737, BL. Add. 32795 fol. 243.

23 Fleury to Louis-Dominique, Count of Cambis, French envoy in London, 11 Dec. 1737, NA. SP. 107/21.

24 Keene to Horatio Walpole, 26 Nov. 1736, NA. SP. 94/126.

25 Waldegrave to Robert Walpole, 21 Nov. 1736, Chewton.

26 On French policy, Black, 'French Foreign Policy in the Age of Fleury Reassessed', *English Historical Review*, 103 (1988), pp. 359–84.

27 John, 2nd Earl of Stair to Sarah, Duchess of Marlborough, no date, BL. Add. 61467 fols 31–33.

28 B. Harris, *A Patriot Press: National Politics and the London Press in the 1740s* (Oxford, 1993).

29 Horatio Walpole to Harrington, 10 Jan. 1736, NA. SP. 84/354 fol. 75.

30 Horatio Walpole to Keene, 12 Jan. 1736, NA. SP. 84/354 fols 129, 127.

31 Thomas Pelham MP to Waldegrave, 19 Jan. (os) 1736, Chewton; *Hyp-Doctor*, 20 Jan. (os) 1736.

32 Reporting letters from London, Gansinot, Wittelsbach envoy in The Hague, to Meerman, Wittelsbach envoy in Vienna, 31 Jan. 1736, Munich, Bayr. Gesandtschaft, Wien 252.

33 Chavigny to Chauvelin, 12 Jan. 1736, AE. CP. Ang. 393 fol. 15.

34 10, 25 Jan., 7 Feb. 1736, Paris, Bibliothèque de l'Arsenal, Archives de la Bastille, Gazetins secrets de la Police, 10165 fols 16, 42, 63.

35 Harrington to Robinson, 3 Feb. 1736, NA. SP. 80/120.

36 Waldegrave to Robert Walpole, 21 Nov. 1736, Chewton.

37 Waldegrave to Newcastle, 24 July 1737, BL. Add. 32795 fol. 168.

38 For additional press sensitivity over Corsica, *York Courant*, 10 Jan. (os) 1739.

39 For reports of British sensitivity about support for Jacobitism, Newcastle to Keene, 11 July 1737, BL. Add. 32795 fols 157–8; Wasner, Austrian envoy in Paris, to –, 8 July 1737, HHStA. Frankreich, Varia 13.

40 Daniel to Waldegrave, 8 Aug. 1736, Chewton.

41 Tilson to Robinson, 12 Aug. 1736, BL. Add. 23798 fol. 439.

42 Tilson to Robinson, 30 Aug. 1736, BL. Add. 23798 fol. 541.

43 Amelot to St Severin, 20 Mar. 1738, Iden Green, Kent, papers of Edward Weston, Under Secretary in the Southern Department, held by his descendant John Weston-Underwood.

44 Charles Emmanuel III to Giuseppe Ossorio, Sardinian envoy in London, 17 Jan. 1739, NA. SP. 107/23.

45 Parliamentary collections of Philip Yorke, BL. Add. 35875 fol. 436.

46 Robinson to Horatio Walpole, 8 Aug. 1736, NA. SP. 80/122.

47 Horatio Walpole to Cyril Wych, envoy in Hamburg, 7 Aug. 1736, NA. SP. 82/57 fol. 159.

48 Horatio Walpole to Guy Dickens, envoy in Prussia, 9 Sept. 1736, NA. SP. 90/41.

49 Dickens to Horatio Walpole, 18 Sept. 1736, NA. SP. 90/41.

50 Trevor to Weston, 6 Jan. 1739, NA. SP. 84/378 fol. 27.

51 Harrington to Trevor, 12 Jan. (os) 1739, NA. SP. 84/378 fols 61–2.

52 Trevor to Walter Titley, envoy in Copenhagen, 19 Feb. (os) 1737, BL. Eg. Mss. 2684 fol. 57.

53 J.M.J. Rogister, 'New Light on the Fall of Chauvelin', *English Historical Review*, 83 (1968), pp. 314–30, and 'A Minister's Fall and its Implications: The Case of Chauvelin, 1737–46', in D.J. Mossop, G.E. Rodmell and D.B. Wilson (eds), *Studies in the French Eighteenth Century presented to John Lough* (Durham, 1978), pp. 200–17.

54　Weston to Titley, 25 Feb. (os) 1737, BL. Eg. Mss. 2684 fol. 72.

55　Horatio Walpole to Trevor, 4 Mar. (os) 1737, Aylesbury, Trevor, vol. 7.

56　Robert Walpole to Waldegrave, 23 Mar. (os) 1737, Chewton.

57　Robert Walpole to Waldegrave, 7 Mar. (os) 1737, Chewton.

58　Waldegrave to Robert Walpole, 13 Ap. 1737, Chewton.

59　Horatio Walpole, 'State of the Negotiations', 8 Nov. 1737, BL. Add. 9131 fol. 163.

60　War of the Polish Succession.

61　Trevor to Harrington, 16 Jan. 1739, NA. SP. 84/378 fols 52–3.

62　Waldegrave to Newcastle, 24 May 1737, BL. Add. 32795 fols 40–4.

63　Keene to Newcastle, 1 July 1737, BL. Add. 32795 fol. 127.

64　Ossorio, reporting conversation with Newcastle, to Charles Emmanuel III, 5 Mar. 1736, AST. LM. Ing. 43; Newcastle to Waldegrave, 5 Jan. (os) 1738, BL. Add. 32800 fols 24–35.

65　Fawkener to Newcastle, 20 Jan. 1739, significantly a copy in the papers of Robert Walpole, CUL. C(H). corresp. no. 2831.

66　Chavanne, Sardinian envoy in The Hague, to Charles Emmanuel III, 5 Feb. 1739, AST. LM. Olanda 36. On the role of the King, Black, ' "George II and All That Stuff". On the Value of the Neglected', 36 *Albion* (winter 2004).

67　Trevor to Harrington, 6 Jan. 1739, NA. SP. 84/378 fol. 1.

68　Trevor to Weston, 14 June 1737, Farmington, Connecticut, Lewis Walpole Library, Weston papers, vol. 11.

69　Dickens to Harrington, 21 June, 8 Feb., 15 Ap. 1738, NA. SP. 90/44.

70　Cambis to Amelot, 27 Mar. 1738, AE. CP. Ang. 397 fols 252–4.

71　Demeradt, Austrian envoy at Berlin, to Prince Liechtenstein, Austrian envoy in Paris, 11 Feb. 1738, HHStA. Frankreich, Varia 13.

72　Cambis to Amelot, 27 Mar. 1738, AE. CP. Ang. 397 fols 252–3.

73　Edward Finch, envoy in St Petersburg, to Walter Titley, envoy in Copenhagen, 23 Feb. 1739, BL. Eg. 2685 fol. 244; Harrington to Trevor, 5 Jan. (os), Trevor to Harrington, 3 Feb. 1739, NA. SP. 84/378 fols 40, 117; *York Courant*, 6 Feb. (os) 1739.

74　Horatio Walpole to Trevor, 26 Aug. 1736, Aylesbury, Trevor 4, no. 70. See also Horatio to Robert Walpole, 18 June 1736, *Christie's Catalogue*, 29 May 1986, p. 42, item 114.

75　Horatio Walpole to Trevor, 19 Aug., 2 Sept. 1736, Aylesbury, Trevor 4, nos. 52, 84.

76　Sarah Marlborough to Stair, 19 Mar. (os) 1738, New Haven, Connecticut, Beinecke Library, Osborn Shelves, Stair Letters, no. 22.

77　Bussy to Amelot, 26 July 1737, AE. CP. Ang. 395 fol. 53.

78　Robinson to Harrington, 30 May 1736, NA. SP. 80/121.

79　Robert Walpole to Waldegrave, 29 Oct. (os) 1736, Chewton.

80　Robert Walpole to Waldegrave, – May (os) 1737, Chewton.

81　Newcastle to Horatio Walpole, 22 July (os) 1737, NA. SP. 36/41 fol. 221.

82　Anon. French memorandum, 5 July 1736, AE. MD. Ang. 6 fols 102–3; Wasner, Austrian envoy, report of 30 Nov. 1736, HHStA. EK. 71.

83　*Reading Mercury*, 21 Feb. (os) 1737; *Gazette d'Utrecht*, 7 Mar. 1737.

84　Tilson to Titley, 1 Nov. (os) 1737, BL. Eg. 2685 fol. 70.

85　Bussy to Amelot, 26 July 1737, AE. CP. Ang. 395 fol. 53.

86　French memorandum, 5 July 1736, AE. MD. Ang. 6 fol. 103; Horatio Walpole to Trevor, 22 Mar. (os) 1737, Aylesbury, Trevor 7.

87　Horatio Walpole to Trevor, 19 Aug. 1736, Aylesbury, Trevor 4, no. 52.

88　Newcastle to Waldegrave, 5 Jan. (os) 1738, BL. Add. 32800 fol. 26; Stair to Alexander, 2nd Earl of Marchmont, 1 Jan. (os) 1738, *A Selection from the Papers of the Earls of Marchmont* (3 vols, London, 1831), II, 94. On this connection,

Stair to Earl of Nottingham, 27 June (os) 1741, Leicester, Leicestershire CRO. Finch Mss. DG/7/4952, and Stair to Robinson, 30 May (os) 1742, BL. Add. 23810 fol. 492.

89 H.M. Scott, ' "The True Principles of the Revolution": The Duke of Newcastle and the Idea of the Old System', in Black (ed.), *Knights Errant and True Englishmen. British Foreign Policy 1600–1800* (Edinburgh, 1989), pp. 55–91; Black, 'The British Attempt to Preserve the Peace in Europe 1748–1755', in H. Duchhardt (ed.), *Zwischenstaatliche Friedenswahrung in Mittelalter und Früher Neuzeit* (Cologne, 1991), pp. 227–43.

6 The crisis of public support, 1740–8

1 Cobbett, vol. 13, cols. 578–9.
2 Chavigny to Schulin, 1 Mar. 1739, Weston Underwood.
3 Newcastle to Dickens, 3 June (os) 1740, NA. SP. 36151 fol. 10; Newcastle to Harrington, 24 June (os), Harrington to Newcastle, 29 June 1740, NA. SP. 43/90; Pelham to Newcastle, 27 June (os) 1740, BL. Add. 32693 fol. 417; F. Frensdorff (ed.), 'G.A. von Münchhausen's Berichte über seine Mission nach Berlin im Juni 1740', *Abhandlungen der königlichen Gesellschaft der Wissenschaften 3u Göttingen*, new series, 8 (1904), pp. 3–87.
4 Harrington to Newcastle, 13 July 1740, BL. Add. 32693 fol. 436.
5 Finch to Harrington, 12 Nov. 1740, NA. SP. 91/26.
6 Dann, *Hannover und England*, p. 26.
7 J.B. Owen, 'George II Reconsidered', in A. Whiteman *et al.* (eds), *Statesmen, Scholars and Merchants* (Oxford, 1973), p. 123.
8 Newcastle to Harrington, 27, 29 July (os), 12 Aug. (os), Harrington to Newcastle, 27 July, 21 Aug., 11 Sept. 1740, P.C. Yorke (ed.), *The Life and Correspondence of Philip Yorke, Earl of Hardwicke* (3 vols, Cambridge, 1913), I, 243, NA. SP. 43/91–3.
9 Dickens to Harrington, 17 Aug. 1740, NA. SP. 90/48.
10 Newcastle to Harrington, 11 Sept. (os), – Sept. (os) 1740, NA. SP. 43/94, 36/52 fol. 145.
11 Anon., *A Letter from Hanover, Showing the True Cause of the Present Broils of Germany and Confusions of Europe* (London, 1744).
12 Harrington to Dickens, 31 Oct. (os) 1740, NA. SP. 90/48.
13 Walpole to Trevor, 19 Dec. (os) 1740, Aylesbury, Trevor 24.
14 W. Mediger, 'Great Britain, Hanover and the Rise of Prussia', in R. Hatton and M.S. Anderson (eds), *Studies in Diplomatic History* (London, 1970), p. 203.
15 Harrington to Trevor, 26 Dec. (os) 1740, NA. SP. 84/388.
16 Thomas Carew MP to Philip Sydenham, 22 Ap. (os) 1742, Taunton, Somerset CRO, Trollop-Bellew papers, DD/TB, box 16, OB 18.
17 Harrington to Newcastle, 2 Aug. 1741, NA. SP. 43/101.
18 Ex inf. Hamish Scott.
19 AE. CP. Br. 49 fols 99–100, 144–6, 149–50, 161–4, MD. Br. 9 fols 164–250.
20 *Champion*, 27 Oct. (os) 1741.
21 W. Mediger, *Moskaus Weg nach Europa* (Brunswick, 1952), pp. 386–8; Blondel, French envoy at the Imperial election, to Bussy, 3 Jan., Wasenberg, Swedish envoy in London, to Gyllenborg, Swedish Chancery President, 2 Feb. 1742, NA. SP. 107/52.
22 Hardenberg to George II, 17 Ap., 7 May 1742, Hanover, Cal. 24 Nr. 2006 fols 51, 58; Bussy to Amelot, 13 Aug. 1742, NA. SP. 107/54.
23 R. Harris, *A Patriot Press: National Politics and the London Press in the 1740s* (Oxford, 1993).
24 G.C. Gibbs, 'English Attitudes towards Hanover and the Hanoverian Succession

in the First Half of the Eighteenth Century', in A.M. Birke and K. Kluxen (eds), *England und Hannover* (Munich, 1986), pp. 33–5.

25 Cobbett, vol. 13, col. 562.

26 Anon., *A Defence of the People: or Full Confutation of the Pretended Facts, Advanced in a late Huge, Angry Pamphlet; called Faction Detected* (London, 1744).

27 Earl of Westmorland, 31 Jan. (os) 1744, Cobbett, vol. 13, col. 566.

28 *Universal Spectator*, 10 Nov. (os) 1744.

29 Anon., *The Mysterious Congress. A Letter from Aix la Chappel, Detecting the late secret negotiations there; Accounting for the extraordinary slowness of the operations of the campaign since the action at Dettingen; and, particularly, for the resignation of the Earl of Stair* (London, 1743), p. 24. See also Anon., *An Important Secret Come to Light. Or, the States Generals' reasons for refusing to guaranty the Electorate of Hanover* (London, 1743).

30 R. Pares, 'American versus Continental Warfare, 1739–1763', *English Historical Review*, 51 (1936), pp. 429–65.

31 *Old England*, 20 Oct. (os) 1744.

32 F.J. McLynn, *France and the Jacobite Rising of 1745* (Edinburgh, 1981).

33 Steinberg to Hyndford, 19 July 1746, Hanover, Cal. Br. 24 Nr. 6618.

34 Rodger, 'Continental Commitment', p. 55. For a similar argument, R. Harding, *Amphibious Warfare in the Eighteenth Century. The British Expedition to the West Indies, 1740–1742* (Woodbridge, 1991), pp. 185–97.

35 Northampton, Northamptonshire L (C) 1734.

36 Harding, *Amphibious Warfare*, pp. 190, 193. I have benefited greatly from discussing this point with Richard Harding.

37 M. Mimler, *Der Einfluss kolonialer Interessen in Nordamerika auf die Strategie und Diplomatie Grossbritanniens während des Österreichischen Erbfolgekrieges 1744–1748. Ein Beitrag zur Identitätsbestimmung des britischen Empire um die Mitte des 18 Jahrhunderts* (Hildesheim, 1983).

38 Henry Legge to Newcastle, 4 Sept. 1758, BL. Add. 32883 fol. 276.

39 Anon., *The Conduct of His Grace The D-ke of Ar-le* (London, 1740), p. 38.

40 AE. CP. Prusse 105 fol. 237; Bussy to Amelot, 17 May 1741, AE. CP. Ang. 412 fol. 52.

41 Mocked by Hervey in *The Patriots are Come* (London, 1742), verse 23.

42 *Universal Spectator*, 26 Mar. (os), 23 July (os), 13 Aug. (os) 1743.

43 John Tucker MP to Richard Tucker, Bod. MS. Don. C. 106 fol. 198.

44 Harrington to Chesterfield, 25 Jan. (os) 1745, NA. SP. 84/408 fol. 87.

45 Trevor to Robinson, 13 Nov. 1745, BL. Add. 23821, fol. 227.

46 Newcastle to Harrington, 21 May (os), 14, 21 June (os), 9 Aug. (os) 1745, NA. SP. 43/37; Trevor to Robinson, 26 Mar. 1746, BL. Add. 23822 fol. 245.

47 Henry to Stephen Fox, 25 Sept. (os) 1745, BL. Add. 51417 fol. 141; *True Patriot*, 27 May (os) 1746.

48 Newcastle to Sandwich, 8 Dec. (os) 1747, BL. Add. 32810 fol. 313.

49 Henry Pelham to Yorke, 15 Oct. (os) 1747, BL. Add. 35424 fol. 9; Newcastle to Cumberland, 25 Nov. (os) 1748, RA. Cumberland Papers 41/238.

50 Ossorio to Charles Emmanuel III, 17 Mar., 19 May 1747, AST. LM. Ing. 53.

51 Newcastle to Sandwich, 27 Oct. (os) 1747, BL. Add. 32810, fol. 211.

52 Anon., *Letters from the Westminster Journal* (London, 1747), ii–iii.

53 Vincent, French agent in Amsterdam, who reported on British affairs, to Puysieulx, French foreign minister, 5 Mar. 1747, AE. CP. Ang. 423 fols 86–7.

54 E. Taillemite, 'Une bataille de l'Atlantique au XVIIIe siècle: la guerre de Succession d'Autriche, 1744–1748', *Guerres et Paix* (Vincennes, 1987), pp. 131–48.

55 Puysieulx to Richelieu, 23 Jan., 22 July 1748, AN. KK. 1372.

56 Intelligence from Lyons, NA. SP. 84/445 fol. 73.

57 Puysieulx to Richelieu, 20 Feb. 1748, AN. KK. 1372.
58 Pelham to Gower, 18 Aug. (os) 1748, NA. 30/29/1/11 fol. 313.

7 Revived tensions, 1748–58

1 A.N. Newman (ed.), 'Leicester House politics, 1750–60, from the Papers of John, Second Earl of Egmont', *Camden Miscellany*, 23 (London, 1969), p. 192.
2 Newcastle to Hardwicke, 21 Nov. 1759, BL. Add. 32899 fols 6–7.
3 Cumberland to Holdernesse, 19 Ap. 1757, BL. Eg. 3442 fol. 19.
4 W. Mediger, 'Hastenbeck und Zeven. Der Eintritt Hannovers in den Siebenjährigen Krieg', *Niedersächsisches Jahrbuch für Landesgeschichte*, 56 (1984), pp. 137–66.
5 H. Wellenreuther, 'Die Bedeutung des Siebenjährigen Krieges für die englisch-hannoveranischen Beziehungen', in *England und Hannover*, pp. 170–2.
6 Holdernesse to Cumberland, 6 May 1757, BL. Eg. 3442; Mitchell to Holdernesse, 4, 7 Ap. 1757, NA. SP. 90/68.
7 Walpole to Mann, 23 Mar. (os) 1749, *Walpole–Mann correspondence* vol. 4, p. 39.
8 'Mr. Pitt's points', 21 Sept. 1753, BL. Add. 32995 fols 29–30.
9 Newcastle to Keith, 6 July 1753, NA. SP. 80/192.
10 Fawkener to Robinson, 19 Ap. 1748, BL. Add. 23827 fol. 356.
11 Newcastle to Münchhausen, 3 Mar. 1752, Hanover, Cal. 11 Nr. 244 fol. 50.
12 Holdernesse to Robert Keith, envoy in Vienna, 27 Feb. 1750, BL. Add. 35468 fol. 40.
13 Newcastle to Holdernesse, 13 Mar. (os) 1750, NA. SP. 84/454 fols 261–2.
14 Loss, Saxon envoy, to Count Brühl, Saxon first minister, 25 Mar. 1750, HHStA. Interiora Intercepte vol. 1.
15 Newcastle to Joseph Yorke, 8 Jan. 1762, BL. Add. 32933 fols 113–14.
16 Perrone to Charles Emmanuel III, 3 May 1753, AST. LM. Ing. 57.
17 Holdernesse to Joseph Yorke, 13 Sept. 1754, NA. SP. 84/467.
18 Joseph to Philip Yorke, 7 Ap. 1752, BL. Add. 53563 fol. 299.
19 Hyndford to Newcastle, 11 Ap. 1752, NA. SP. 80/190.
20 U. Dann, *Hannover und England, 1740–1760* (Hildesheim, 1986); A.M. Birke and K. Kluxen (eds), *England und Hannover* (Munich, 1986).
21 J.C.D. Clark (ed.), *Memoirs and Speeches of Lord Waldegrave* (Cambridge, 1985), p. 207.
22 Ossorio to Charles Emmanuel III, 25 Ap. 1740, AST. LM. Ing. 46; Bussy to Rouillé, French foreign minister, 29 July 1755, AE. CP. Br. 52 fol. 19.
23 Viry to Charles Emmanuel III, 12 May 1756, AST. LM. Ing. 60.
24 AE. MD. Ang. 1.
25 J.M. Black, 'International Relations in the Eighteenth Century: Britain and Poland Compared', *Diplomacy and Statecraft*, 13 (2002), pp. 83–112.
26 Newcastle to Holdernesse, 29 Aug. 1755, BL. Add. 32858 fol. 333.
27 Hanbury-Williams to Robinson, 20 Oct., 17 Nov. 1747, BL. Add. 23826 fols 113, 188.
28 Sandwich to Newcastle, 22 Dec. 1747, BL. Add. 32810 fol. 324.
29 Chesterfield to Sandwich, 17 Feb. (os) 1747, BL. Add. 32807 fol. 127; Farmington, Connecticut, Lewis Walpole Library, Horace Walpole's Commonplace Book.
30 Newcastle to Sandwich, 5 Ap. (os) 1748, BL. Add. 21817 fol. 19.
31 Newcastle to Sandwich, 13 July (os) 1748, BL. Add. 32813 fols 5–7; Pelham to Gower, 18 Aug. (os) 1748, NA. 30/29/1/11 fol. 313; Legge to Newcastle, 24 Ap. 1748, BL. Add. 32812 fol. 41.
32 *Correspondence of William Pitt, Earl of Chatham* (4 vols, 1830–40) I, 64.

33 Holdernesse to Earl of Rochford, envoy in Turin, 4 Oct. 1751, NA. SP. 92/59 fol. 170.
34 Joseph to Philip Yorke, 23 Mar. 1753, BL. Add. 35363 fol. 324.
35 Referring to the Bavarian subsidy issue, Perrone to Charles Emmanuel III, 19 Mar. 1750, AST. LM. Ing. 56.
36 Newcastle to Gerlach Adolf von Münchhausen, 29 Nov., 9 Dec. 1748, Hanover, Cal. 24 Nr. 1740 fols 1, 9; Münchhausen to Austrian minister, Khevenhüller, 23 Mar. 1749, BL. Add. 32816 fol. 247; H.M. Scott, ' "The True Principles of the Revolution": The Duke of Newcastle and the Idea of the Old System', in J.M. Black (ed.), *Knights Errant and True Englishmen: British Foreign Policy, 1660–1800* (Edinburgh, 1989), pp. 69–71; Newcastle to Hardwicke, 24 Oct. 1754, Newcastle to Holdernesse, 11 July 1755, BL. Add. 32737 fol. 191, 32857 fol. 54.
37 Newcastle to Joseph Yorke, envoy in The Hague, 20 Ap. 1753, NA. SP. 84/463.
38 Count Viry, Sardinian envoy, to Charles Emmanuel III, 23 Sept. 1757, reporting conversations with both ministers, AST. LM. Ing. 62.
39 AE. CP. Autriche 254.
40 For examples, Sir Robert Wilmot to William, 4th Duke of Devonshire, 30 Sept. 1755, Chatsworth, History of Parliament Transcripts; Richard Rigby to 2nd Earl Gower, 1 Oct. 1755, NA. 30/29/1/14.
41 Fox to William, 4th Duke of Devonshire, 24 Jan. 1756, Chatsworth, History of Parliament Transcripts.
42 L. Schilling, *Kaunitz und das Renversement des Alliances* (Berlin, 1994).
43 Mitchell to Holdernesse, 27 May 1756, NA. SP. 90/65.
44 Andrew Mitchell, envoy to Frederick II, to Holdernesse, 2 Jan. 1757, NA. SP. 90/68; Frederick II to Michell, Prussian envoy in London, 8 Jan. 1757, *Polit. Corr.* 14, p. 187.
45 Puysieulx to Mirepoix, French envoy in London, 14 Mar. 1750, AE. CP. Ang. 428 fols 207–8.
46 Haslang to Preysing, 7 Jan., Haslang to Wachtendonck, 11 Jan. 1757, Munich, Bayr. Ges. London 233.
47 Starhemberg, Austrian envoy in Paris to Kaunitz, 12 Oct. 1756, Kaunitz to Starhemberg, 9 Jan. 1757, J.C. Batzel, 'Austria and the First Three Treaties of Versailles, 1755–1758' (PhD, Brown, 1974), pp. 236, 265.
48 Frederick II to Mitchell, 7 Feb., 29 Mar., Mitchell to Holdernesse, 8 Feb. 1757, BL. Add. 6843 fols 67–8, 88, Eg. 3460 fol. 173, Add. 6832 fol. 112, NA. SP. 90/68; Project for a neutrality treaty, AE. CP. Br. 52 fols 86–96; *Polit. Corr.* vol. 14, pp. 278–80; Batzel, *Treaties*, pp. 282–5.
49 Titley to Holdernesse, 19 Feb. 1757, NA. SP. 75/102; Haslang to Preysing and Wachtendonck, 15, 29 Ap. 1757, Munich, Bayr. Ges. London 233.
50 *Polit. Corr.* vol. 14, pp. 517–18.
51 Maria Theresa to Starhemberg, 5 Mar. 1757, Batzel, *Treaties*, p. 290.
52 Holdernesse to Cumberland, 17 May 1757, BL. Eg. 3442 fols 78–9; Mitchell to Holdernesse, 12 May 1757, NA. SP. 90/68.
53 AE. CP. Br. 52 fols 119, 130–1. Correspondence of Duke of Richelieu, Paris, Bibliothèque Victor Cousin, Fonds Richelieu, vol. 58 fols 86, 100–1, 109–10, 135, vol. 59 fol. 101.
54 Anon., *A Letter to the People of England, upon the Militia, Continental Connections, Neutralities, and Secret Expeditions* (2nd edn, London, 1757), p. 20.
55 Mitchell to Holdernesse, 11 Nov. 1757, NA. SP. 90/70.
56 BL. Add. 6843 fol. 140.
57 Newcastle to Fox, no date, Earl of Ilchester (ed.), *Letters to Henry Fox* (London, 1915), p. 86.
58 *Monitor*, 25 Aug. 1759.

59 Choiseul to the Count of Choiseul, envoy in Vienna, 9 Jan. 1760, AE. CP. Autriche 275 fol. 19.
60 J.M. Black, 'Naval Power and British Foreign Policy in the Age of Pitt the Elder', in J.M. Black and P. Woodfine (eds), *The British Navy and the Use of Naval Power in the Eighteenth Century* (Leicester, 1988), pp. 100–3; M. Schumann, 'Anglo-Prussian Diplomacy and the Baltic Squadron, 1756–1758', *Forum navale* 59 (2003), pp. 66–80.
61 Mitchell to Holdernesse, 23 July, 4 Nov., 9 Dec. 1756, 2 July 1757, Joseph Yorke to Holdernesse, 11 Ap. 1758, NA. SP. 90/65, 67, 69, 71. See also Frederick II to Michell, 14 May, Frederick II to Podewils, 11 June 1757, *Polit. Corr.* 15, pp. 36, 161.
62 Holdernesse to Mitchell, 17 July 1757, NA. SP. 90/69; Holdernesse to Cumberland, 7 Sept. 1757, BL. Eg. 3442 fol. 236.

8 Hanover to the background, 1759–71

1 Mitchell to Holdernesse, 31 Mar. 1757, NA. 90/68.
2 Chavigny to Chauvelin, 18 Feb. 1732, AE. CP. Ang. 376 fol. 235.
3 T.C.W. Blanning and C. Haase, 'Kurhannover, der Kaiser und die Regency Crisis von 1788–9', *Blätter für Landesgeschichte*, 113 (1979), pp. 432–49.
4 Hanbury-Williams to Henry Fox, 17 June 1751, BL. Add. 5193 fol. 52.
5 R.R. Sedgwick (ed.), *Letters from George III to Lord Bute 1756–1766* (London, 1939), pp. 28–9, 78–9, 177.
6 George III, draft, BL. Add. 32684 fol. 121.
7 Rockingham to Sir George Saville, 30 Oct. 1760, Bod. Ms. Eng. Lett. c. 144 fol. 284.
8 Newcastle to Mitchell, 8 Sept. 1760, BL. Add. 6832 fol. 51.
9 Haslang to Baron Wachtendonck, Palatine foreign minister, 10, 31 Mar. 1761, Munich, Bayr. Ges. London, 238.
10 Bussy to Choiseul, 11 June, Choiseul to Bussy, 19 June 1761, AE. CP. Ang. 443 fol. 176, 180, 445 fol. 10; Choiseul to Ossun, envoy in Madrid, 19 Feb. 1760, AE. CP. Espagne 527 fol. 235.
11 Bussy to Choiseul, 26 June, 9 July, Choiseul to Bussy, 27 June 1761, AE. CP. Ang. 443 fol. 277, 339, 445 fol. 17; Choiseul to Ossun, 30 July 1761, AE. CP. Espagne 533 fol. 173; Viry to Charles Emmanuel III, 30 June 1761, AST. LM. Ing. 66.
12 Bussy to Choiseul, 26 July 1761, AE. CP. Ang. 444 fols 67–8; Haslang to Wachtendonck, 28 July 1761, Munich, Bayr. Ges. London 238; Viry to Charles Emmanuel III, 23 Oct. 1761, AST. LM. Ing. 66; WW. R1–22.
13 Cabinet minute, 6 Jan. 1762, NA. 30/47/21.
14 Newcastle to Joseph Yorke, 8 Jan. 1762, BL. Add. 32933 fols 113–14.
15 K.W. Schweizer, 'Lord Bute, Newcastle, Prussia, and the Hague Overtures', *Albion*, 8 (1977), pp. 72–97, esp. 79–81.
16 K.W. Schweizer, 'The Bedford Motion and the House of Lords Debate, 5 February 1762', *Parliamentary History*, 5 (1986), pp. 108–23.
17 F. Spencer, 'The Anglo-Prussian Breach of 1762: An Historical Revision', *History*, 41 (1956), pp. 100–12; K.W. Schweizer and C.S. Leonard, 'Britain, Prussia, Russia and the Galitzin Letter: a Reassessment', *Historical Journal*, 26 (1983), pp. 531–56; Schweizer, 'Lord Bute and the Prussian Subsidy, 1762', *Notes and Queries* (Mar. 1989), pp. 58–61, and *Frederick the Great, William Pitt, and Lord Bute. The Anglo-Prussian Alliance, 1756–1763* (London, 1991).
18 Yorke to Weston, 5 Jan. 1762, BL. Add. 58213 fol. 64.
19 Bute to Wilhelm, Count of Schaumburg-Lippe, 2 Nov. 1762, BL. Add. 36797 fol. 19.

20 Ossun to Choiseul, 19 Ap. 1762, AE. CP. Espagne 536 fol. 86.
21 AE. CP. Espagne 533 fol. 452, 475.
22 Newcastle to Hardwicke, 26 Sept. 1761, BL. Add. 35421 fol. 97.
23 Choiseul to Ossun, 12 Jan. 1762, AE. CP. Espagne 535 fol. 56.
24 Ossun to Choiseul, 1 Feb. 1762, AE. CP. Espagne 535 fol. 139.
25 Choiseul to Ossun, 17 Ap. 1762, AE. CP. Espagne 536 fol. 60.
26 Frederick II to George III, 22 Jan. 1762, San Marino, California, Huntington Library, Stowe papers ST6 vol. 1, p. 133.
27 *London Evening Post*, 17 Ap. 1762.
28 Newcastle to Hardwicke, 15 Nov. 1761, BL. Add. 35421 fol. 141–2.
29 William Copeland to Charles, 2nd Earl of Egremont, Secretary of State for the Southern Department, 4 Sept., George Oake to Egremont, 19 Dec. 1762, New Haven, Beinecke Library, Osborn Shelves, Anglo-Portuguese Relations.
30 Choiseul to Ossun, 3 Oct. 1762, AE. CP. Espagne 537 fol. 208.
31 *Briton*, 10, 24 July, 22 Oct., 4 Dec. 1762. On costs, C. Eldon, *England's Subsidy Policy Towards the Continent During the Seven Years War* (Philadelphia, 1938).
32 See, for example, *Royal Magazine*, Dec. 1762.
33 Bute to Bedford, 18 Jan. 1763, BL. Add. 36797 fol. 30.
34 Nivernais to Louis XV, 17 Feb. 1763, AE. CP. Ang. 449 fol. 353.
35 K.W. Schweizer and J. Bullion, 'The Vote of Credit Controversy, 1762', *British Journal for Eighteenth-Century Studies*, 15 (1992), pp. 175–88.
36 Haslang to Wachtendonck and to Count Preysing, the Bavarian foreign minister, 7 Sept. 1762, Munich, Bayr. Ges. London 239.
37 Nivernais to Choiseul, 24 Sept. 1762, AE. CP. Ang. 447 fols 146–8.
38 Newcastle to Hardwicke, 31 July 1762, BL. Add. 32941 fol. 126.
39 Newcastle to Hardwicke, 1 July 1762, BL. Add. 32940 fol. 180.
40 Yorke to Newcastle, 5 Jan., Newcastle to Yorke, 16 Jan. 1753, NA. 84/462.
41 Nivernais to Praslin, French foreign minister, 11, 17 Dec. 1762, 5, 8 Jan., 13 Feb., 21 Ap. 1763, Chatelet, French envoy in Vienna, to Praslin, 3, 25, 31 Aug., 11, 21 Sept., Praslin to Chatelet, 16 Sept. 1763, AE. CP. Ang. 448 fols 268, 325, 449 fols 40, 67, 306, 309–10, 450 fol. 287, AE. CP. Autriche 295 fols 135, 240–6, 266–8, 303–4, 330–1, 310–11.
42 Nivernais to George, 2nd Earl of Halifax, Secretary of State for the Northern Department, 12 Feb. 1763, Mount Stuart, papers from Cardiff Public Library, 10/129; Nivernais to Praslin, 13, 17 Feb. 1763, AE. CP. Ang. 449 fols 306–10, 353–4; Haslang to Preysing, 11 Mar., Preysing to Haslang, 17 Mar. 1763, Munich, Bayr. Ges. London 241.
43 Haslang to Preysing, and to Wachtendonck, 11 Mar. 1763, Munich, Bayr. Ges. London 241.
44 G.M. Ditchfield, *George III. An Essay in Monarchy* (Basingstoke, 2002), p. 24.
45 S. Conrady, 'Die Wirksamkeit Königs Georgs III für die hannoverschen Kurlande', *Niedersächsisches Jahrbuch für Landesgeschichte*, 39 (1967), pp. 150–91.
46 E.g. re Bentheim and Osnabrück, Nivernais to Praslin, 14 Mar., 5 Ap. 1763, AE. CP. Ang. 450 fols 89, 194.
47 H. Wellenreuther, 'Von der Interessenharmonie zur Dissoziation. Kurhannover und England in der Zeit der Personalunion', *Niedersächsische Jahrbücher für Landesgeschichte*, 67 (1995), p. 55.
48 Haslang to Baron Baumgarten, 7 May 1765, Munich, Bayr. Ges. London 243.
49 Sheffield, Archives, Wentworth Woodhouse muniments, R1–692, 694; Newcastle to Rockingham, 17 Sept. 1766, BL. Add. 32977 fol. 92; *St. James's Chronicle*, 27 Sept. 1766.
50 Zeedhuitz to Haslang, 11 June, 22 July, Haslang to Zeedhuitz, 30 June, 7 July, Munich, Bayr. Ges. London 247.

51 H.M. Scott, 'Aping the Great Powers: Frederick the Great and the Defence of Prussia's International Position, 1763–86', *German History*, 12 (1994), p. 290.
52 Yorke to Weston, 15 Mar. 1763, BL. Add. 58213 fol. 218.
53 Diede, Danish envoy, to Osten, Danish minister, 15 Sept. 1772, Copenhagen, Danske Rigsarkivet, Department of Foreign Affairs, 1953.
54 H.M. Scott, *British Foreign Policy in the Age of the American Revolution* (Oxford, 1990).
55 Porter to Weston, 29 Jan. 1763, BL. Add. 57927 fol. 23.
56 Anon., *The True Interest of the Princes of Europe, at this Present Juncture* (London, 1739), pp. 11–12.
57 Yorke to Weston, 1 Ap. 1763, BL. Add. 58213 fol. 224.
58 See e.g. Viry to Charles Emmanuel III, commenting on George III, 14, 28 Ap. 1763, AST. LM. Ing. 68; Newcastle to Rockingham, 17 Sept. 1766, BL. Add. 32977 fol. 93; Louis, Count of Châtelet, French envoy, to Choiseul, reporting Shelburne, 27 May 1768, AE. CP. Ang. 484 fol. 86.
59 N. Tracy, *Navies, Deterrence and American Independence: Britain and Sea Power in the 1760s and 1770s* (Vancouver, 1988); Scott, *British Foreign Policy*.
60 M.M. Escott, 'Britain's Relations with France and Spain 1763–1771' (PhD, Wales, 1988), pp. 154–5, 170.
61 M. Peters, *'Monitor'*, p. 70.
62 Bedford to Bute, 9 July 1761, Mount Stuart, papers of the 3rd Earl of Bute, 1761 corresp. no. 478.
63 1 Dec. (os) 1740, Cobbett, vol. 11, p. 713.
64 AE. CP. Espagne 523 fols 6, 15, 18, 527 fol. 235, 532 fol. 334, 536 fol. 17; AN. KK. 1351 no. 88.
65 Harcourt to Thomas, 3rd Viscount Weymouth, Secretary of State for the Southern Department, 8 Feb. 1769, NA. SP. 78/277 fol. 117.
66 Instructions from the borough of Preston, 19 Mar. (os) 1742.
67 E.g. *York Courant*, 16 Jan. (os) 1739.
68 Draft to Stormont, 28 Feb. 1766, Bury St Edmunds, West Suffolk Record Office, Grafton papers 423/235; Perrière (reporting comments of Henry Conway, Secretary of State for the Southern Department) to Charles Emmanuel III, 16 May 1766, AST. LM. Ing. 72.
69 F. Crouzet, 'Mercantilism, War and the Rise of British Power', in P.K. O'Brien and A. Clesse (eds), *Two Hegemonies. Britain 1846–1914 and the United States 1941–2001* (Aldershot, 2002), p. 79.
70 Nivernais to Praslin, 27 Jan. 1763, AE. CP. Ang. 449 fol. 216.
71 Yorke to Weston, 22 Feb. 1763, BL. Add. 58213 fol. 208.
72 Châtelet to Choiseul, 27 May 1768, AE. CP. Ang. 483 fol. 63; Rochford to Shelburne, 7 July 1768, NA. SP. 78/285 fol. 122.

9 Interventionism, George III and the Hanoverian connection, 1772–93

1 Carmarthen to William Pitt the Younger, 28 Oct. 1785, NA. 30/8/151 fol. 29.
2 Haslang to Beckers, Palatine foreign minister, 14 June, 19 Aug. 1774, Beckers to Haslang, 10 Dec. 1774, Ritter, envoy in Vienna, to Beckers, 27 Ap., 3, 24, 31 Aug., 7 Sept., 5, 26 Oct. 1774, Munich, Bayr. Ges. London 252, Wien 702; *Westminster Journal*, 3, 17 Sept., 1 Oct. 1774.
3 For the value of a long-term perspective, M. Howard, *The Continental Commitment* (London, 1972) and D. Baugh, 'British Strategy during the First World War in the Context of Four Centuries: Blue Water versus Continental Commitment', in D.M. Masterson (ed.), *Naval History: The Sixth Symposium of the U.S. Naval Academy* (Wilmington, 1987), pp. 85–110.
4 N.A.M. Rodger, 'Continental Commitment', p. 50.

5 C. Wilkinson, *The British Navy and the State in the Eighteenth Century* (Woodbridge, 2004).

6 Champeaux to Rouillé, 16 Ap. 1755, AE. CP. Ang. 438 fol. 413. For a different view, Rouillé to Marshal Noailles, 21 July 1755, AE. CP. Ang. 439 fols 264–5; Maria Theresa to Starhemberg, 27 Sept. 1755, Batzel, *Treaties*, p. 97.

7 Perrone to Charles Emmanuel III, 7 Aug. 1755, AST. LM. Ing. 59.

8 Frederick II to Knyphausen, 9 Aug. 1755, *Polit. Corr.* XI, p. 244.

9 Bernis to Aubeterre, 3 Jan. 1758, AE. CP. Espagne 523 fol. 6.

10 E. Buddruss, *Die französische Deutschlandpolitik, 1756–1789* (Mainz, 1995), pp. 73, 227.

11 Hugh Elliot, envoy in Copenhagen, to Keith, 11 Aug. 1778, Joseph Yorke to Keith, 9 Oct. 1778, Keith to Stormont, 4 Dec. 1779, BL. Add. 35514 fol. 242, 35515 fol. 154, 35517 fol. 311; Scott, *British Foreign Policy*, pp. 37, 269–70.

12 Kaunitz to Kageneck, 9 Mar., 13 Nov. 1784, HHStA., EK. 129.

13 York to George III, 28 Feb. 1785, A. Aspinall (ed.), *The Later Correspondence of George III* (Cambridge, 1962), I, p. 178.

14 Draft in George's Hand, RA 6071.

15 Blanning, '*Fürstenbund* of 1785', pp. 321–6.

16 Cobbett, *Parliamentary History*, vol. 20, columns 1019–20.

17 J. Richard, *A Tour*, pp. 185–7.

18 For example, *Daily Universal Register*, 2, 3, 5 Jan., 4, 15, 22, 26 July, 14 Aug., 1 Sept. 1786.

19 Kageneck to Kaunitz, 18, 25 Oct. 1785, Kaunitz to Reviczky, 3 Ap., 27 July 1786, HHStA. EK 124, 129; K. Aretin, *Heiliges Römisches Reich, 1776–1806* (2 vols, Wiesbaden, 1967), I, 178; Fox to Richard Fitzpatrick, – Nov. 1785, BL. Add. 47580 fols 126–7.

20 Kageneck to Kaunitz, 1 Feb. 1785, HHStA. EK 124.

21 J.W. Marcum, 'Vorontsov and Pitt: The Russian Assessment of a British Statesman, 1785–1792', *Rocky Mountain Social Science Journal*, 10 (1973), pp. 50–1; York to George III, 1, 8 June 1787, Aspinall, *George III*, I, p. 370; F.C. Wittichen, *Preussen und England in der europäischen Politik, 1785–1788* (Heidelberg, 1902), p. 117.

22 Joseph Ewart, envoy in Berlin, to George Aust, senior clerk at the Foreign Office, 14 Oct. 1791, private collection of the author.

23 P. Glanvill, *The King's Silver: George III's Service in Hanover and England* (Waddesdon Manor leaflet, 2003).

24 Trevor to Carmarthen, 8 Ap. 1786, NA. FO. 67/5; Rose to Wilberforce, 27 Sept. 1787, Bod. Wilberforce Mss. d 17/1 fol. 19.

25 Richmond to Pitt, 5 July 1787, NA. 30/8/170 fol. 82.

26 Pitt to George III, and reply, both 16 Sept. 1787, Aspinall, *George III*, I, pp. 324–5, Manchester, John Rylands Library, Eng. Mss. 912 no. 37.

27 Luzerne, French envoy in London, to Montmorin, French foreign minister, 13 May 1788, AE. CP. Ang. 565 fol. 160.

28 George III to Prince and Princess of Orange, both of 6 June 1788, Aspinall, *George III*, I, pp. 376–7.

29 F.K. Wittichen, *Preussen und England in der europäischen Politik 1785–1788* (Heidelberg, 1902).

30 Elliot to Carmarthen, 29 Nov. 1788, NA. FO. 22/10 fol. 423.

31 George III to Pitt, 19 Oct. 1788, Aspinall, *George III*, I, p. 485; Lord Hawkesbury to Duke of Dorset, 28 Oct. 1788, Maidstone Kent Archive Office, Sackville papers U269 C 182.

32 S. Conway, 'Continental Connections: Britain and Europe in the Eighteenth Century', *History*, 90 (2005).

33 George III to George, 2nd Earl Spencer, 1st Lord of the Admiralty, 3 Oct. 1794, BL. Add. 75817.
34 G.S. Ford, *Hanover and Prussia, 1795–1803. A Study in Neutrality* (New York, 1903).
35 George III to Marquis Cornwallis, 1 Nov., Hawkesbury, Foreign Secretary, to Cornwallis, 1 Nov. 1801, C. Ross (ed.), *The Correspondence of Charles, First Marquis Cornwallis* (3 vols, London, 1859), pp. 384–5, 388–9.
36 D.S. Gray, 'The French Invasion of Hanover in 1803 and the Origins of the King's German Legion', *Proceedings of the Consortium on Revolutionary Europe* (1980), pp. 198–211.
37 Grenville to Sir Morton Eden, envoy in Vienna, 9 Sept. 1798, BL. Add. 73765.

10 Conclusions

1   Anon. memo. Northumberland CRO. 650/C/18/3 p. 19.
2   Townshend to Horatio Walpole, 27 Aug. 1725, BL. Add. 48981 fol. 106.
3   Newcastle to Horatio Walpole, 23 May (os) 1726, BL. Add. 32746 fol. 133; Chance, *Alliance of Hanover*, p. 287.
4   See, for example, Diemar to Prince William of Hesse-Cassel, 2 July 1726, Marburg, England 194.
5   Chance, *The Alliance of Hanover*, pp. 708–25.
6   Draft with Townshend's views for Horatio Walpole, – May (os) 1727, BL. Add. 48981 fol. 214.
7   Jean Le Chambrier, Prussian Resident in Paris, to Frederick William I, 4 Mar. 1727, AE. CP. Prusse 83. The French had considerable success in intercepting this correspondence.
8   R. Hutton, 'The Making of the Secret Treaty of Dover, 1668–1670', *Historical Journal* 29 (1986).
9   Graham to Hay, 30 Nov., 7 Dec. 1726, RA. Stuart Papers 99/103, 130.
10 Project of Count Henning Friedrich von Bassewitz, first minister of Charles Frederick of Holstein-Gottorp, 30 Nov. 1726, *Sbornik imperatorskago Russkago istoricheskago obshchestva* (148 vols, St Petersburg, 1867–1916), 64, p. 453.
11 Giacinto Fiorelli, Venetian envoy in London, to the Venetian government, 9 Aug. 1726, Venice, Archivio di Stato, LM. Ing. 96 fols 338–9.
12 Townshend to Charles Du Bourgay, envoy in Berlin, 22 Ap., Edward Finch, envoy to Saxony-Poland, to Townshend, 15 Oct. 1726, NA. SP. 88/33, 90/20. See also Magnan, French envoy in St Petersburg, to Morville, French foreign minister, 9 Nov. 1726, *Sbornik* 64, pp. 443–5.
13 Chammorel, French envoy, to Morville, 10 Ap. 1724, AE. CP. Ang. 347 fol. 169.
14 Edward Finch, envoy in Stockholm, to Harrington, 29 Aug., Harrington to Robinson, 30 Nov. (os) 1733, NA. SP. 95/64, 80/101; Diemar to Dornberg, 29 Nov. 1733, Marburg, England 203; Frederick I of Sweden to Diemar, 24 Nov. 1734, HHStA. GK. 85a; Black, 'International Relations in the Eighteenth Century: Britain and Poland Compared', *Diplomacy and Statecraft*, 13 (2002), pp. 83–112.
15 Martine to Landgrave Karl of Hesse-Cassel, 1 Nov. 1723, Marburg, Frankreich 1586 fol. 216.
16 Pelham to Hardwicke, 14 Nov. 1748, BL. Add. 35423 fol. 80.
17 Horatio Walpole to Newcastle, 6 Feb. 1726, BL. Add. 32746. See also, Horatio Walpole to Townshend, 10 Sept. 1725, in reply to Townshend's of 27 Aug., BL. Add. 48981 fols 115–24, 105–14.
18 N.A.M. Rodger, 'Seapower and empire: cause and effect?', in B. Moore and H. van Nierop (eds), *Colonial Empires Compared: Britain and the Netherlands, 1750–1850* (Aldershot, 2003), pp. 97–111.

19 Newcastle to George Lyttleton, 1 Nov. 1755, *Sotheby's Catalogue*, 12 Dec. 1978, catalogue of the Lyttleton papers, p. 135.
20 For example, R. Jervis, *Perception and Misperception in International Politics* (Princeton, 1976); A.I. Johnston, *Cultural Realism: Strategic Culture and Grand Strategy in Chinese History* (Princeton, 1995).
21 For example, E. Ringmar, *Identity, Interest and Action: A Cultural Explanation of Sweden's Intervention in the Thirty Years War* (Cambridge, 1996); G. Parker, *The Grand Strategy of Philip II* (New Haven, CT, 1998).
22 T. Claydon, *William, William III and the Godly Reformation* (Cambridge, 1996).
23 Zöhrern to Sinzendorf, 3 Nov. 1741, NA. SP. 107/50.
24 *Groans*, p. 31.
25 *Groans*, pp. 30–2.
26 *Groans*, pp. 24–5.
27 Hendrik Hop, Dutch envoy, to Fagel, 8 Dec. 1741, NA. SP. 107/51.
28 Bolingbroke to George Lyttelton, 4 Nov. 1741, R. Phillimore (ed.), *Memoirs and Correspondence of George, Lord Lyttelton, from 1734 to 1773* (2 vols, London, 1845) I, 194–200.
29 N.A.M. Rodger, 'Continental Commitment', p. 55.
30 Palm to Charles VI, 20 Feb. 1726, NLA. Mss. 1458/9/9/18.

Selected further reading

Unless otherwise stated, place of publication is London.

Anderson, M.S., *The War of the Austrian Succession 1740–1748* (1995).
Baugh, D.A., 'Great Britain's "Blue-Water" policy, 1689–1815', *International History Review* (1988).
Baugh, D.A., 'Withdrawing from Europe: Anglo-French maritime geopolitics, c. 1750–1800', *International History Review* (1998).
Baxter, S.B., 'The Myth of the Grand Alliance', in Baxter and P.R. Sellin (eds), *Anglo-Dutch Cross Currents in the Seventeenth and Eighteenth Centuries* (Los Angeles, 1976).
Baxter, S.B. (ed.), *England's Rise to Greatness, 1660–1763* (Berkeley, 1983).
Bertram, M., *Georg II. König und Kurfürst* (Göttingen, 2003).
Birke, A.M. and Kluxen, K. (eds), *England und Hannover* (Munich, 1986).
Black, J.M., *The Collapse of the Anglo-French Alliance, 1727–1731* (Gloucester, 1987).
Black, J.M., *British Foreign Policy in an Age of Revolution* (Cambridge, 1994).
Black, J.M., *The Hanoverians. The History of a Dynasty* (2004).
Blanning, T.C.W., ' "That horrid Electorate" or "Ma patrie germanique"?: George III, Hanover and the *Fürstenbund* of 1785', *Historical Journal* (1977).
Blanning, T.C.W., and Haase, C., 'Kurhannover, der Kaiser und die Regency Crisis von 1788–89', *Blätter für Landesgeschichte* (1979).
Brewer, J., *The Sinews of Power: War, Money and the English State, 1688–1783* (1989).
Browning, R., 'The Duke of Newcastle and the Imperial Election Plan, 1749–54', *Journal of British Studies* (1967–8).
Browning, R., *The Duke of Newcastle* (New Haven, CT, 1975).
Butterfield, H., 'British Foreign Policy 1762–65', *Historical Journal* (1963).
Chance, J.F., *George I and the Northern War* (1909).
Chance, J.F., 'George I and Peter the Great after the Peace of Nystad', *English Historical Review* (1911).
Chance, J.F., *The Alliance of Hanover* (1923).
Cobban, A., *Ambassadors and Secret Agents: The Diplomacy of the First Earl of Malmesbury at The Hague* (1954).
Conway, S., 'Continental Connections: Britain and Europe in the Eighteenth Century', *History* (2005).
Cunningham, A., 'The Oczakov debate', *Middle Eastern Studies* (1964–5).

Dann, U., *Hanover and Great Britain 1740–1760* (Leicester, 1991).

Doran, P.F., *Andrew Mitchell and Anglo-Prussian Relations during the Seven Years' War* (New York, 1986).

Duchhardt, H., *Balance of Power und Pentarchie: Internationale Beziehungen 1700–1785* (Paderborn, 1997).

Dull, J.R., *A Diplomatic History of the American Revolution* (New Haven, CT, 1985).

Dunthorne, H.L.A., *The Maritime Powers 1721–1740: A Study of Anglo-Dutch Relations in the Age of Walpole* (New York, 1986).

Ehrman, J., *The Younger Pitt: The Years of Acclaim* (1969).

Eldon, C.W., *England's Subsidy Policy towards the Continent during the Seven Years War* (Philadelphia, PA, 1938).

Ellis, K.L., 'The Administrative Connections between Britain and Hanover', *Journal of the Society of Archivists* (1969).

Gerhard, D., 'Kontinentalpolitik und Kolonialpolitik im Frankreich des ausge-henden ancien régime', *Historische Zeitschrift* (1933).

Gibbs, G.C., 'Britain and the Alliance of Hanover, 1725–1726', *English Historical Review* (1958).

Gibbs, G.C., 'English Attitudes towards Hanover and the Hanoverian Succession in the First Half of the Eighteenth Century', in Birke, A.M. and Kluxen, K. (eds), *England und Hannover*.

Gregg., E., *The Protestant Succession in International Politics 1710–1716* (New York, 1986).

Harris, B., *Politics and the Nation: Britain in the Mid-Eighteenth Century* (Oxford, 2002).

Hartley, C., *Charles Whitworth. Diplomat in the Age of Peter the Great* (Aldershot, 2002).

Hatton, R., *George I* (1978).

Hatton, R., *The Anglo-Hanoverian Connection 1714–1760* (1982).

Hertz, G.B., 'England and the Ostend Company', *English Historical Review* (1907).

Horn, D.B., 'The Origins of the Proposed Election of a King of the Romans', *English Historical Review* (1927).

Horn, D.B., *Sir Charles Hanbury-Williams and European Diplomacy 1747–58* (1930).

Horn, D.B., 'The Cabinet Controversy on Subsidy Treaties in Time of Peace', *English Historical Review* (1930).

Horn, D.B., *British Public Opinion and the First Partition of Poland* (1945).

Horn, D.B., *Great Britain and Europe in the Eighteenth Century* (Oxford, 1967).

Horn, D.B., 'The Duke of Newcastle and the Origins of the Diplomatic Revolution', in Elliott, J.H. and Koenigsberger, H.G. (eds), *The Diversity of History* (1970).

Jones, G.H., *Great Britain and the Tuscan Succession Question, 1710–1737* (New York, 1998).

Konigs, P., *The Hanoverian Kings and their Homeland* (Lewes, 1993).

Lodge, R., *Great Britain and Prussia in the Eighteenth Century* (Oxford, 1923).

Lodge, R., 'The First Anglo-Russian Treaty, 1739–42', *English Historical Review* (1928).

Lodge, R., *Studies in Eighteenth Century Diplomacy, 1740–1748* (1930).

Lodge, R., 'Russia, Prussia, and Great Britain, 1742–44', *English Historical Review* (1930).

Mackesy, P., *The War for America 1775–1783* (1964).

Madariaga, I. de, *Britain, Russia and the Armed Neutrality of 1780* (1960).

Marshall, P.J. (ed.), *The Oxford History of the British Empire. II. The Eighteenth Century* (Oxford, 1998).

McKay, D., 'The Struggle for Control of George I's Northern Policy, 1718–19', *Journal of Modern History* (1973).

McKay, D., *Allies of Convenience: Diplomatic Relations between Great Britain and Austria 1714–1719* (New York, 1986).

Mediger, W., *Moskaus Weg nach Europe: der Aufstieg Russlands zum europäischen Machtstaat im Zeitalter Friedrichs des Grossen* (Brunswick, 1952).

Mediger, W., *Mecklenburg, Russland und England-Hannover 1706–1721* (Hildesheim, 1967).

Mediger, W., 'Great Britain, Hanover and the Rise of Prussia', in Hatton, R., and Anderson, M.S. (eds), *Studies in Diplomatic History* (1970).

Metcalf, M.F., *Russia, England and Swedish Party Politics 1762–1766* (Stockholm, 1977).

Michael, W., *England under George I: The Beginnings of the Hanoverian Dynasty* (1936).

Middleton, R., *The Bells of Victory: The Pitt-Newcastle Ministry and the Conduct of the Seven Years' War 1757–1762* (Cambridge, 1985).

Minchinton, W. (ed.), *Britain and the Northern Seas* (Pontefract, 1988).

Murray, J.J., *George I, the Baltic and the Whig Split of 1717* (1969).

Naumann, H., *Österreich, England und das Reich 1719–32* (Berlin, 1936).

Niedhart, G., *Handel und Krieg in der Britischen Weltpolitik, 1738–1763* (Munich, 1979).

Pares, R., 'American versus Continental Warfare 1739–1763', *English Historical Review* (1936).

Peters, M., *Pitt and Popularity: The Patriot Ministry and London Opinion during the Seven Years' War* (Oxford, 1980).

Raven, G.J.A., and Rodger, N.A.M., *Navies and Armies. The Anglo-Dutch Relationship in War and Peace 1688–1988* (Edinburgh, 1990).

Reading, D., *The Anglo-Russian Commercial Treaty of 1734* (New Haven, CT, 1938).

Richmond, H., *Statesmen and Sea Power* (Oxford, 1946).

Richter-Uhlig, U., *Hof und Politik unter den Bedingungen der Personalunion zwischen Hannover und England* (Hanover, 1992).

Roberts, M., *Splendid Isolation 1713–1780* (Reading, 1970).

Roberts, M., *Macartney in Russia* (1974).

Roberts, M., *British Diplomacy and Swedish Politics, 1758–1773* (1980).

Rodger, N.A.M., *The Command of the Ocean: A Naval History of Britain 1649–1815* (2004).

Schroeder, P.W., *The Transformation of European Politics 1769–1848* (Oxford, 1994).

Schweizer, K.W., 'The Non-renewal of the Anglo-Prussian Subsidy Treaty, 1761–1862', *Canadian Journal of History* (1978).

Schweizer, K.W., *England, Prussia and the Seven Years' War* (Lewiston, NY, 1989).

Schweizer, K.W., *Frederick the Great, William Pitt and Lord Bute: The Anglo-Prussian Alliance, 1756–1765* (New York, 1991).

Scott, H.M., *British Foreign Policy in the Age of the American Revolution* (Oxford, 1990).

Scott, H.M., 'Britain as a European Great Power in the Age of the American Revolution', in Dickinson, H.T. (ed.), *Britain and the American Revolution* (Harlow, 1998).

Scott, H.M., *The Emergence of the Eastern Powers, 1756–1775* (Cambridge, 2001).

Taylor, S., and others (eds), *Hanoverian Britain and Empire* (Woodbridge, 1998).

Tracy, N., *Navies, Deterrence, and American Independence: Britain and Sea Power in the 1760s and 1770s* (Vancouver, 1988).

Ward, A.W., *Great Britain and Hanover: Some Aspects of the Personal Union* (Oxford, 1899).

Williams, B., *Carteret and Newcastle* (Cambridge, 1943).

Index